Second to None

Second to None

The Fighting 58th Battalion of the Canadian Expeditionary Force

Kevin R. Shackleton

THE DUNDURN GROUP
TORONTO · OXFORD

Copy-Editor: Andrea Pruss
Design: Jennifer Scott
Printer: University of Toronto Press

National Library of Canada Cataloguing in Publication Data

Shackleton, Kevin R
The Fighting 58th Battalion of the Canadian Expeditionary Force / Kevin R. Shackleton.

ISBN 1-55002-405-1

1. Canada. Canadian Army. Battalion, 58th--History. 2. World War, 1914-1918--Regimental histories--Canada. I. Title. II. Title: Fighting Fifty-eighth Battalion of the Canadian Expeditionary Force.

D547.C2S395 2002 940.4'1271 C2002-902297-5

1 2 3 4 5 06 05 04 03 02

We acknowledge the support of the **Canada Council for the Arts** and the **Ontario Arts Council** for our publishing program. We also acknowledge the financial support of the **Government of Canada** through the **Book Publishing Industry Development Program** and **The Association for the Export of Canadian Books**, and the **Government of Ontario** through the **Ontario Book Publishers Tax Credit** program.

Care has been taken to trace the ownership of copyright material used in this book. The author and the publisher welcome any information enabling them to rectify any references or credit in subsequent editions.

J. Kirk Howard, President

Printed and bound in Canada.
Printed on recycled paper.

www.dundurn.com

Dundurn Press	Dundurn Press	Dundurn Press
8 Market Street	73 Lime Walk	2250 Military Road
Suite 200	Headington, Oxford,	Tonawanda NY
Toronto, Ontario, Canada	England	U.S.A. 14150
M5E 1M6	OX3 7AD	

Second to None

Table of Contents

Preface		9
Prologue		13
One:	February and March 1916 *Entering the Zone of Stealth*	29
Two:	April 1916 *Taking the Strain*	37
Three:	May 1916 *Dishing it Out*	45
Four:	June 1916 *Battle for Mount Sorrel*	55
Five:	July 1916 *More of the Same*	67
Six:	August 1916 *A Veteran Battalion*	73
Seven:	September 1916 *Into the Meat Grinder*	79
Eight:	October 1916 *Expendable*	87
Nine:	November 1916 *Recovery*	97
Ten:	December 1916 *Anatomy of a Trench Raid*	103
Eleven:	January 1917 *Winter Sets In*	111
Twelve:	February 1917 *Preparation for Something Big*	115
Thirteen:	March 1917 *Keeping the Enemy Off Balance*	119
Fourteen:	April 1917 *The Battle for Vimy Ridge*	125
Fifteen:	May 1917 *Keeping the Pressure On*	135
Sixteen:	June 1917 *Leading the Way*	139
Seventeen:	July 1917 *Relative Calm*	149

Eighteen:	August 1917 *Hill 70 and Lens*	153
Nineteen:	September 1917 *A Temporary Reprieve*	161
Twenty:	October 1917 *Passchendaele: The Third Battle of Ypres*	167
Twenty-one:	November 1917 *Passchendaele Retained*	183
Twenty-two:	December 1917 *Restoring the Edge*	195
Twenty-three:	January 1918 *The Perfect Raid*	201
Twenty-four:	February 1918 *The Calm Before the Storm*	211
Twenty-five:	March 1918 *The Storm Breaks*	215
Twenty-six:	April 1918 *The Storm Passes*	221
Twenty-seven:	May 1918 *Preparations for the Counter Stroke*	225
Twenty-eight:	June 1918 *Honing the Edge*	229
Twenty-nine:	July 1918 *Ready!*	233
Thirty:	August 1918 *Testing the Edge*	239
Thirty-one:	September 1918 *The Edge is Blunted*	263
Thirty-two:	October 1918 *One Last Effort*	271
Thirty-three:	November 1918 *The End*	275
Thirty-four:	December 1918 – March 1919 *Going Home*	281
Epilogue		289
Endnotes		305
Honour Roll		321
Index		353

Preface

On May 18, 1939, the Historical Committee of the 58th Battalion wrote to the Records Section of the Department of National Defence, asking for copies of the various documents necessary for the writing of the battalion's history. War clouds were already gathering over Europe and the Pacific, and the start of the Second World War, twenty-one years after the Great War had ended, quickly put the project on hold. If the history had been written at that time, the story that might have been told would be much different from the one unfolding in this volume. Major Warner Elmo Cusler, one of the original officers of the 58th, was the chairman of the committee. Two other originals — the last commanding officer of the battalion, Lieutenant Colonel Robert Alexander Macfarlane, and Major Henry E. Rose, the author of large sections of the battalion War Diary — were members of the committee.[1] Together, this trio had been involved with virtually all of the battalion's major actions, and they would have brought to the history an intimate knowledge of the men and the battles that they had undertaken. With war looming, and with it having broken out so soon after the project began, they might have felt a sense that the sacrifice of so many lives had been futile. This belief would have given to the history a tone very different from that which it might have had if the narrative had been written soon after the Great War.

Two decades later, Sergeant George Thomas Bell, secretary of the Historical Committee, offered the battalion's records to Major D.J. Goodspeed when the major was writing the history of the Royal Regiment of Canada, published in 1962. In *Battle Royal*, Goodspeed included chapters on the Canadian Expeditionary Force battalions perpetuated by the Royal Regiment and indicated that there was enough material for a volume on the 58th alone, but that he did not have space for the whole story. A history of the 58th written at this time might have concentrated on the valour of the men and the waste of life, as Goodspeed did in his other book, *The Road Past Vimy*.

The project could still have been revived, but the next decade would see the war in Vietnam and the rise of anti-war sentiment among the grandchildren of the Great War veterans. Historical reappraisal of the Great War in light of the Second World War and the Cold War with communist countries would make the Great War seem like a futile bloodbath in which men's lives were squandered needlessly. Sergeant Bell still had the battalion's files at this point, and there would have been survivors to interview if someone had resumed the project, but it would have been a race against time to complete it before these old soldiers faded away. The climate of the time was not supportive of a project that looked at a war from so long ago when the Second World War was still foremost in Canadian minds.

This current book stems from my rising interest in genealogy. In an effort to learn more about what happened to my grandfather and his brother-in-law in the Great War, I began to probe their military records and those of their battalion. I was looking for material that would put the 58th Battalion into the context of the war in which it served. I could not find much in published sources. Because the battalion had been formed from a number of other units and did not continue as a separate regiment for long after the Great War, as did two of the other battalions in the 9th Brigade, the 58th had essentially dropped from sight. This is most unfortunate because, while there were many battalions formed during the war (numbering ran up to the 252nd), the 58th was one of only fifty that saw action in Belgium and France. Most of the others were broken up to provide reinforcements for the units already at the sharp end of the war.

The War Diary has provided the skeleton of the story. Finding people with more information to bring the memory of the men back to life has been a hit and miss process. Personal sources would have been more easily available a generation ago. The advantage is that I have not been overwhelmed with material. I have tried to include in my narrative every reference to any individual in the War Diary in order to help their relatives learn where their ancestors were at any given time. I have also tried to include all available material on the O.R.s, the other ranks or non-officers, who are so often nameless in the Diary. I apologize to other authors of battalion histories who have included in their texts the names of as many men as possible. I used to find this very distracting. Now, however, in the light of my own efforts, I can appreciate what they were trying to do. I hope the current reader will bear with me as I create historical narrative out of the War Diary, the files of the battalion, and a variety of personal sources.

I have been very fortunate to have a number of people offer to help me with my project. My business associate, Brent Robinson, was kind enough to allow me time to visit the National Archives in Ottawa and the battlefields of the Western Front. John McLean read my first draft and suggested the idea of publishing a photograph of men from the 58th in the "Where are they now" column of the *Toronto Star*, which opened many new doors to information on the men of the 58th. Bill Rawling was also kind enough to read the first draft, making a number of suggestions and pointing me to additional sources from men of the battalion. Ian Waldron, youngest son of Private David H. Waldron, and Gord MacKinnon, nephew of Corporal Archie MacKinnon, embraced the project as their own, and together we resurrected the Historical Committee for the 58th. Ian was extremely generous with his time, editing the book three times before it was fit for a publisher. The Waldron family kindly allowed me frequent access to the collection of mementos left by David Waldron. Gord was always willing to check various libraries, archives, and cemeteries to trace leads on men from the battalion. He read several drafts of the manuscript to correct errors and make suggestions, which only helped to improve the finished product. John Haslam, of the Central Ontario branch of the Western Front Association, put me in touch with the Luce Maple Leaf Committee in France. As well, he lent me several books on the Canadians in the First World War. Marc Pilot and Captain Jean Mroz guided me over the battlefield at Hourges. Alain Bouten, co-host of the Protea Bed and Breakfast in Zonnebeke, Belgium, kindly showed me the Bellevue Spur and Vindictive Crossroads battlefields. Jane Cusler, daughter of Elmo Cusler; Geoff Stead, nephew of Dick Joyce; Doug Ware, grandson of Gerald Cosbie; and Don Jukes, nephew of Homer Jukes, contributed significant resources to this work. Major Robert Ritchie (Ret.) made numerous trip to the National Archives for me. They are just a few of many families who shared memories and memorabilia of their fathers, grandfathers, and uncles and helped me to bring this slim volume to life. And, of course, I must thank my wife, Linda, and my children, who kept me from becoming one of the troglodytes of the Great War in my basement dugout and helped me stay in touch with the present while I was so focused on the past. Any errors in the text are my sole responsibility.

Kevin Shackleton
March 2002

Prologue

Raising the Battalion

The original order to form the 58th Battalion was issued by the Minister of Militia in May 1915, and its ranks were filled with 1,151 men by the middle of July. Major Goodspeed suggested that the valiant stand of the Canadian First Contingent at the Second Battle of Ypres in April 1915 had raised the enthusiasm of the volunteers and brought them flooding to the recruiting offices.[2] At Ypres, the Canadians withstood the first use of poison gas as a weapon of war and prevented the Germans from capturing the last major Belgian town in Allied hands. While this enthusiasm may have increased the desire to enlist, it is also possible that the men had already made up their minds to join and were in militia regiments waiting their turn to be selected for overseas service. The May order directed the active infantry regiments of the 2nd Military District to recruit quotas of between twenty and seventy-five officers and men to fill the battalion's ranks.[3] Lieutenant Colonel Harry Genet of the 38th Dufferin Rifles circulated through the district to locate officers to staff the battalion. By June 21, the men began to arrive at Paradise Camp, situated just outside Niagara-on-the-Lake, Ontario.

The nominal roll of those who made the journey to England records the name of each soldier, any previous military experience, the name and address of next of kin, and the country of birth. It reveals that almost 56 percent of the men had some military experience. Of these, 103 listed experience with the Imperial Forces or Territorial units from Britain. For a country without a military tradition or a significant standing army constantly maintained by new draftees, as was the case in the French, German, and Russian armies, this seems truly remarkable.[4] Most of the officers were born in Canada, and all but two of them had military experience. Lieutenant Colonel Harry A. Genet, of London, England,[5] had five years of experience with the 2nd (South) Middlesex Territorial Regiment and over seventeen years with the 38th Dufferin Rifles of the Canadian Militia. The second-in-command, Major Panayoty P. Ballachey, had also served with the 38th. He had established his dentistry practice in Brantford after graduation from the University of Toronto in 1899 and was serving as school trustee before enlisting in the C.E.F. Lieutenant George H. Cassels, a Toronto lawyer and a graduate of Royal Military College in Kingston, had served with the 48th Highlanders before being posted to the 58th and appointed to command B Company. Cassels was part of the Canadian upper class. His father was Sir Walter Gibson Pringle Cassels of Montreal, and his wife was Cecil Vivian Kerr, the daughter of Senator T.K. Kerr.[6] Captain John D. Mackay of Haileybury, Ontario, a South African War veteran, commanded D Company. By contrast, Captain Waring Gerald Cosbie, the medical officer, was a recent graduate of the University of Toronto Medical School. Lieutenant Warner Elmo Cusler, a twenty-six-year-old banker from Thorold, Ontario, came from United Empire Loyalist stock. He joined the battalion just before it left the Niagara area, having served earlier with the 19th Regiment.[7] He would play a prominent part in several of the battalion's actions. Lieutenant Henry E. Rose, another British-born officer in the unit, had also been a banker in civilian life. Lieutenants William A.P. Durie[8] and John Egerton Ryerson[9] had banking experience and connections to the Canadian elite. They, along with Lieutenant Ayton R. Leggo, had been educated at Toronto's Upper Canada College. Durie's father had founded the Queen's Own Rifles of Canada, and Durie himself had served in that regiment in the pre-war years. Leggo and another officer, Lieutenant Richard H. Joyce, would keep diaries to record their experiences with the battalion. This was officially for-

Officers of the
58th Battalion Canada
3rd Contingent.

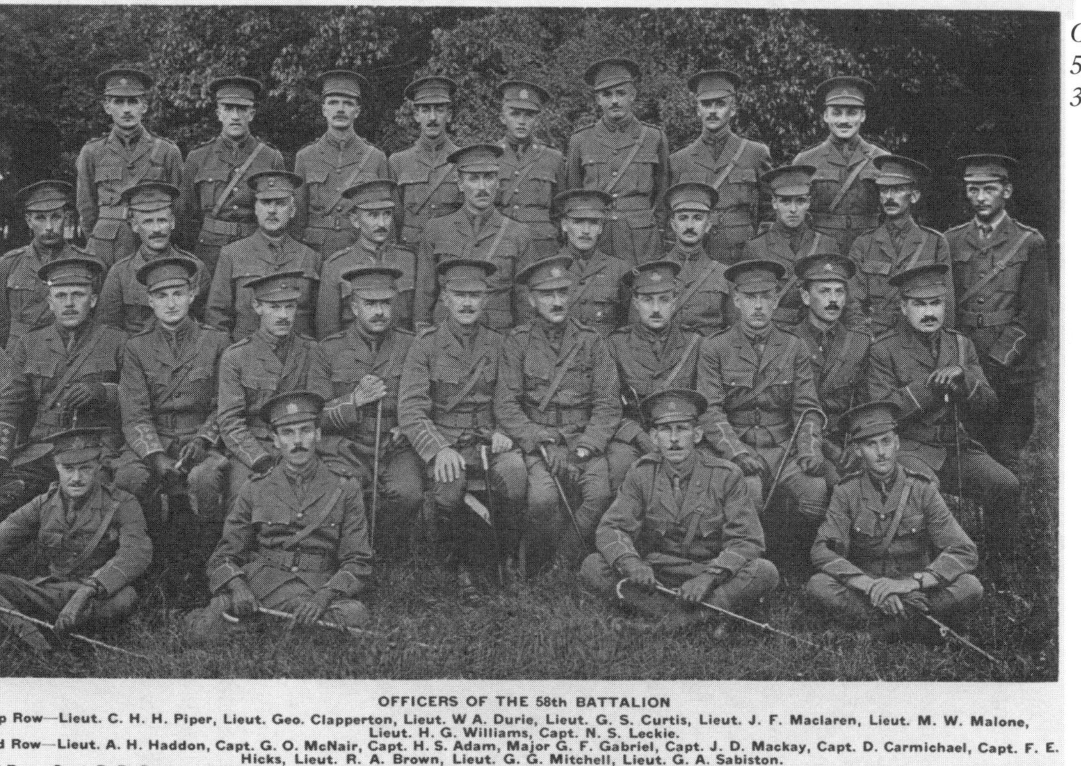

OFFICERS OF THE 58th BATTALION

Top Row—Lieut. C. H. H. Piper, Lieut. Geo. Clapperton, Lieut. W A. Durie, Lieut. G. S. Curtis, Lieut. J. F. Maclaren, Lieut. M. W. Malone, Lieut. H. G. Williams, Capt. N. S. Leckie.

2nd Row—Lieut. A. H. Haddon, Capt. G. O. McNair, Capt. H. S. Adam, Major G. F. Gabriel, Capt. J. D. Mackay, Capt. D. Carmichael, Capt. F. E. Hicks, Lieut. R. A. Brown, Lieut. G. G. Mitchell, Lieut. G. A. Sabiston.

3rd Row—Capt. D. D. Gunton, Q.M.; Capt. H. G. Cosbie, M.O.; Capt. S. T. Blackwood, Adj.; Major P. P. Ballachey, Senior Major; Major F. L. Bunton jr. Major; Lieut. Col. H. A. Genet, O.C.; Capt. T. W. Forwood, Paymaster; Lieut. J. A. Pearce, Sig. Officer; Lieut. King Eager, M.G.O.; Lieut. D.L. McKeard, Asst. Adjutant.

Front Row—Lieut. M. E. Gardner, Lieut. J. E. Ryerson, Lieut. F. H. N. Casey, Lieut. A. W. Macdonald.

Canada 3rdContingent.

bidden in case the keeper should be captured and the contents of the diary prove useful to the enemy.

The other ranks came from varied backgrounds. Nearly half had been born in England. When those of Irish, Scottish, and Welsh birth were added to the total, over half of the battalion was British-born. Native-born Canadians made up only about a third of the unit's strength when it sailed for Britain. This was very much the case with the entire Canadian Expeditionary Force at this stage in the war.[10] There was also a small handful of men born in other places in the Empire; British Guiana, South Africa, India, and the British West Indies were included in the list of birthplaces. Sixteen Americans were also recorded on the nominal roll, and one has to wonder why they volunteered for service overseas. Perhaps they felt their own country was too slow to take up a just cause, or perhaps they had family ties to the British Empire.[11] Could it be that they, like some of the other men, enlisted simply for the adventure of going off to war? There were additional Americans in the battalion, but they chose to hide their nationality. David Waldron, for example, was only sixteen, so he lied about both his age and his country of birth. He had bought his first pair of long trousers to make himself appear older when he presented himself at the recruiting office. He joined the battalion with Walter Matthews and Chester Baker, boyhood friends from his neighbourhood in Toronto's east end. His good friend Lorne Craig also listed his birthplace as Canada, but he had been born in Waukegon, Illinois, and his parents were living in New York State. Waldron would keep a diary of his experiences, from his arrival in France in February 1916 until the end of the war.

There were few members of the battalion who fit the romantic conception of Canadians as rugged outdoor types, such as ranchers, lumberjacks, and prospectors. One pair that may have fit that stereotype was James Douglas Rutherford and Herbert Ray Scott. Close friends, they came from New Ontario, as northern Ontario was known at the time. Rutherford was of pioneer stock: his family was homesteading in the Clay Belt around New Liskeard. An examination of the nominal roll reveals at least twenty pairs of brothers in the original list of volunteers, and possibly two father-and-son pairings. James

Henry Hookey Senior and Junior of 26 Markham Street, Toronto, were certainly one pair. It is possible that George Fretwell and George William Fretwell, both of 44 Hamilton Street in Toronto, were a second pair. One reason that these fathers and sons went to war may have been their interest in soldiering. All four men had been in the militia before the war.[12] The family of Emily Calver of Toronto provided six men for the battalion: three sons and three sons-in-law. One of them was fifteen-year-old Andrew J. Calver. He would go to England with the battalion, but eventually his mother would request his return home. Another was son-in-law Private James Farr, who had stopped in Toronto as he emigrated to Australia to visit his boyhood friend Percy Calver. On meeting his friend's sister Ruth, James decided to end his migration in Toronto.

The volunteers ranged in age from boys in their mid-teens to men in their fifties. Robert McKee, the author's grandfather, was a single man just shy of his thirtieth birthday. His parents had died before the war, and he was living with some of his siblings and their families. He seems a little old to have been swept up by the spirit of adventure. It may have been that he had a desire to "get away from it all" and the war provided his chance to break the strings that held him in Toronto. Fred Rosser, his future brother-in-law, was born in Oxford, England and had come to Canada in 1912. He married in Canada in 1914, but had no children. Perhaps he saw it as a means to return to the old country at government expense. Robert had enrolled in the 48th Highlanders, and Fred had served with the Governor General's Bodyguard; it may have been a sense of duty that caused them to volunteer for service overseas with the Canadian Expeditionary Force (C.E.F.). They, like so many others, left no record of the process by which they made the decision that would place them in the trenches of Flanders fields.

The battalion gathered at Paradise Camp in Niagara-on-the-Lake from June 23 to October 29, 1915. Equipment and uniforms were still in short supply. Initially, the men were issued clothes that made them look like Latin American farm workers. Several photographs show them in large floppy hats on route marches or relaxing around the camp. The route march involved going for long hikes, at times

Courtesy Waldron family.

The 58th on a route march, a staple of training at Paradise Camp, Niagara-on-the-Lake

Courtesy Waldron family.

The 58th Battalion at Paradise Camp, Niagara-on-the-Lake.

thirty-two kilometres, over a predetermined route. It was designed to build up the strength and condition of the men, for infantry units would move mainly on foot. Route marches became a specialty of the battalion, and there was great inter-company and inter-battalion rivalry as each unit strove to complete its march the fastest without

Courtesy Waldron family.

The 58th Battalion at Paradise Camp, Niagara-on-the-Lake.

losing any men along the way. George Cassels, later acting commanding officer of the battalion, considered this friendly rivalry to be the basis of the battalion's fine esprit de corps.[13] The men would spend hours on close order drill, where they would march around the parade grounds under the command of officers and noncommissioned officers (NCOs) to grow accustomed to acting as a unit and responding to commands without thinking. Because the tactics at the time expected men to close with the enemy and use the bayonet, time was spent stabbing straw-filled dummies with that knife-like weapon attached to the rifle. It is unlikely that the men were trained in map reading or the use of bombs or machine guns at this stage, for these essentials of modern warfare were not readily available for the units in the field even a year after the war began. The men were also inoculated against a variety of diseases during this period.

On August 11, the battalion was called on to send reinforcements to France for other units already in action. A smaller percentage of the 5 officers and 250 other ranks selected for the draft had military backgrounds (compared to the men who would go to England in the fall), but a greater proportion of those who did have experience had seen service with British units.[14] A number of men who were physically unfit or who could not stand the training were released during this period. One who had been rejected in the initial selection process returned on August 11. John "Pinky" Campbell had had his varicose veins treated before returning to the camp and dealt with the issue of his poor teeth by telling the medical officer he intended to shoot Germans, not bite them. On his own admission that he could play the piccolo he was accepted into the band.[15]

On August 22, the men posed for pictures sorted into their various sub units.[16] This series of photographs is particularly interesting because it is one of the few documents placing men in specific units. The Signaling Section shows the desperate shortage of equipment for training: the men are seen clutching semaphore flags. If these were ever to be used in the trenches, only tens of metres from the enemy, they would have brought certain death. There is only one Colt machine gun with the Machine Gun Section, although the normal scale of issue for a battalion was two. It is possible, of course, that the gun was only a prop for the photograph. Field telephones, trench mortars, and rifle grenades are nowhere in evidence.

Canada 3rd Contingent.

Signaling section 58th Battalion Canada 3rd Contingent.

Canada 3rd Contingent.

Machine Gun Section 58th Battalion Canada 3rd Contingent.

The 58th, along with the 34th, 35th, 37th, No. 2 Field Service Unit, and No. 2 Field Ambulance men, was also captured on film for Canada 3rd Contingent from 1st & 2nd Divisions Ontario.

September was a month of parades. On Labour Day, the battalion sailed from Niagara-on-the-Lake to Toronto to march in a parade through the city and return home again by ship. On September 22, Sir Sam Hughes, Minister of Militia, paid the camp a visit and inspected the troops. Not to be outdone by his minister, Sir Robert Borden, prime minister of Canada, also inspected the men and met the officers on September 25. These visits gave some weight to rumours that the battalion would be headed for England in the near future.[17] In late October, the 58th and the two other battalions training with it in the Niagara area marched to Toronto for the next stage of their training. The march was in the nature of a tactical exercise, and the men were ordered to treat it as if they had broken through the enemy defences and were in pursuit of the foe. Spirits were running high, and the defenders were inclined to take the exercise very seriously. On one occasion, they attacked the scouts by firing off blank ammunition inside the car the scouts were using, nearly blinding some of the occupants.[18] All of the men of the unit completed the 112-kilometre march without dropping out along the route. Training similar to that undertaken in Paradise Camp continued within the Exhibition Grounds.[19]

Courtesy Jane Cusler.

Final kit inspection before the 58th marched to Toronto from Niagara-on-the-Lake on October 29, 1915.

In preparation for the march to Toronto, the men were issued the Ross rifle. Sir Sam Hughes, minister of militia and a South African War veteran, preferred this rifle to the Lee-Enfield issued to British troops because of it greater accuracy as a target rifle. Until the march from Niagara-on-the-Lake, the men had been issued only belts and bayonets. They received Oliver harnesses for carrying equipment before the march. This was the same device used in the South African War, and it had not been very effective then, as while it was holding the men's equipment it tended to rise up and choke them.[20] They had dispensed with their floppy hats and were now in the standard Canadian battledress uniform with its stiff collar and peaked cap. In October the battalion received forty men from the 74th Battalion, and in November it received fifteen men from the 75th Battalion to make up for part of the draft sent to France as reinforcements.[21] Among them was Toronto-born Private Archie MacKinnon. Archie would send home a number of descriptive letters about life in the trenches. The last ten days in Toronto were spent on more route marches, which were recognized by all as a way of marking time before they shipped out for England.[22] The battalion boarded the Grand Trunk Railway train to Montreal early on a rainy November 20 and was seen off by the men of the 37th, 74th, and 75th Battalions.[23] Major General Logie, commander of the Exhibition Camp, saw a soldier on the platform with the 58th and forced him to board the train, even though he was from another unit. Because the guards would not let him off the train, he went all the way to England with the 58th and was taken on strength.[24] From Montreal, the Inter-Colonial Railway transported the men to Halifax. Private Doug Rutherford sent home a letter after arriving in England in which he specifically mentioned the good beds and food on this leg of the trip. The men had little to do other than play cards.

The train journey was in pleasant contrast to the sea voyage to England aboard the S.S. *Saxonia*, a converted Cunard liner — a journey that commenced on November 22.[25] The battalion arrived in the afternoon of that day and was immediately loaded on board. Captain Cosbie sent home a letter describing the trip and recorded the scene as the men clambered up the gangway: "There was a great crowd of people at the dock, and a band playing cheerful music, while the men crowded the rigging and whooped and howled to their hearts' content. It certainly is a wonder to me where they will ever put all the troops, about 3,000 in all. Well anyway at 5:27 we slipped out and were on our way."[26]

The 58th traveled with the 54th Kootenay Battalion and Number 1 Siege Battery of Halifax. The ship could comfortably carry eleven hundred troops; for this journey, it was packed with about twenty-four hundred. Lieutenant Colonel Genet noted the crowded conditions on board and described the meals as bad.[27] Lieutenant Ayton Leggo had a different opinion on the food he received, comparing it to that served in fine hotels, and in large quantity.[28] Private Rutherford's view was more in keeping with his commanding officer. Two days out of harbour, he was complaining about the meals in his letter to his sister: "...supper wasn't as good as it should be and the dinner was bum. For dinner we had potatoes cooked with their great

Courtesy Waldron family.

Troops aboard the S.S. Saxonia.

coats on and boiled meat, which I think came from the steer Noah had in the Ark." Captain Cosbie reported that the crew of the ship was selling sandwiches to the hungry men at three for twenty-five cents. The next day, Rutherford recorded the comment of one officer that the men had been treated too well in Niagara, and he wondered how this officer would fare when he tried to lead his men in France. Finally, on November 29, the men raided the canteen for a supply of good food. After that, the meals improved, and Rutherford wished they had taken action on the third day of the voyage. The ship was too crowded to do much but eat and play cards, which may account for the emphasis on food in Rutherford's letter.[29] The threat of enemy submarine attacks near the coast of Ireland added to the discomfort of the voyage and created some of the tensions that the men would feel next as they approached the battlefield. They were ordered to sleep in their clothes and wear their life belts at this point in the voyage. The stress of the warning affected the chaplain, Captain Charles Jeakins, to the point where he approached Captain Cosbie for a remedy to his sleeplessness. The ship traveled at a slower pace each day than at night and was without escort until it approached Ireland, where it was joined by two destroyers as protection against the submarine threat. When the men heard that a transport loaded with horses had been torpedoed recently within twenty-four kilometres of their route, they were all glad to come ashore.

The *Saxonia* arrived at Plymouth, England with its escort on December 1. The men boarded a train for Liphook, Hampshire the next day. Captain Cosbie noted the reception they received as the train moved to its destination. "All along the way the people came to doors and windows, or stopped on the streets as the train rushed by and took of [sic] their hats and cheered, some old women putting out their washing would drop it, pick up a shirt and wave it."[30] After arrival at Liphook they walked twelve kilometres with full packs and empty stomachs through rain and mud to Bramshott Camp.[31] They did not follow the First Contingent's trail to the muddy Salisbury Plain. Instead, they moved into the area vacated by Lord Kitchener's New Army. This was fortunate, for it turned out to be another rainy winter, with mud fifteen centimetres deep, even at Bramshott.[32] The men went into barracks, but there were no quarters for the officers, who were taken in by the officers of the 60th Battalion.[33] Initially, the battalion trained under the 4th Canadian Division. The syllabus was very similar to that which the battalion had followed in Canada, with much marching, physical training, bayonet fighting, musketry, and parade ground drill. However, bombing with hand grenades (at this point in the war these were homemade affairs known as "hair brush" or "jam tin" bombs, soon to be replaced by the more reliable Mills bomb), machine gun tactics, and signalling also became important parts of the syllabus. Lieutenant Joyce's diary contains references to bombing and machine gun courses, which took him away from the regular training with the battalion. In a letter to his family dated December 13, Lieutenant Cusler mentions spending six hours a day in physical training. Discipline was tough, and Private Rutherford's letter mentions that offences that would result in two days' punishment in Niagara would now get ten at Bramshott.[34] Since a large percentage of the officers and men had been born in Great Britain, the stay in England was a homecoming for many. About half the men were able to enjoy Christmas with their families, but others had to be content with the army-issue Christmas dinner of turkey and pudding and the minstrels brought in by the officers for their entertainment. All appreciated the frequent granting of leave; the men could visit family and friends or simply take the time to visit London and its famous attractions. When the men were not on active training, there was time to write letters home or use some of the recreational facilities provided within the camp. The unit's first casualties came in England. On January 3, Private Oscar Gallagher of D Company died of spinal meningitis and was buried on January 5.[35] On January 6, twenty-two-year-old Bugler Harry Rance fell victim to the same illness. Even today, this disease is often reported among groups of young people in high schools who share drinks or cigarettes; so perhaps it is not surprising that it would fell some healthy young soldiers. It had been a problem for the First Contingent as well.[36] Gallagher and Rance would not be the last men to die of disease while in the service of their country, but the incidence of this type of casualty would turn out to be much lower than in previous wars, despite the appalling conditions the men would face in the trenches. The unit made good progress in its training, and by mid-January the word began to circulate that the 58th had been selected to go to France.[37] On January 27, there was a reassignment of officers, with Major Cassels taking command of A Company and Captain Carmichael moving to C Company. This move was seen by Joyce as "a rotten piece of work all round. If this shiftyness and wire pulling goes on the 58th will crack up."[38] Joyce was particularly upset by the actions of Captain McKeand, the adjutant, who, like Captain MacKay, was also a veteran of the Boer War. In February, the unit was officially selected for inclusion in the new 9th Brigade of the 3rd Canadian Division, along with the 43rd from Winnipeg, the 52nd from Port Arthur, and the 60th from Montreal. It would be in France just eight months after its formation, less time than many battalions took to reach England. There was some additional shuffling of officers to new appointments, and not all of them would go to France immediately. The officers and men were issued British army web equipment to replace the inefficient Oliver harness, and Lieutenant Leggo found it more comfortable than the old leather material.[39] As the battalion prepared to leave England, Lieutenant Cusler wrote home to his family to assure them that he now had some familiarity with machine guns and grenades and the methods of delivering the latter type of weapon.[40] When the battalion moved to France, both Cusler and Leggo were left behind, along with Lieutenants Durie, Macdonald, Walker, and Curtis.[41] Leggo would eventually be transferred to the Cavalry Corps, then to the Royal Flying Corps, and would be shot down over France in 1917. Archie MacKinnon wrote a short note to his family letting them know he was "...going to France or trenches this afternoon. I have 120 rounds of ammunition now and bayonet sharpened already for anybody."[42] The band put its instruments in storage, and the persistent Pinky Campbell and his fellow bandsmen went to France as stretcher-bearers. On February 20, the battalion moved to Southampton prior to crossing the English Channel to Le Havre and France.

On arrival in France, the 9th Brigade would join the 7th and 8th Brigades of the 3rd Division. The 7th contained the Princess Patricia's Canadian Light Infantry, the Royal Canadian Regiment, the only regular battalion in the pre-war Canadian Army, and the 42nd and 49th Battalions. The 8th Brigade was composed of the 1st, 2nd, 4th, and 5th battalions of the Canadian Mounted Rifles, which were converted to infantry units before being sent to France.

A short poem that was printed just before the battalion left for France seems to catch the mood of the men as they headed for the front:

> There's a dear old spot in Canada,
> That's where I'd like to be,
> But while the war is raging,
> This is the place for me.
>
> They said "Young Man we need you,
> We like the looks of you,
> Here, sign your name, three times,"
> The Doctor said, "You'll do."

They gave me a new uniform,
My Room and Board were free,
A dollar ten for nothing,
That's the life for me.

They sent me to Niagara,
To get in fighting trim,
That, when I'd meet the Kaiser,
I'd put one over him.

Then they sent me over to England,
To get some further training,
Old England is a fine place,
But it's nearly always raining.

We'll soon be going to the Front,
To meet Old Hans and Fritz,
They say it's very cold o'er there,
So send some socks and mitts

Don't worry about me at the Front,
We'll stop the Germans noise,
If anybody can do it,
The 58th are the Boys.

But I must leave off writing,
I hear the Cook-house blow,
I'm with a bunch of hungry guys,
So it don't pay to be slow.

But just before we part again,
Let us both rise and sing,
The Maple Leaf for ever,
And then God Save the King.

Anonymous

Chapter One

February and March 1916
Entering the Zone of Stealth

There had been continuous fighting along the Western Front since August 1914, and Canadian troops had been in the thick of it since April 1915. The 58th Battalion would now take its place in the order of battle. On February 20, 1916, the unit began moving to France from Bramshott Camp. The troops embarked at Southampton on February 21, arriving in France on the twenty-second. They landed the day after the Germans began a major offensive against the French at Verdun. This attack had limited territorial objectives, but it was designed to bleed the French Army white as it fought to retain control of a place with powerful symbolic meaning for France. Verdun and its fortresses held the gate to the Champagne Plain and controlled the direct route to Paris. During the Franco-Prussian War of 1870, the fortress garrisons there were the last to surrender to the Prussians. In 1914, they had survived the German onslaught and had given the French time to create the so-called miracle of the Marne, when the troops in Paris rushed to the Marne River by taxi and autobus in order to stop the German drive to the capital city.

The battalion moved by train from Le Havre to Godersvelde (modern day Godewaersvelde) in Belgium. Private Waldron wrote of riding in a boxcar with twelve men and three horses. The body heat of the horses kept the rest of them warm on a cold day.[43] On the twenty-third, the unit was billeted in farms near St. Sylvestre-Cappel, a short distance southwest of Godersvelde. It was now near the base of the roughly isosceles triangle that was the murderous Ypres salient. A salient is a sharp bulge in a defensive line that protrudes into enemy positions. As a result of their determination to hold this slice of Belgian territory, the British were vulnerable to artillery fire from German guns on either side of the salient, and it was artillery fire that would cause many, if not most, of the casualties suffered by the 58th during its time at Ypres. The Canadian 1st Division had held the line here after the first poison gas attack of the war on April 22, 1915, in what was known as the Second Battle of Ypres. The routine for the next five days included company drills and route marches in preparation for moving to the front lines.

The prevailing weather was cold and clear. The land was very flat, with some of the prominent tactical features being only sixty metres above sea level. Such high points as Hill 60, Hill 62, and Observatory Ridge were key to the defence of the British line, as they prevented the Germans from seeing all of the British positions and allowed the British to view the German positions. The area inside the salient had become a wasteland. The villages had been damaged to the point that it was difficult to find even rubble on the ground. The closer one moved toward the front, the less the trees looked like trees and the more they resembled matchwood. The smell of death permeated the salient.

The month of March eventually brought the battalion into contact with the enemy, after they were introduced in stages to the harsh realities of war on the Western Front. For ten days, they camped at Aldershot Huts, where they were given a more realistic expectation of what life in the trenches would be like. It seems probable that they were introduced to trench mortars, stand-tos, sniping posts, field telephones, and other essentials of war on the Western Front. Now, in the "zone of stealth" — a band of territory about six kilometres wide extending from the Belgian coast on the North Sea to Switzerland — they would make all of their moves into and out of the line at night, using communication trenches dug from one line of trenches to another. Movement above ground in daylight anywhere in the zone of stealth would attract small arms or artillery fire and would invite an early death. Fortunately, there were trench maps to make order out of a maze of deep ditches. The trenches all had names; usually, groupings of trenches had the same first letter (Able, Acorn, and Acre, for example), but often they were named after a place or event of significance to the unit that dug them. Whatever their names, they were difficult to negotiate in the dark. This meant units coming into the line needed a guide. Because the confusion that accompanied the relief of one unit by another often created an opportunity for the enemy to attack, it had to be carried out as quietly as possible to avoid drawing an enemy response. For their first experience of the front, the men were sent on working parties with more experienced battalions from the 1st Division and then placed in the lines with these units, two platoons at a time. One entry in Private Waldron's diary records that he spent time burying telephone cable to protect it from enemy artillery fire, and another entry describes the weather as so cold that he "nearly froze to death" while in the line.[44] Meanwhile, the senior officers and Battalion Sergeant Major Quinn attended a course at Ash House. On March 10, the battalion moved from the Aldershot Huts to Fletre. There were two more days of instruction, this time in the art of bombing with hand grenades and in the use of gas masks. Throwing a hand grenade was not like throwing a baseball. Rising out of the trench to make a pitch-like throw would likely be fatal. Rather, a soldier had to use his arm as a kind of catapult, lobbing the grenade out of the trench and over the sandbagged parapet. A gas mask had to be worn properly to be effective, and the men usually tried the device in a hut filled with tear gas to see they had donned it properly. Tears in their eyes would tell them if they had not learned their lessons well.

The 58th was at that time attached to the 4th Brigade, which was in the line at Vierstraat, about five kilometres south of Ypres. The next move was from Fletre to an overnight billet in Loker, before marching to Vierstraat on March 16 in order to relieve the 52nd Battalion. The next six days would give these untried soldiers their first taste of trench warfare. The opposing forces held trenches that were less than seventy metres apart, and Waldron described the ground of No Man's Land as "flat as a billiard table." The trench routine usually started with a "stand-to" at dawn. All the soldiers would be on the firing step of the trench to watch for a surprise enemy attack. Some units would practice a "mad minute" and fire off their weapons in the general direction of the enemy lines, hoping to hit an unsuspecting enemy well behind the front. The morning rations would be brought forward from the battalion kitchen. Usually, there would be a rum issue to restore the men after a cold, damp night in the trenches. After breakfast, the men who had been on duty the night before would try to get some rest in the shallow scrapes or "funk holes" along the side of the trench. The rest of the unit would work on repairing or improving the trench or would organize and ready themselves for attack or defence. The evening meal would come up near dark, and again the unit would stand to in case of an attack as the sun went down. Those chosen for sentry duty would remain at their posts. Some men might be tasked for patrols in no man's land or for carrying and working parties. These jobs were best performed at night to avoid enemy observation and interference in the form of shelling or small arms fire.

The first day in the front line on March 17 saw heavy rifle and machine gun fire, but there were no casualties. Waldron recorded his experience of being shot at by enemy machine gunners as he went back for rations; he had to lie between the rails of the tramway and watch sparks fly from the rails as the bullets struck.[45] The first casualty occurred during the clear, mild morning of the next day when Lance Corporal William Clare was killed. Born in England, Clare had served in the Governor General's Bodyguard, a Toronto militia unit, and had joined the 58th in that city on July 1, 1915. The battalion had to sit and take it when the Germans started a heavy artillery attack in the early morning of March 19, but it suffered no casualties. Captain Cosbie's first letter to his mother after arriving in the salient sought to reassure her he was in no danger. He was located at a Casualty Clearing Station in an old brewery protected by sandbags almost five hundred metres behind the front line.

> Life in the trenches themselves is comparatively safe, as up there the parapet completely protects you, and the German trenches are so close (only sixty yards away at one spot) that their artillery cannot shell us without the danger of hitting their own trenches. The Germans are great boys for putting up Star lights and the line certainly looks like the Exhibition fire works at night.
>
> The work of the aeroplanes is wonderful. All the artillery fire on both sides is directed by them, or else from great captive observation balloons. The German aeroplanes come over three or four times a day and the Anti Aircraft guns crack and the British planes go up after them, but up to the present I have not seen a real scrap in the air.[46]

Private Waldron recorded in his diary that the men tried to kill some of the hordes of rats sharing the trenches with the soldiers by baiting their bayonets with cheese and then stabbing or shooting the hungry rodents.[47] Private George Fretwell of D Company died of wounds on the twentieth. From the information in the nominal roll, it appears that he joined the battalion in July 1915, and his son joined the following month. Lieutenants Joyce and Howard spent the early morning hours of March 21 attacking the German trenches with machine gun fire and grenades. Canadian artillery joined in at 5:00 A.M. with a thirty-minute barrage.[48] Lieutenant Joyce's diary gives a description of the last day in the line before the battalion's relief on March 22.

> They gave us some nasty H. E. [high explosive] Shells all day on C. Co.'s frontage and continued to put shrapnel into Bois Carre but no casualties. One hole in our parapet. Thirteen men hurt last night in the com'n trench. We came out tonight pitch dark rain & cold and got to billets at S. A very miserable night.[49]

While the battalion was at billets in Lokre, Archie MacKinnon wrote to his sister, giving her a glimpse of life in the trenches after the 58th's first tour:

> I have been here at the front for 6 weeks and only been in the Front Line of trenches 6 days. We are having a good time here although it has been a little tough. I am in good health & working every day. Today is Sunday & I work all day but still we like it. Old Fritz is badly beaten but I should worry he won't last long.[50]

During March, the headlines of the Toronto and Hamilton papers were dominated by the French success in repulsing the German attack at Verdun. The issue of conscription was being discussed at this stage of the war, even before Canadian casualties hit their peaks later in the conflict. At this time, the numbers of Canadian dead and wounded were low enough that the papers could identify casualties by their units. Before the end of June, the volume of dead and wounded increased to the point that men were simply listed in alphabetical order. The *Daily Mail and Empire* for March 20 listed Private Arthur A. Allen among the wounded and identified Lance Sergeant Frederick Mellor, also wounded, on the twenty-first. On the twenty-third and twenty-fourth, the men attended their first bath parade, just over a month after their arrival on the Western Front. The official record makes no mention of lice, but Captain Cosbie quoted Captain Adam in a letter to his mother writing that "there is no rest for the wicked or lousy. Of the former I know nothing quoth Cap. but of the latter I know it to be true,"[51] so this scourge of the front-line soldier had infested the men of the 58th. Since the seams of the men's clothes were likely to be the site of the lice and their eggs, it was difficult for the men to remove them. As a result, they were often given fresh clothing, which didn't always fit, and they were able to concentrate on the removal of the lice from their persons, not always successfully. It was important to keep the lice under control because they were the host of the bacteria, Bartonella quintana, that caused "trench fever" in the men.[52] This disease could lead to gangrene and death. The men were also entertained at a concert in a local cinema. The rest was short, and, on the twenty-ninth, the unit was in brigade reserve at the Railway Dugouts. Here they again supplied working parties and held several strong points. Lieutenant Durie had rejoined the battalion at this time and went up to the front lines for the first time with one of these working parties. The unit was subjected to heavy shelling by the enemy on March 31, and there were five more casualties from shell splinters.

The Human Balance Sheet

Killed	2
Wounded	6

Chapter Two

April 1916
Taking the Strain

On April 1, the battalion returned to the front-line trenches in relief of the 43rd Battalion. The War Diary describes the occupied area as "the left sub-sector of the Left Sector," still in the Ypres area. They were north of the area they had occupied in March and near the village of Hooge. From here, the men of the battalion were able to overlook the enemy trenches and observe movements back to Clonmel Copse and Stirling Castle, two enemy positions south of the Menin Road. Private Waldron and two friends went on a tour of the enemy front line that night. During this front-line assignment, casualties were light, reflecting only harassing fire from the enemy. The Diary records sniper fire on two days out of four. Private Waldron's diary notes the death of Private Frank Richard Graham, who was shot by an enemy sniper and died on April 4. Lieutenant Durie wrote to his sister Helen, giving her a good picture of what he was doing.

> My dearest Helen
>
> I am writing you this letter from a dugout in the trenches. We are on our last day and are going out tomorrow for a short rest. While I am writing there is a sanguinary bombardment going on.

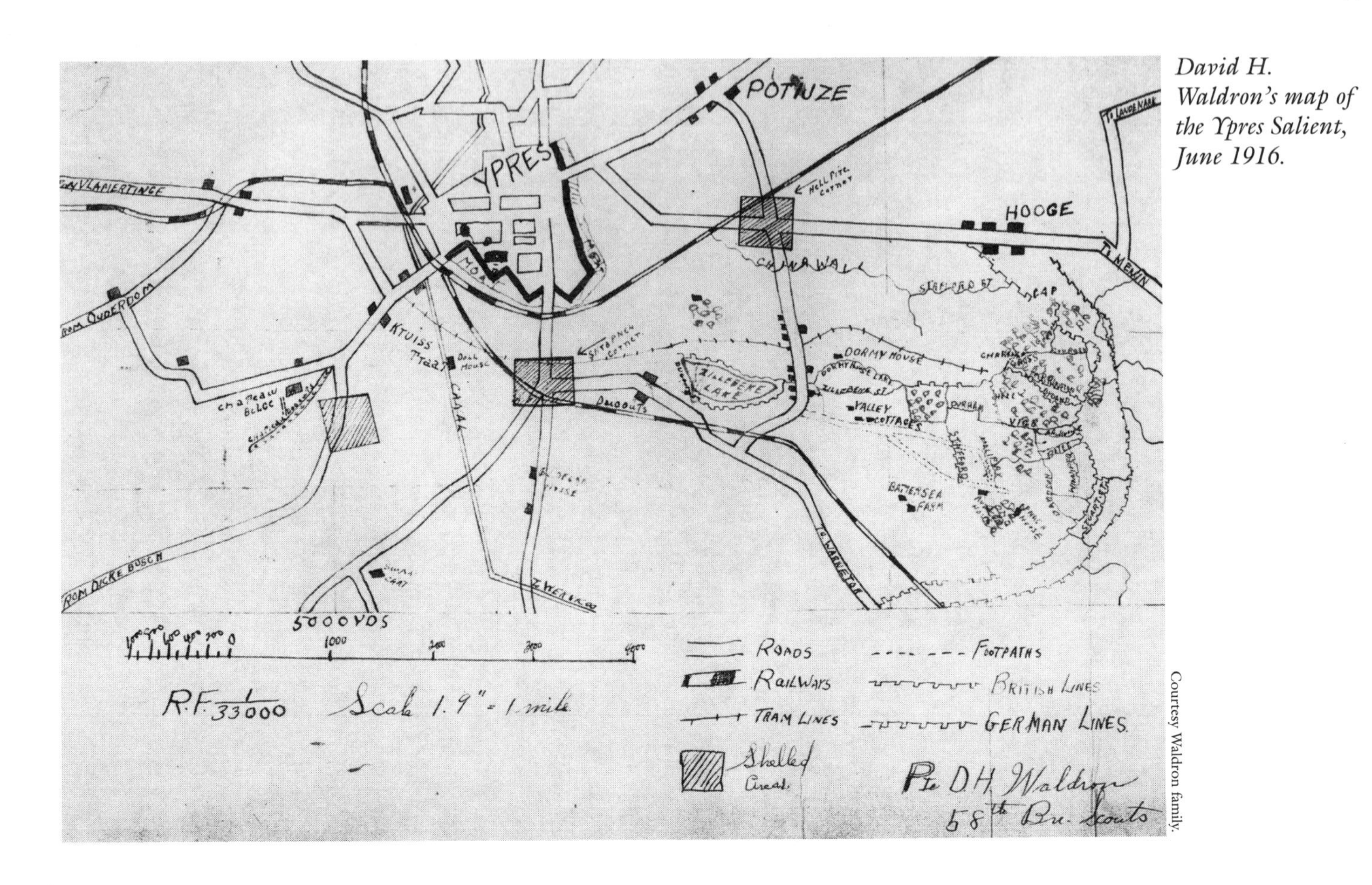

David H. Waldron's map of the Ypres Salient, June 1916.

Courtesy Waldron family.

I have been on two working parties, and I have been twice in No-Man's Land visiting a listening post at night. You have to jump over the parapet. The first time I did it I had a queer feeling, but I was not afraid. If you go into No Man's Land and a flare comes you stand perfectly still. If you see the flare in time you flatten on the ground. It seemed so strange to be out in front, though I was only about fifty or a hundred yards out, and to see our men and the Germans firing at one another. So far I have been on night work, that is walking up and down the front line seeing that the sentries are on the job.

I shall probably write to-morrow and as often as much as I can, and I wish you would write to me as often as possible.

Your affectionate brother,
W.A.P. Durie[53]

The battalion remained in the front line until relieved by the 43rd on the night of April 5 and 6. They marched back to Camp E to serve as brigade reserve. The next three days were spent in physical training, route marches, and musketry or rifle practice. The unit's firepower was increased on the receipt of four Lewis guns, or light machine guns.[54] The Lewis gun would eventually replace the Colt medium machine guns the battalion had originally brought to France. It weighed about 16 kilograms with a loaded magazine holding 47 rounds of ammunition and, in the hands of a capable operator, could fire 150 rounds a minute.[55] The battalion also managed a soccer match against the 1st Canadian Mounted Rifles, which they won by a score of three to one. They marched back into the trenches on April 9. Action was more intense, and the unit's experience of trench warfare was growing. The Diary reports that the enemy shelled the trenches with 5.9-inch shells.[56] Lieutenant Joyce was reassigned to D Company and was mildly disappointed by the move. On the night of April 11, he stayed awake and threw grenades into a crater held by the Germans. His comment in his diary was that the lines were only forty yards apart at some points.[57] This spell in the front line cost the battalion three dead and five wounded.

Waldron was out on patrol on the eleventh and twelfth.[58] Sometimes patrols were small affairs with only three or four men. Waldron reports on the eleventh that he was in the company of his friend Chester Baker and George Rollo. The following night, Doug Rutherford, Ray Scott, and another soldier joined him. Patrols were used to locate weaknesses in the enemy defences prior to a raid, or to deter enemy patrols from coming too close to the Canadian lines. Often the men started out with a compass bearing or a wire to guide them in the direction of the enemy lines. They ran a real danger of becoming lost in No Man's Land, since the ground was constantly changing as shells exploded and new trenches and saps were dug. They generally had to crawl about on all fours to avoid being silhouetted against the horizon. They would have to freeze into immobility if either side fired an illumination flare, as sentries easily detected movement. On the first night, the Canadian trio was surprised by a German patrol, but Waldron and his friends managed to return safely to their own lines. The next night they turned the tables on the Germans and ambushed them, killing two with hand grenades.

Lieutenant Joyce's entry in his diary for April 12 gives a good snapshot of trench life and mentions a problem that affected the performance of the Ross rifle.

> Turned in at 4:30 A. M. and got up at 11 A. M. cold and rainy. The men are sleeping around on the firing step in the open owing to the lack of dugout accomodation [sic], very rotten. Quite a lot of shelling on our right. We are now in the apex of the Ypres Salient. Some S.A.A. [Small Arms Ammunition] marked U. S. is rotten. The bullet can be pulled from the cartridge case with the fingers and the cordite [explosive] instead of being stranded & wadded pours out like black powder. We canned the lot. On duty til midnight.[59]

The battalion was relieved by the 1st Canadian Mounted Rifles on the night of April 13, and four of Lieutenant Joyce's men were slightly wounded by shrapnel in the process of moving out of the front line trenches to the "safer" support areas. The battalion was slow leaving the front line trenches and so missed a ride back to their billets on the narrow-gauge railway, as the train stopped running near dawn. On the first night out of the line, the men were entertained by a band at the local cinema.[60] While in the rest area, they had their second bath. They provided working parties of about half the battalion on one day and one night and managed to win another soccer match against the 52nd Battalion by a score of two to zero. Again the men were billeted in farm buildings. One man was so tired and wet from the working party that he lay down to sleep in the cow stable. He awoke with a bump when the cow sharing the billet with him gave birth to a calf, soaking his great coat with amniotic fluid. He had to go on parade without his coat, since it was soaking wet, and this led Major Cassels to question him and learn the story.[61] On the seventeenth, Joyce was again assigned to the Machine Gun Section. Before they returned to the trenches, they had an inter-company soccer match, which was won by B Company.

On April 21, they began the move back into the trenches. Part of the battalion moved into Zillebeke Bund, just under a kilometre southeast of Ypres. The balance of the unit went to the Belgian Château, about two kilometres west of Ypres, in brigade support. Joyce described it as "a rotten place filthy with mud and cold."[62] Two days later, the unit was subjected to heavy German shelling, and one of the dugouts received a direct hit from a 5.9-inch (150mm) high explosive shell. Major Norman Leckie and three other ranks were killed, and Captain Mitchell and nine soldiers were wounded. "Tout" Leckie had joined the battalion as a captain and had been promoted in England. The son of the Hamilton City Treasurer, he had graduated from Queen's University as a mining engineer and had a prominent career as a football player at college and with the Toronto Argonauts.[63] It is likely that another of the casualties was Sergeant William Warwick, a fire captain, also from Hamilton. His death was reported in the *Spectator* on May 1. For the first time, the Diary notes casualties from shell shock, just two months after the battalion's arrival in France. "Shell shock" was the term to describe what in the Second World War would be known as "battle fatigue" and in the present day as "post-traumatic stress disorder." It was not well understood at the time, and medical opinion linked it to the effects of the concussion from exploding shells. Captain Cosbie, the medical officer, mentioned two cases in a letter to his father. "The effect of what are known as H.E.s or High Explosives is terrific. They simply blow things to smithereens, and two of the men in one of the huts, which was hit are pitiable examples of shell shock, which happily is not a long existing condition, they generally get over it in a few days, but at present are sitting dazed and muttering to themselves, quite unconscious of their surroundings."[64] Since many personal accounts of action at the front refer to men being buried by exploding shells, the connection seems a reasonable one. Symptoms of the illness include an unwillingness to return to the trenches, a raving madness, or a comatose condition. American psychiatrists accompanying combat troops into action during the Second World War noted that men reached their most effective state for combat about three weeks after reaching the front. By the time the men had spent six weeks in action, they had already begun to see their death as inevitable, and their ability to function was impaired. The condition could be brought on by the stress of combat or constant shelling and the exposure to the elements. The Americans came to the conclusion that, after about 200 to 240 days in action, everyone would break down. Private Archie MacKinnon provides an example of how some men saw their future even after only a few months in the trenches. In a letter written to his family in March, he had expressed the belief that the Germans would soon be finished. In a letter dated April 19, less than a month later, he writes:

> Well I have been writing this letter for 3 or 4 days now this is Easter Sunday & is a dandy day only Old Fritz is handing over some eggs & is making us look out. He has been shelling us all day. We have had 12 days of rain and everything is very muddy & lots of water. Well we are going to celebrate the battle that

> took place here last year soon. I am getting along fine & in good health. I wish I could go out on a motor-cycle these fine mornings but I should worry. I suppose you people are wondering when the war will be over but I guess it will last another week anyway. I don't think it will last very long for me cause I am expecting it [death or wounding] every day.[65]

One way to prevent the total collapse of a unit's fighting effectiveness was to give it time out of the line in more amenable conditions, allowing the men to rest and restore their spirits.[66] Unfortunately, because psychiatry was a new profession in the First World War, the idea of treating soldiers well when they appeared to be malingering was not commonly accepted. The High Command of the British army feared that all soldiers would seek a diagnosis of shell shock as an "easy way out" and that there would be no one left to defend the trenches. Harsher treatments, like electric shock therapy, were prescribed for those who exhibited extreme symptoms of the illness.[67] Another way to keep up a unit's fighting efficiency was to supply fresh reinforcements to replace the inevitable casualties. One could assume that the reason more units did not disintegrate was that many men were killed or wounded before they could suffer psychological breakdown.

On April 24, the battalion was again subjected to a shelling by 5.9-inch guns and suffered four more casualties, including three from shell shock. These losses occurred while the unit was in brigade support, providing working parties that could be involved in road building, trench digging, or carrying supplies to front line troops. They were shelled again on the twenty-fifth. On April 26, there was a major shelling of the Belgian Château area about eight kilometres behind the forward Canadian positions, and again there were casualties. That evening, the unit was subjected to a combined shrapnel and tear gas attack, its first exposure to one of the new horrors of trench warfare. Joyce gives an account of the strafe:

> At 6:30 pm a terrific bombardment began, the Huns shelling all our routes. I started with a working party

> for Hooge but was turned back in YPRES and arrived home O.K. All working parties held up. Poor Herbie Daw got through with his party and was killed. There was fighting also at St. Eloi. It was a rough night.[68]

Lieutenant Herbert Daw, second in command of B Company, was killed, and three other ranks were wounded. Daw was a Hamilton lawyer whose death was reported on the same day as that of Sergeant Warwick under the headline, "Lieutenant Daw and Sert.-Major Warwick Make Sacrifice."[69] On April 27, B Company and two sections of bombers moved up to Zillebeke Bund. On the twenty-eighth, the unit was subjected to another early morning artillery attack, and this time the 5.9s were joined by 8-inch (21cm) howitzer shells. Fortunately, there were no casualties. Lieutenant Colonel Genet and Captain McKeand inspected the trenches. On the twenty-ninth, the battalion went into the front line in relief of the 43rd Battalion and suffered one casualty. They were not molested by the enemy on the thirtieth, despite an attack on the 2nd Division to their right.

The Human Balance Sheet

	April	**Cumulative**
Killed	12	14
Wounded	37	43
Shell Shock	7	7

Chapter Three

May 1916
Dishing it Out

May 1 marked the first time the battalion was directly attacked by enemy infantry. It had returned to the front line the day before. The weather was clear and mild, with winds from the northeast. At 3:30 in the afternoon, the Germans shelled two of the battalion's strong points with shrapnel from 77mm field artillery, wounding one soldier. At 6:30 P.M., Trench 63 and the support and communication trenches behind it were subjected to fire from trench mortars firing 250mm mortar bombs weighing anywhere from 25 to 95 kilograms. This mortaring was the prelude to a trench raid. It did serious damage to the trenches and the telephone wires back to the artillery. Communications were maintained by runner Private Campbell making three trips through heavy fire to deliver messages. At 8:15 P.M., the shelling ceased, and the enemy was seen to leave his trenches. Battalion rifle and machine gun fire, supported by field artillery, drove the Germans back to their trenches before they could penetrate the front line of the battalion. According to the Diary, Captain Adam remained cool and kept the situation in hand at all times, despite being blown off his feet three times by exploding shells. Lieutenant Robert A. Macfarlane was one of the first to notice the Germans leaving their trenches and was reported to have jumped up on the parapet of the trench to fire at them with his revolver. Sergeant Harry G. Edmison sent home a first hand account of the action:

> For two days it was quiet, and then on May 1st (a big holiday in Germany) things were let loose. About four o'clock in the afternoon they started to shell our trench over about a mile of front, and for four hours they put over everything they owned, from 3-inch shrapnel to 15-inch Jack Johnsons, besides everything in bombs, grenades and trench mortar stuff that was ever invented. Old timers of the First Division [C.E.F.] and Imperial Forces tell us it was the heaviest bombardment they ever saw while it lasted. The only thing that saved us was that our front lines are only about 50 yards apart,[70] and they had to put most of the heavy stuff into our support lines to avoid their own. As it was I lost one-third of my platoon [about ten men]. Suddenly their artillery stopped entirely, as it had got fairly dark, and their famous Prussian Guards swarmed over the parapets in their old mass style. Our fellows waited until a bunch of them got over, and then mowed them down. Of the hundreds that came out and started, only one that I know of got to our trench. He was a Prussian Guard captain, and they brought him in, wounded in three places. I don't know what their casualties could have been, for we buried more-and they were only the ones close up to our trench-than we lost in our wounded and killed together. When we got them chased well back, our artillery started, and what they gave us was only a joke to what our guns poured into their lines.[71]

The rifles and machine guns of Sergeant Edmison's men were effective to about eighteen hundred metres, and the soldiers were expected to fire them accurately to ranges of over five hundred metres.

It should have been no surprise that they inflicted heavy casualties on the Germans at a range of less than forty-five metres.

Archie MacKinnon brought his family up to date on life in the trenches and included a few comments about the same action.

> Dear Sister
>
> Recd your letters & 3 parcels O.K. & certainly was pleased to rec them. I have been very busy lately & had some experiences. You say I am a lot fatter in picture. Gee you ought to see me now. You seem to think I have an awful load to carry but that is only 3 parts of it. I certainly can stand some awful knocking around. We were in trenches for 16 days counting Reserves & Front Line & am out for 16 days rest as they call it. I think when the 58 comes back Ray will be saying My Archie isn't there. It only takes 1 small bullet. It is too bad about Ray being sick. I hope he never stutters. Too bad about Mac McArthur. Gee there seems to be a lot of fellows enlisting. I can tell them something & I hope from the bottom of my heart Ronnie [his brother would arrive in Flanders the next month] never gets hear [sic]. You want to know what to send me well biscuits or cake anything to eat & all kinds of Keatings [anti-lice powder] this is some place for lice, Good night.... You asked me if I were scared when I first went in trenches well no I wasn't. I thought nobody could wish for a better place until I seen wounded fellows & fellows getting killed along side of me and have to pick up pieces & put them in blanket for to be buried. War is no joke. I have been hit five times but not serious it was shrapnel.[72] I was hit 4 times in a battle were [sic] your girl's friend was wounded. All Canadian bn are here together. I was buried in & cover clean up once & my friends dug me out. So you can imagine how I like warfare but don't think

> I don't get back at them. They shelled us hard for 2 hours & tried to take our trench. When they come over the parapet believe me I put bullets & bombs into them as fast as I could but they didn't get our trench we were only 35 yds apart so you know how quick we act. Poor Old Fritz dead men laid in No Man's Land all that night & next day. We only got 15 prisoners and 2 were officers. I went after them and I was so excited I didn't know what to do only give it to them. So you think [the] 58 ain't in those battles. Well I am glad [to] be on this side [of the] firing line any way....[73]

The result of the mortar attack and the repulse of the enemy raid was the highest one-day casualty total for the battalion since coming to France. Captain George O. McNair and eight other ranks were killed. Fourteen men were wounded. Private Waldron wrote that he and his friend Frank Cormack were blown over and that Cormack went back to hospital as a result.[74] Six more men were victims of shell shock, and, for the first time, twelve soldiers were missing. While it was possible that some of the missing would turn up later, it was a feature of trench warfare and constant shelling that some men would be hit by shells and their bodies totally blown apart. Alternatively, their bodies could be battered beyond recognition after they fell, or they could be buried by the soil thrown up as more shells continued to land in the same small area. Even if their comrades managed to locate and bury them with some measure of dignity, graves near the front were often obliterated by the constant shelling and all trace of them forever lost.

The battalion remained in the lines until May 7, but the remainder of the week was relatively uneventful in comparison to the first day. Each day brought some shelling and the threat of gas attacks, but the enemy remained in his trenches. Lieutenant Durie was wounded in the chest and right lung by a stray round while riding on horseback behind the lines on the night of May 4. He had been acting as paymaster while Captain Forwood was in England.

He survived to be evacuated to hospital. On the sixth, the Germans carried out a rifle grenade attack on the Appendix, a section of trench on the eastern side of Sanctuary Wood that faced the enemy position known as Stirling Castle. The rifle grenade provided the infantry with a means of launching a small anti-personnel bomb a longer distance than could be achieved by muscle power. The grenade was attached to a wooden or metal rod, and the rod was inserted in the barrel of a rifle. It was propelled out of the rifle by the firing of a blank rifle cartridge. During the grenade attack, Lieutenant Henry R. Thomson and one man were wounded, and two other ranks were killed.

On the night of May 6, there was a gas alert, the first mention of one in the Diary. It was recorded at 11:35 P.M. The Germans' tactic was to send the gas over when it was less visible and might find men sleeping and unprotected by their gas masks. The first such attacks had used chlorine gas. The Germans later introduced phosgene gas on the Russian Front and brought it to the Western Front in December 1915. There were no casualties attributed to gas during this alert although it did not end until the eighth, when the unit was back in the reserve area. On May 7, the enemy carried out a heavy bombardment of Trench 63 with 5.9-inch shells. They did serious damage to the communication and support trenches. In retaliation, the Canadian heavy artillery commenced counter-battery fire,[75] resulting in the cessation of enemy shelling. The battalion was relieved that night by the 4th Canadian Mounted Rifles of the 8th Brigade and was at Camp D at 6:00 the next morning

The battalion now began an extended absence from the front lines. It was times like these that gave the men a chance to restore their spirits and add to their reserves of courage for the eventual return to the front. The first two days in the rear area passed quietly with no major activities. The acting brigadier of the 9th C.E.F. Infantry Brigade inspected them. On the eleventh, they had a bath parade and supplied working parties. On the twelfth, they again played football with the 52nd Battalion and defeated them three to zero. On the fifteenth, they moved further to the rear to brigade reserve Camp E. Here they checked their equipment, trained, did physical drill, and generally restored themselves after two months in the line. Despite the distance from the front line, the men were still harassed by the enemy, now in the form of early morning raids by enemy aircraft dropping bombs.[76] The men were also available for working parties to bring out the wounded, bury the dead, and build trenches. Joyce wrote in his diary, "The usual Sabbath strafe with 4 casualties, none serious. The soil we dig and move here consists largely of the deceased of a year ago."[77]

Of note during this absence from the front were two Field General Courts Martial held in the unit, one for three members of the 9th Brigade and one for two noncommissioned officers of the battalion, Company Sergeant Major Drysdale and Sergeant Clayton. Unfortunately, it was not possible to learn the outcome of the trials. It may have been about this time that Lieutenant Maurice R. Henderson joined the battalion from the 33rd Battalion in England. His family was strongly in favour of the war effort, and he had joined up before completing his degree at the University of Toronto.

On May 23, the unit moved up to the front, effecting the relief of the 43rd Battalion by 1:00 A.M. on the following day. It was in the same sector where it could observe German movements in Clonmel Copse. Lieutenant Joyce gives an account of the benefits of being able to see into the enemy lines:

> Thursday 25 4/15. They shelled us intermittently from 5 am to dark, but they got more than they gave including our trench mortar. This afternoon we caught a relief going in and got after them with the machine guns and our 18 pdr [pounder] battery. Our observer said we broke up the gang. We get splendid observation here on our right which commands all our Bn frontage. Our supporting artillery here is good – very good.[78]

Waldron's diary refers to a steady stream of men and munitions moving into the woods and to the Germans digging "T" saps, or short trenches from their front line into No Man's Land, as a prelude to constructing a new line. No doubt with some dismay, he noted that nothing was done to disrupt these preparations, and he hoped that the enemy did not attack while the 58th was in the line.[79] The battalion remained in this position until the end of the month. There were no infantry attacks on them during that time, but the battalion was subjected to shelling every day as the enemy appeared to be registering his guns for an impending attack. The 2nd Battalion of the 1st Division was also in the line at this time, further south. Their War Diary describes the period as quiet or extremely quiet each day, but their historian says it was the type of quiet that engendered uneasiness.[80] The 58th's diarist's knowledge of the enemy's weapons continued to improve; he recorded shelling by 5.9- and 4.2-inch guns as well as 77mm field guns. He also noted the variety of weapons used by the Canadian artillery units to retaliate: "heavies, trench mortars & F[ield] A[rtillery]."

During this period, Lieutenant Joyce went on an impromptu patrol with Pinky Campbell. Campbell had turned out to be an expert at navigating the warren of trenches and was invaluable as a runner carrying messages between companies and headquarters. A friend of Joyce's batman, he spent a lot of time with the Machine Gun Section. A discussion about a feature on a map led Pinky to dare Joyce to follow him out to No Man's Land to see the feature Pinky claimed was a fence. Joyce took the dare and, after a rapid slither over the mud and debris, found himself looking at the head and shoulders of a German sentry. Pinky was all for killing the man on the spot, but Joyce vetoed that idea, preferring to turn a machine gun on the spot the next night.[81] On May 27, Lieutenant Cusler sent home a letter describing life in the trenches:

> My dear ones at home. All is fine and I have a very comfortable dugout. You see it is cheaper to move than pay rent and the rats were few in my last place but here there are quite a number of the long tailed residents & they seem to be very prolific all having large families. This is the place where you get to know your men for you see them & live with them in

> the stress & rigour of Trench life & it is wonderful the spirit of the men as a whole. Of course once a man has been shell shocked it gets to him & he cannot stand it but those cases are few. No man can honestly say he likes shell fire for if he does he is insane, but on the other hand you fall into a routine and I know in my own case as long as the shells miss me I am happy, for a miss is as good as a mile. The birds sing quite merrily & seem to take it as the ordinary course of events. I got the orderly corporal to come in with me. He is a fine chap & is a wonderful boy & I like to have him handy. We are all quite sporty here. Fine ferns growing on our parapets quite like a garden & the parados likewise. [Cusler sent home samples of the fern and the other plants growing in the area] You know we have a lot of fun more cheer than hardship. It['s] much different than I had expected but the life on the whole is not a very strenuous one. We have as good a meal as any man could wish sometimes a little delayed. I know one day a shell blew up our kitchen but they dug it out & only delayed the game an hour. Of course a few bits of Belgium or piece of Sand in the sugar is harmless and makes the works go better. Must go to bed & get a snooze as morning breaks early, at 2:30 it is quite light & it is now nearly ten. Will write a few lines more in the morning. Elmo.[82]

On most days during this assignment, the casualties were light, but on May 28, a heavy artillery bombardment killed ten other ranks, wounded four, and caused a shell shock casualty. There were casualties again on the thirty-first as the battalion was being relieved; Captain W.G. Cosbie and five other ranks were wounded, and two other ranks were killed. Cosbie's wound was slight and he remained with the battalion. Captain H.S. Adam was reported sick on the twenty-eighth; then on the thirtieth, he was recorded as a shell shock casualty. Upon relief by the 1st Canadian Mounted Rifles, the battalion proceeded to Camp C and arrived there on the morning of June 1.

The Human Balance Sheet

	May	**Cumulative**
Killed	27	41
Wounded	25	68
Shell Shock	16	23
Missing	12	12
Reinforcements	5	5

Chapter Four

June 1916
Battle for Mount Sorrel

June 1 saw the battalion resting at Camp C. Three men were killed and six wounded during the night of the relief. Enemy action would make the period of rest much shorter than the battalion expected. On June 2, the men were put on notice to be ready to move in an hour, then on half an hour's notice, and then at 5:00 P.M. they were told to move to Camp F. When they arrived at Camp F, they were told to move again to the Belgian Château, west of Ypres. At the Château, the men took up positions in trenches west of Kruistraat Road. At 7:30 P.M. the unit moved again to the south side of Ypres at Ypres Ramparts and was placed under the command of the 7th Brigade. The battalion was now in reserve during a major German attack to capture a key sector in the Ypres Salient. Ypres was the major town in a salient in the British line formed in the first months of the war.[83] The British and Germans had tried to outflank each other in the move to the sea that eventually saw the Western Front formed. Fighting for the area in 1914 had cost the British army many of its professional soldiers, and the German Army many of its student volunteers. In April 1915, during the Second Battle of Ypres, the Germans had used chlorine gas for the first time and had forced the retreat of the unprepared soldiers of two French units. This created a gap six and a half kilometres wide in the Allied front. Resolute action by the First Contingent of the Canadian Expeditionary Force and the Princess Patricia's Canadian Light Infantry, a Canadian unit then serving with the British Expeditionary Force, had stopped the Germans from exploiting the hole that their new weapon had created in the front line. Now the Germans were making their third attempt to wrest from the Allies this small portion of Belgium not under their control.

Courtesy Geoff Stead.

Looking back (north) from Observatory Ridge, Ypres Salient.

The new attack began with a ferocious artillery barrage that coincided with an inspection of the 3rd Division's front line by Major General Mercer and Brigadier General Williams commanding the 8th Brigade on the early morning of June 2. Mercer had seen many reports indicating that the Germans were preparing to attack, and the new corps commander, Julian Byng, had asked him to make a reconnaissance to see if a spoiling attack could be launched to stop those preparations.[84] Mercer was killed in the storm of steel and high explosive that rained down on the Canadian lines, and Williams was wounded and captured as the Germans assaulted the trenches in Armagh Wood. The shelling lasted four hours, and in that time it erased the trenches of the 4th Canadian Mounted Rifles and most of the men in them.[85] At 1:00 P.M., the Germans exploded four mines and launched the attack to capture Mount Sorrel and Hill 62. They next proceeded along Observatory Ridge until the 5th Canadian Mounted Rifles stopped them at Maple Copse, just west of the ridge. The Princess Patricia's were again spoilers of German plans when they held up the attack for eighteen hours at Sanctuary Wood, north of Maple Copse.

On June 2, as already noted, the 58th was in reserve at Ypres Ramparts. The following day it moved east to the Zillebeke area, with B and C Companies at Zillebeke Switch, and A and D Companies and Headquarters at Zillebeke Bund. The battalion was under heavy shellfire for hours at a time. Private Waldron described it as hell. They were not directly involved in the fighting of the first Canadian counterattack, but they provided parties of men to carry up hand grenades, small arms ammunition, rations, and other supplies to the front line troops. In this role, the unit suffered sixteen casualties.

On June 5, B and C Companies were moved into the front line trenches from the Tramway to Zillebeke Church. Major Hicks used good judgement to keep the troops sheltered in the trenches during the shelling and kept casualties to a minimum. Unfortunately, he was wounded before the day was done. During the night, A and D Companies moved up to replace B and C Companies in Zillebeke Village. Enemy shelling had demolished its buildings. June 6 saw Major MacKay, the Boer War veteran, take command of the forward companies that now came under the command of the 43rd Battalion. They moved to the area of Maple Copse in the centre of the 3rd Division's position to reinforce the 43rd. B Company moved to Zillebeke Switch. Enemy shelling continued to be heavy, and the unit suffered six killed and eleven wounded.[86] One of the dead was David Waldron's childhood friend, Lance Sergeant Walt Matthews. Waldron confided to his diary that the shock of losing his friend made him "feel

Courtesy Waldron family.

Corporal 451266 Walter Frank Matthews, killed in action in the Ypres Salient on June 6, 1916, and Private David Henry Waldron.

anything but well."[87] The two of them had enlisted while underage, anxious to participate in the adventure of war. They shed their short pants to enter the army, but it was still like being in Boy Scouts, at least until the dying started. Working parties were provided that night to reconstruct the communications trench, clear the battlefield, and carry the wounded to dressing stations. Lieutenant Joyce rejoined the battalion after attending a machine gun course.

On the morning of the seventh, the enemy's shelling was heavy enough to confine the soldiers to their positions. Three soldiers were killed in the barrage and nine were wounded, including one through shell shock. Waldron mentions nearly being killed as he took a message to Dormy Huts.[88] The battalion positions were shelled heavily again from 6:30 P.M. to 9:00 P.M. Again, the unit was not involved directly in the fighting. It provided cover for Pioneers working in the trenches and working parties to clear the battlefield and reconstruct the trenches. Although the German effort was nearly spent by this time, the diarist described the usual early morning shelling that claimed three lives and wounded fifteen soldiers on the eighth.[89] Wounded in the shelling of June 6, Lieutenant Cusler sent home a short note to let his family know he was well:

> My dear ones at home, I am in great shape but will admit we have had one mighty hard time of it. I have seen war at its highest & trench life in mud to the hips but if the Good Lord permits I hope to some

Courtesy Geoff Stead.

Dormy House, Ypres Salient, located west of Maple Copse in the sector held by the 58th during the spring of 1916. Photo taken in 1919.

Shelters, Sanctuary Wood, Ypres Salient. Photo taken in 1919.

> day have a reunion with the dear ones at home. We must fight it to a finish & have a permanent peace & then Oh! the Joy. So long for now.
>
> Your loving Bro Elmo.[90]

The 52nd Battalion relieved portions of the unit, but retained two platoons of A Company in the forward line. The next day saw a similar routine, and two more soldiers were wounded. Shelling on the morning of the tenth produced eight more casualties before the 43rd Battalion completed the relief of the unit. During that relief, completed on the morning of the eleventh, one soldier was killed and six wounded. The battalion spent the day in the area of the Belgian Château, west of Ypres, before returning to the front line in relief of the 43rd Battalion, the unit that had relieved it the day before. A and B Companies were in the front line, with headquarters at Dormy House, and C and D Companies were in support and reserve at Maple Copse. One officer and seven soldiers were wounded during the relief. While in the front line, the battalion was ordered to participate in an attack to recapture the old front line in Sanctuary Wood in conjunction with an attack by the 1st Division to recapture Tor Top and Mount Sorrel.

The artillery preparation for this attack began on June 9 as the weather cleared enough to allow the Royal Flying Corps to observe the fall of artillery shells.[91] It continued off and on until June 12 in twenty- to thirty-minute bombardments designed to keep the enemy guessing about the actual start of the attack. General Haig, British commander in chief, had not been able to add any infantry units to the assault force, as he was preparing for the beginning of the Battle of the Somme on July 1. He did make available the 2nd Dismounted Cavalry Brigade as a counterattack force if the situation deteriorated further before the Canadians could retake their positions. He also allowed the Canadians access to British, South African, and Indian artillery units, and this concentration of firepower, the heaviest yet produced by the British, was devastating to the German troops. On June 12, there was a bombardment on all German positions between Hill 60 and Sanctuary Wood that lasted ten hours. Archie MacKinnon described the scene from the Canadian trenches: "Nobody can imagine what kind of a night it was June 12th. When you see 5 acres of bush going up in the air there is something doing. Big trees and everything in the air at once."[92] At 8:30 P.M. there was another half hour of intense shelling of the German front line while the troops moved up to the start line.

Lieutenant Joyce mentions a small attack by the Germans on his trench while his unit was cut off from the other companies, but they killed all those who entered the trench.[93] Following a final heavy artillery barrage, and under the cover of a smoke screen and rain, the assaulting units moved forward in waves. In another letter home, MacKinnon described the way he felt before the attack began:

> It certainly is an awful place especially when you are told you are going to make an attack at 12 midnight and they start smashing trenches up at 9 o'clock and stay there 3 hours in bombardment and you get the word, "Over the top in one minute". Your heart

> comes clean out of your mouth and then away you go and you don't know anything until you wake up in hospital or a couple of hours afterwards when things are quiet again. I wish some people could understand what it is like.[94]

Lieutenant Charles M. Howard led his platoon of A Company in the attack at 1:30 in the morning on the thirteenth. The men left the shelter of the shattered trenches and scattered shell holes of Maple Copse and moved at a walk across the gently sloping open ground east to Sanctuary Wood. The diarist described it as "a complete success." He recorded that twenty-eight unwounded prisoners were captured and there were many enemy casualties. One enemy machine gun was knocked out. The other three battalions of the First Canadian Division (3rd, 16th and 13th) also captured their objectives.

There were heavy casualties among the officers of A Company, and Lieutenant Joyce was ordered to leave the Machine Gun Section and take temporary command. He sent Pinky Campbell back to headquarters to ask for supplies and reinforcements to enable the company to hold the recaptured positions. Pinky was able to bring a platoon from another company into the front line before being killed by a shell burst.[95] In the advance to the old trenches the men had retaken a dressing station, where they found the body of a padre and several of the wounded with fresh bayonet wounds. In this fierce fighting, Joyce "turned a machine gun on about 50 — they were lost and trying to surrender" and used these discoveries as his justification for doing so.[96] His diary does contain an entry for the fourteenth indicating that he took forty prisoners as the Germans counterattacked his position. Howard was awarded the Military Cross for his consistent good work as battalion bombing officer and for successfully leading the attacks on the Hill Street, Warrington, and Bydand Avenue trenches in the Sanctuary Wood area. Lieutenant Joseph A. Pearce, signal officer, received the Military Cross for his efforts to scout the front line and visit the trenches captured by Howard's force immediately after the attack in the face of heavy shelling. Two scouts, Waldron's friend Lance Sergeant Lorne B. Craig and Private Alexander D. McGregor, who conducted reconnaissance on the front line and carried messages to maintain communication with the forward troops, were awarded Military Medals. David Waldron was also recommended for the Military Medal for his work carrying dispatches and orders to various units and for the daylight patrol he went on with Sergeant Le Seur, but it was not granted.[97] Waldron noted the patrol in his diary and wrote that he "would not do it again for a fortune."[98] Lance Corporal William Hubbard, who took over his section after Corporal Albert Hitchcock was killed and fought off an attack by twenty-five Germans with the remaining six men, three of whom were wounded, was also recommended for the Military Medal. Once the Germans realized their infantry had been ejected from the old Canadian lines, they retaliated by shelling the battalion's reserve positions at Maple Copse and the restored front line. An enemy shell burst killed Major Ballachey as he moved about the new positions the next day. Privates Archie MacKinnon and James McKellar were partially buried by another shell burst. MacKinnon managed to dig them both out and attend to McKellar's wound, but to no avail, for a second shell arrived, cutting McKellar in two.[99]

By late on the fourteenth, the cost to the battalion was clearer. Initially, the only casualties the battalion recorded on the thirteenth were the deaths of Lieutenants Clapperton and Nicol. They were standing in a trench bay conferring and about to move forward when a high explosive shell landed, killing them as well as Company Sergeant Major D.G. Wright of A Company and a runner.[100] As the situation became clearer, it was learned that, in addition, Lieutenant Henderson[101] and twenty-six other ranks had been killed. Seventy-four soldiers were wounded and another twenty-three put out of action through shell shock. Forty men were reported missing, and they would likely be either dead or prisoners of war.[102] On June 21, one soldier reported missing was reported safe, and that left only six men unaccounted for.

Much of the old front line had been recaptured in this operation — the first large-scale, deliberately planned attack by the Canadian Corps. The price of this success was eight thousand casualties. The relief was completed at 5:15 A.M. on the fifteenth, the unit suffering only two more wounded as it left the front line. Over the next few days, it was withdrawn from the support trenches to rest and replace its losses. Sergeant Edmison's letter home, dated June 17, gives an account of the events described above:

> You will have my note of the 11th inst. perhaps, by this time. When I wrote we thought we were going back up for a rest, but we moved back up the line that night, after only a few hours' rest, and were in the thick of the fight for four more days — a total of twenty-two days in the firing line. We had several chases after the enemy, and one morning, just at daylight, I got my platoon right in amongst them, but they didn't fight. They either tried to retreat and got shot for it, or dropped their rifles and held up their hands. We got well in advance of our own lines, and stayed there for several hours, coming out without a casualty. The German artillery sometimes gains them some ground, but their infantry usually loses it again for them. The remnants of our battalion and our division came back to our base camp night before last. We will have to have a draft of at least 50% before we can go up the line again. It is certainly a relief to get back from the noise of the guns.[103]

Reinforcements were received on the nineteenth while the battalion was out of the line. Captain Parsons and 151 other ranks were posted to the companies. Lieutenant Joyce was ordered to report to the Machine Gun School at Grantham, England.[104] The process of integrating them into their new platoons began with route marches, drills, sports, and specialized training, such as bombing schools and gas helmet practice. At this time, it is possible the men were being trained in the use of the P (for phenate) Helmet, a chemical-soaked bag with two eye pieces drawn over the head with the bottom of the bag tucked into the collar of the soldier's clothing. These helmets were effective unless wet, but they were also uncomfortable to wear. They would also make it difficult for the soldier to carry out strenuous physical activity as they reduced the flow of air to the lungs.[105] There were a number of false gas alarms during this period. The men would be roused from sleep by a cacophony of rattles, whistles, and gongs to stand to until the all clear was given. They would put on their masks and wait for that signal. Fred Noyes gives a graphic description of what it was like to put on and wear one of them.

> And what uncomfortable, stifling contraptions they were particularly those first pullover affairs we were issued. The eye-pieces soon became opaque. Slobbers of saliva drooled from mouth-corners and dripped from sweating chins. Sense of direction was quickly lost, and then it was "To hell with the mask! — I'd rather be gassed!" It would be ripped off and, more often than not, the air outside would be found sweet and clean compared to that inside the detested respirator.[106]

The battalion took time to mark the anniversary of its birth on June 23 and 24 with dinners, first for the officers and then for the sergeants. One platoon of the battalion was in attendance at the funeral of Major General Mercer, whose body had been recovered from Armagh Wood. The next day, the corps commander, Lieutenant General Sir Julian Byng, future governor general of Canada, inspected the battalion. On the twenty-seventh, the officers met the new divisional commander, Major General Louis Lipsett. Lipsett was a regular British army officer who had been in Canada at the outbreak of the war. He first commanded the 8th Battalion, then the 2nd Brigade, before being promoted to command the 3rd Division. He made it a point to visit the front line soldiers and, as a result, had a high reputation with the troops.[107] On June 28, the unit received a warning order to replace the 42nd Battalion in the area of Zillebeke Bund on the night of June 30. The relief was completed at 11:30 P.M. on a night described by the diarist as quiet.

The Balance Sheet

	June	Cumulative
Killed	43	84
Wounded	143	211
Shell Shock	28	51
Missing	40	52
Reinforcements	152	157

Chapter Five

July 1916
More of the Same

Dominion Day was spent in reserve, but the Diary makes no special mention of the day. As usual, the battalion was shelled by the enemy, and, as was the pattern in reserve, it provided a large number of its men for working parties, this time under the direction of the Royal Engineers. This routine was repeated for two more days before the battalion returned to the front lines in relief of the 43rd Battalion. On July 2, the unit received a draft of six replacement officers: Lieutenants F.H. Richardson, E.A. Simpson, E.P Jensen, J.E. Sutherland, H.V. Hearst, A.C. Williams, and J.L. Dashwood.

On July 4, the unit was subjected to three serious artillery attacks in the course of the day, but only three men were wounded. No doubt there was an element of luck in these low casualty numbers, but they also reflect a growing experience of life in the front lines and, particularly, the knowledge of how to take advantage of the shelter offered by the trenches at the first sign of such an attack. That night, the unit moved back into the trenches to relieve the 43rd Battalion. The first day in the line was spent cleaning up the battlefield and restoring the trench system. There was assistance from men of the 5th Canadian Mounted Rifles. July 6 saw the battalion subjected to artillery attacks, one just after noon and the other in the evening. The first saw an estimated three hundred rounds from 5.9-inch heavy artillery firing high explosive shells and 77mm field guns firing shrapnel shells fall in about two and a half hours. There were four casualties during the first attack; three men were wounded and one was a victim of shell shock. In the second attack, damage was done to the headquarters kitchen, but there were no casualties. While the Diary describes the seventh as a quiet day, there were casualties even though there was no mention of shelling; three soldiers were killed and five wounded. The unit provided another large working party, and the transport unit took out four loads of material from the cleanup effort of July 5.

On July 8, the battalion participated in a trench raid. This type of action was designed to promote cooperation among the men before a major attack, and it served to gather intelligence about enemy positions and keep them off balance. All working parties were cancelled, except for the ration party and a group of thirty men working to repair damage to Dormy House, the site of the damage to headquarters the day before. That night, a party of riflemen and bombers under the command of Lieutenant C.M. Howard were sent out into No Man's Land to attack a German bombing position. A second party, under the command of Lieutenant J.A. Pearce, was to open covering rifle fire from the Gourock Road bombing block. There was a heavy bombardment of the German lines by friendly artillery. Lieutenant Howard's party found their objective empty of enemy, and Lieutenant Pearce reported that the enemy strongly held trenches running from Gordon Road to the Loop. Both parties returned to their trenches without casualties.

The next day began with a heavy barrage on the enemy's front line. The Germans retaliated by shelling the Warrington, Hill Street, and Maple Copse trenches. Captain H.S. Parsons was able to move the rations forward, despite the shelling. Two officers, including Lieutenant Pearce of the previous night's raid, and eleven other ranks were wounded in the shelling, and one soldier was killed. Private Fred Render was struck by machine gun fire and died before he could be taken to the Casualty Clearing Station. That night, the 43rd moved forward in relief of the battalion, but, even before the relief was started, the area was subjected to another intense artillery bombardment. The pounding of 5.9-inch, 4.2-inch, and 77mm guns and heavy trench mortars lasted three hours. The Allied artillery replied in kind. The brigade to the right of the battalion suffered an even heavier bombardment on its positions on Observatory Ridge and Mount Sorrel. Five soldiers were killed during the relief and eight were wounded. The following day, the battalion moved out of brigade reserve at Zillebeke Bund to a quieter location further behind the lines at Camp C Toronto.

On the twelfth of July, the battalion moved back to St. Lawrence Camp, and on July 13, it moved back to billets in the Steenvoorde area for an extended period of training. These moves were accomplished without casualties. The training began on the fourteenth and usually lasted six hours per day. The four companies carried out extended order drill, and the specialists attended bombing and machine gun courses. The soldiers were inoculated against an unspecified disease that afflicted the company sergeant major of A Company. On July 21, there were practice attacks on the Bombing School Trenches, first by companies, and then by the whole unit. There is no reference in the Diary to the tactics being taught. At this point in the war, attacks usually saw the men leave their trenches and move through a gap in their own wire and then spread out to form a long open line parallel to their trench before walking across No Man's Land to the enemy trench. The rationale behind this type of formation was that the new soldiers had not had time to learn the skirmishing formations and tactics of the regular British army. The British High Command observed that, while one line or wave of attackers usually failed to capture the objective, two lines sometimes succeeded, and three lines generally succeeded.[108] One soldier was accidentally injured during this exercise.

The battalion moved from the Steenvoorde area to Camp Erie on July 23. It was allowed to rest that afternoon. The next day, it went through the usual drills before having a bath parade. Private Waldron's diary contains an entry for July 24, which reports that he was off to scouting school with some of the other scouts. He would return to the battalion on August 13, having learned some "good points." On July 25, the battalion again participated in drills. That night, it moved by train to Ypres to relieve the Princess Patricia's Canadian Light Infantry. By this time in the war, Ypres had been heavily damaged by German artillery fire. The unit moved on that night to Zillebeke Bund to relieve the 5th Canadian Mounted Rifles. While 498 officers and men were involved in working parties, the remaining company commanders, machine gun and bombing officers, and 19 NCOs moved up to the trenches held by the 4th C.M.R. prior to the battalion relieving that unit the following night. The relief was begun at 8:30 P.M. when guides were met at Zillebeke Village, just slightly east and south of Ypres, and completed at 12:25 A.M. The Diary carefully notes the disposition of each company in specific trenches.

July 28 was a quiet day, with only one soldier wounded in sporadic trench mortar attacks. For the first time, the Diary mentions kite balloons overlooking the battalion's trenches. The enemy would have tethered these small balloons to winches on the ground so that they could be pulled down when attacked by Allied aircraft. The site would also be ringed with anti-aircraft guns to protect the balloons. Observers suspended in a basket below the kite balloon would be able to view the Allied lines and detect troop movement and could direct the fire of German artillery on the trenches. In the middle of the night, there was a trench mortar attack on the A Company area, and three soldiers were wounded. The next morning, there were still six balloons above the front, and the A Company position in Trench 46 was subjected to a heavy artillery and trench mortar attack from 6:00 until 8:00 that evening. During the shelling of B Company's section of the line, Lieutenant J.E. Sutherland was killed by a sniper, less than a month after he had arrived from England. The next two days were quiet, and there appear to have been no new casualties. Brigadier General Hill of the 9th Canadian Infantry Brigade commented favourably on the work done by the battalion in clearing up the Right Sector on July 5.

The Human Balance Sheet

	July	Cumulative
Killed	10	94
Wounded	39	250
Shell Shock	2	53
Missing	0	52
Reinforcements	7	164

Chapter Six

August 1916
A Veteran Battalion

The first day back in the line passed quietly without mention of any enemy shelling. Despite this, one soldier was killed and six were wounded. The Diary comments that the unit had improved the trenches in its sector and mentions several discoveries of buried small arms ammunition and hand grenades. It was common to leave supplies like these in the trenches so that each relieving unit would not be overburdened on its move to the front. These would then be buried in the shellfire and confusion of this heavily contested area. At the time of writing, these caches of arms, as well as unexploded artillery shells, are still being recovered from the battlefields of the First World War.[109]

August 2 was another quiet day with no mention of enemy activity, but there were two casualties. The third was a definite change from the first two days back in the line. At 1:30 A.M., the men in Trench 53 noticed an enemy working party repairing the trench opposite. They attacked with hand grenades and drove them off with casualties. Similarly, the Germans drove off a brigade wiring party from the area in front of Sap F, a portion of trench extending into No Man's Land. The battalion responded by attacking the enemy trenches with grenades and Stokes mortar bombs. The Stokes mortar had come into use with the British army in 1915. It fired a three- or four-inch shell in a high arc to land on the enemy positions. Relatively light and simple to operate, it gave infantry units control of another close support weapon for use within the trenches. One soldier was wounded in these exchanges. That afternoon, Canadian Corps commander Lieutenant General Byng visited the battalion headquarters. He was regarded as one of the best officers in the British army. He did not remain in a headquarters chateau, but came to the front to see conditions first-hand. During the night, the battalion on the right of the 58th detonated two camouflets, or explosive-filled caverns, at the end of tunnels extending from Trench 39 toward the enemy front. Such devices, when detonated, were designed to disrupt enemy tunneling toward the British lines. The explosions were followed by heavy artillery bombardment by friendly artillery, which drew a response from the enemy. Likely the enemy saw the detonation of the camouflets as the prelude to an attack and tried to disrupt it with artillery fire. No damage was reported, and things were quiet by 11:30 P.M. The battalion was relieved on the fourth and proceeded to the Cavalry Barracks at Ypres. It had suffered three wounded during the day.

On August 5, six new officers reported for duty. From the fifth to the seventh, the unit supplied working parties totaling 9 officers and 550 other ranks. The work was often heavy, involving the carrying of timber, metal sheets, and sandbags for filling to maintain and improve the trenches. It usually resulted in exposure to enemy fire, as supplies and building materials were too awkward to be moved through the trenches and had to be carried overland. The month of August was relatively dry, and this would have made trench maintenance easier than in the wet spring and winter months, but the constant shelling would have made it necessary to carry out regular repairs. Participating in working parties, particularly during the short summer nights, deprived the soldiers of rest after they came out of the front line, where sleep would have been difficult to obtain. The battalion was able to avoid work parties for the next three days and was moved into divisional reserve at Camp Winnipeg on August 11.

The battalion's Diary gives no hint of complaint or dissatisfaction, but on August 11, the unit's Ross rifles were replaced with the British Lee-Enfield. The Ross had been controversial from its acceptance by the Canadian Expeditionary Force. It was a Canadian-designed and manufactured weapon and favoured by Minister of Militia Sir Sam Hughes. It was generally despised by Canadian troops for a number of reasons. It was longer than the Lee-Enfield and thus more awkward to use in the trenches. Its ammunition had to be a precise fit for its breech, or it jammed. It was also incapable of being used in a rapid-fire situation as it overheated, causing its metal parts to expand and jam its bullets in the breech. Keeping the Ross clean was difficult in the trenches, and dirt was another cause of jamming. Private Fraser of the 31st Battalion found a Lee-Enfield lying in front of his unit's trenches in October of 1915. It had been there for ten months when its original owner had been killed in the First Battle of Ypres. It was cleaned up in half an hour or so and was fired safely.[110] The only saving grace of the Canadian weapon was its accuracy, and it continued to be used by snipers for that reason.

Starting on the twelfth, the unit participated in four days of training and drill. Particular attention was paid to instruction in the use of hand grenades, which was given at the First Division's Bombing School. Even in the reserve area, the battalion had to be ready to defend itself from gas attacks. There was a gas alert on the night of the twelfth. On the fifteenth, advance parties from the battalion moved into the line with the 43rd Battalion in order to prepare for the return to the front of the rest of the battalion on August 16. The move was made after 7:00 P.M. on a quiet, rainy night. Two casualties were reported.

The unit's return to the front line began with a gas alert, which coincided with completion of the relief of the 43rd. The alert was cancelled at 2:10 P.M. It seems there were two casualties during the day. In the evening, enemy shellfire and trench mortar bombs landed near Stafford Street and X trenches without doing any damage. The next morning, the unit to the battalion's right, the Royal Canadian Regiment, carried out a trench raid under cover of an artillery bombardment. Things remained quiet on the battalion's front, and only three men were wounded.

On August 19, Captain Tryon of the 73rd Battalion joined the unit for an introduction to trench routines prior to his own unit's deployment at the front. This could be taken as a sign that the 58th was a competent fighting unit, which could provide the officers of new units a good opportunity to learn the ropes of trench warfare. It turned out to be an active day for the introduction of a newcomer to the battlefield. At 9:45 A.M., the enemy detonated small a camouflet charge under Sap C, causing casualties among the Tunneling Company. The surviving tunnelers suspected that the enemy was continuing work on more such threats to their tunneling. B Company was ordered to stand to in case there was an enemy attack through the tunnels. Bombing and consolidating parties took up positions to counterattack. The enemy increased the tension by firing trench mortar bombs on the front line and support trenches at 2:20 P.M. Friendly artillery retaliated, and the front was quiet that night. The twentieth was a day of heavy casualties despite the diarist's comments that the morning and night were quiet. There was a gas alert for about four hours that morning. Nine men were killed, and Lieutenant Dashwood and sixteen men were wounded, along with four men disabled by shell shock. That night, the unit went into brigade reserve when relieved by the 43rd Battalion.

Although the battalion was in reserve for the next three days, there were more casualties, likely from artillery fire, but possibly from stray small arms rounds, which could travel up to eighteen hundred metres from the guns that fired them. One man was killed and four were wounded on August 21, and one was killed and two were wounded on the twenty-second. The unit provided working parties both days. On August 23, the 1st Battalion Seaforth Highlanders viewed the unit's positions. Another British Regular Army unit, the 1st Royal Warwickshire Regiment, relieved the 58th later the same day and then the battalion proceeded by train to Poperinghe, a reserve area ten kilometres due west of Ypres. The battalion remained at Poperinghe for the rest of the month. Time was spent on training and lectures. 58th Battalion files in the National Archives contain a memo giving very detailed instructions about how this training should be conducted. There would be three periods of training of three days each. The first period would be centred on sections and platoons. The next period would deal with company training. The last would deal with battalion training. If time allowed there would be brigade training as well. The periods began with all ranks being instructed in what the training was designed to accomplish. At the conclusion of each exercise the lessons learned were reviewed. The specialists in the battalion were to train in their specialties, but also work in conjunction with the remainder of the unit. The final point was to stress the need for "young Officers" to be instructed in map reading, the use of the compass, the making of reports, and the writing of notes.[111]

The weather changed; there were frequent showers and heavy rainstorms, which sometimes necessitated moving the training program indoors. B Company had a soccer match with an entrenching battalion and continued its winning ways with a three to two victory. On the twenty-sixth, Major General R.E.W. Turner, the commander of the 2nd Division, gave Lieutenant Colonel Genet and his company commanders a lecture on the lessons from the Battle of the Somme, which had begun on July 1. The British army suffered almost sixty thousand casualties on this first day of fighting, its heaviest one-day total ever.[112] Whole units were virtually wiped out as they walked forward into withering machine gun fire from the enemy trenches. One of the most famous incidents occurred when the 1st Newfoundland Regiment attacked Beaumont Hamel, losing 26 officers and 658 men without ever reaching the enemy trenches.[113] The Battle of the Somme would continue until November and give the Canadians, including the 58th, their first experience of a major offensive.

The Human Balance Sheet

	August	Cumulative
Killed	12	106
Wounded	48	298
Shell Shock	5	58
Missing	0	52
Reinforcements	1	165

Chapter Seven

September 1916
Into the Meat Grinder

At the start of September, the battalion was out of the line, west of Ypres. For the next six days, it was involved in training for and rehearsing an attack to be launched later in the month. Brigadier Hill observed the battalion's efforts. On the same day, September 5, the officers met the army commander. On the sixth, they carried out a battalion practice attack, which was described in the diary as very successful. On the seventh, the unit began its move south to the Somme front. The men marched first to Bavinchove Crossing, then from there traveled by truck to Fort Rouge Crossing. A short march from that hamlet brought them to Arques Station, where they boarded trains — thirty-six men to a boxcar — for Auxi-le-Château.

The battalion arrived at Auxi at 4:30 A.M. It detrained in good order and moved off at 6:10 A.M. in sluggish fashion after a night in rough rolling stock. With a tea break at eight o'clock, spirits were revived, and the march to billets at Maison Rolland finished at noon without any marching casualties. The men were treated to a band concert that night.

From the ninth to the fifteenth, the unit moved a number of times, proceeding through a string of small French villages to a position just behind the Canadian front lines at Usna Hill near La Boiselle, east of Albert on the road to Bapaume. The Canadian Corps' three divisions were now in the Somme sector. On July 1, the British Expeditionary Force had begun its largest offensive of the war in the valley of the Somme River, attacking with nineteen British divisions and three French divisions on a front of twenty kilometres. The attack was preceded by an artillery bombardment of almost three million shells that rained down on the German positions for a week. Designed to crush the German defensive positions, it served only to alert the Germans to the coming attack and allow them to position reserves for a counterattack. The attack was launched with roughly 128,000 men rising from the British trenches in successive lines, or waves, and attempting to cross No Man's Land at a steady walking pace, each man burdened with at least 30 kilograms of equipment. The German dugouts, thirty feet deep in the chalk soil of the Somme Valley, protected the defenders and allowed them to emerge almost unscathed, set up their machine guns, and execute incredible slaughter on the advancing British. In the first hours of the attack, sixty thousand men were killed, wounded, or went missing. With this expenditure of human capital, the British could not call off the attack with no breakthrough and only insignificant gains of territory. The French were still fighting to retain Verdun and wanted the British to maintain their attack in order to draw the Germans away from that area. Looking for a breakthrough that would not come, Haig and the British General Staff continued the assault on the Somme Front. They drew upon fresh divisions from quiet sectors, using up their fighting capacity, and then sending them back to quiet sectors to rebuild, until virtually every division in the B.E.F. was used up. The attack finally ended when winter made it impossible to continue any longer. The combined casualty totals for the British, French, and German armies in this battle extending over four and a half months were 1.2 million killed, wounded, and captured.[114] Two and a half months after the battle had begun, the Canadians were to play their part. On the fifteenth of September, the 2nd and 3rd Divisions of the C.E.F. participated in a major British attack to capture the village of Courcelette. It seems more than a little ironic that, on the day before a major action by the battalion, it should participate in a pay parade, but that was the case. The men heard the sound of the heavy guns firing in support of the attack as they moved into the line. The reports from the front were good and, by the standards of the day, the Canadian units staged a successful attack; with the assistance of tanks, used here for the first time, they captured the town of Courcelette and gained a foothold on the next line of enemy trenches known as Fabeck Graben.

September 16 dawned clear and cool with a wind from the northwest. The unit expected an order to move that morning, but nothing happened until 12:10 P.M., when it moved to the Chalk Pit near Contalmaison to wait for instructions. The operation order came from 9th Brigade Headquarters at 4:30 P.M. and placed the battalion in support of an attack by the 52nd and 60th Battalions on a line through to the Zollern Redoubt. They were to go into the attack after the 7th Brigade captured the Zollern Graben trench. After the initial successes of the first day, the advance slowed as the men grew tired, the enemy brought in reserves, and the artillery support became less effective. An attack by the 7th Brigade failed to achieve its objective, and the 9th Brigade dug in on a line north of the Sunken Road, only a short distance outside the village of Courcelette. Prior to the proposed attack, the battalion had become lost in the tangled web of trenches, hindered by poor guiding and a lack of time to allow for proper reconnaissance.

The battalion had to change its location again the next day. There was plenty of action at the front, both sides striving to improve their positions. Heavy shelling caused many casualties as the enemy tried to prevent the battalion's working party from completing a jumping off trench between Fabeck Graben and Zollern Graben. Lieutenants Hearst, Bunting, and Harris were wounded, along with Majors Anderson and Forster and sixty-three other ranks. Thirteen men were killed, and three were reported missing. The next day, the unit moved into the front line trench in preparation for an attack on Zollern Graben, and again it was subjected to heavy artillery fire, although there were fewer (but still heavy) casualties. The tally included four dead, Captains McKeand and Macfarlane and thirty-three other men wounded, and three missing.

It was during this two-day period of heavy enemy shelling that Archie MacKinnon was wounded. He was promoted to corporal on

Courtesy Gordon MacKinnon.

Private Archie MacKinnon, wounded at the Somme in September 1916.

September 2 and placed in charge of a machine gun section. He had been buried by shellfire in June, but managed to dig himself and a comrade out. This time, the concussion of the shell hurled him into the air and caused his left leg to be wrapped around his neck. He lost a lot of blood from three wounds in his right arm. He had the "Blighty," the wound that would take him out the trenches. He was lucky. The rest of the men in his section were killed.[115]

The day before the bombing attack, the situation seemed to be quieter: there were only nine casualties in total. One of them was Captain John Ryerson, the trench mortar officer with the battalion, who was struck down by sniper fire. He was responsible for two of the eight light trench mortars attached to the 9th Brigade. Ryerson wrote home in April describing how he ducked as each bullet "sang by" during his first few days back in the line.[116] It may have been that the enemy shelling had reduced the protection provided by the trenches, or that he was preoccupied with preparing the mortars to support the next day's attack and forgot to keep his head down.

At 5:00 A.M. on September 20, the battalion launched what was supposed to be a surprise bombing attack up Zollern Graben trench in concert with the 43rd battalion. The enemy was alert and prepared for the attack. The men of the battalion moved about seventy metres up the trench before they encountered an

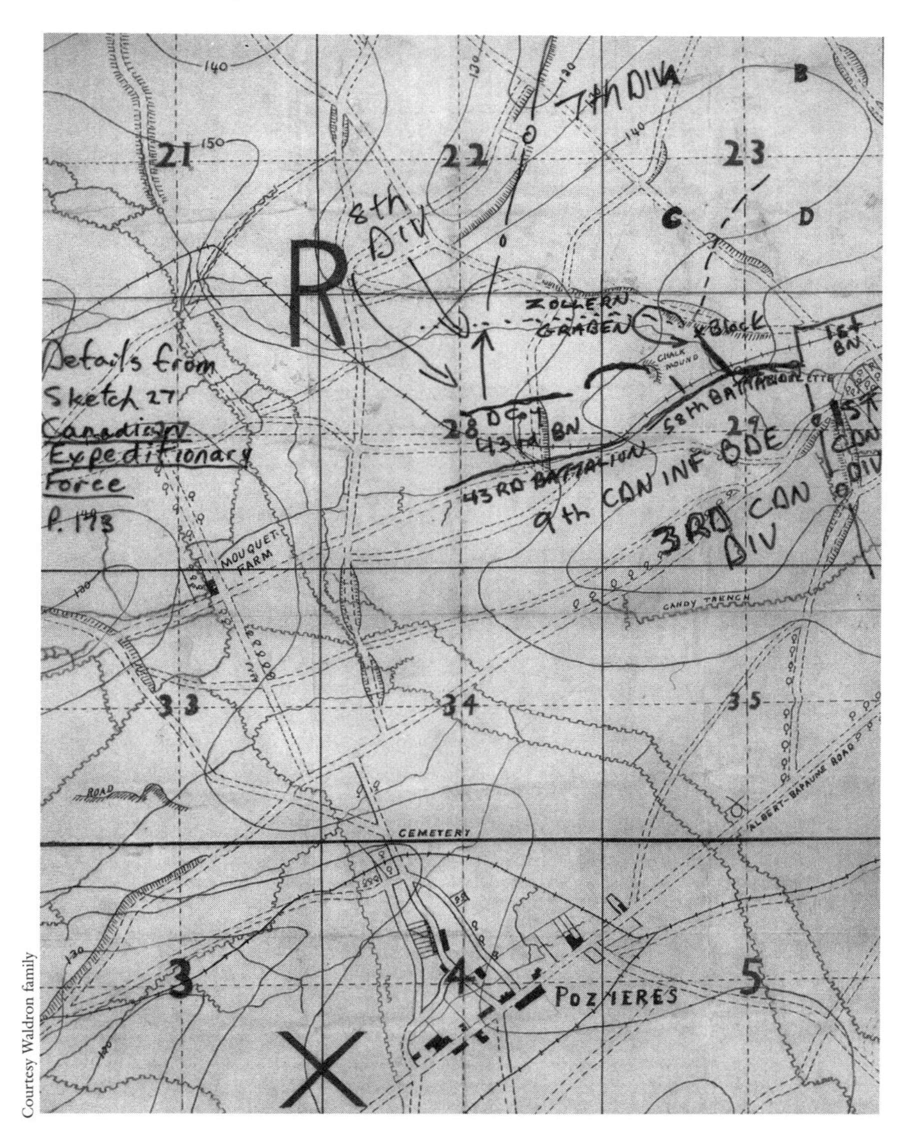

Courtesy Waldron family

Zollern Graben Raid, the Somme, September 20, 1916. Map by David H. Waldron, details from Sketch 27 Canadian Expeditionary Force, p. 173.

enemy bomb block, an earth-and-wire obstacle across the trench that halted their progress. The enemy soldiers opened a heavy machine gun and rifle fire at close range on the men trapped in a confined space. Casualties among the attacking platoon were very heavy, with the leading two sections of about sixteen men wiped out. Lieutenant Joseph T. Walker was probably killed at this stage. Lieutenant Roy W. Parke was wounded as he tried to restart the attack, and his place was taken by Lieutenant Wallace, who moved the survivors twenty-five metres away from the enemy block to construct one for the battalion. A large portion of the attacking company became casualties. In addition to Lieutenant Walker, eight other ranks were killed. There were thirty-four wounded, including the previously mentioned Lieutenant Parke. Private Waldron, who had returned from scout and reconnaissance training with the Australians on September 7, recorded in his diary that the operation had failed because the 58th attacked an hour after the two flanking battalions. He blamed the Divisional Command for the mistake.[117] The official history makes no mention of the waiting Germans, but indicates that a new regiment of the 7th Division counterattacked under cover of smoke and drove the Canadians out of the sections of trench they held in a fight that lasted all morning.[118]

The next day, the Germans counterattacked the front line of the 2nd Battalion on the unit's right flank and penetrated into the trenches in front of Courcelette before being driven out. There was a heavy artillery bombardment in support of this attack, and it struck the unit's trenches, killing Lieutenant E. A. Simpson. Simpson had been wounded at the Belgian Château near Ypres in April and returned to the battalion only in July. Four more men were wounded before the relief by the 52nd Battalion was completed. The battalion was at the Chalk Pit by 2:30 A.M. on the twenty-second and moved further to the rear at 3:00 P.M. These moves exposed the battalion to further heavy casualties, as the front was very active. Seven soldiers were killed, five went missing, and twenty-six were wounded as they marched back to the Brickfields near Albert, about three kilometres behind the front line. The diarist's initial casualty tally for five days in the line, including those out of the line for illness, was three hundred. This number was revised upward as the men rested in the Brickfields on the twenty-fourth before moving back along the route followed when the battalion had moved into the line earlier in the month. Sixteen new officers joined the unit at Warloy. The next day, the men marched past Lieutenant General Sir Julian Byng on their way to Herisart. On the twenty-sixth, the battalion was addressed by Major General Lipsett. That day there was a further adjustment to the casualty figures, which reduced the number of missing to nineteen and took one off the wounded total.

On September 27, the battalion received 163 replacements for some of its 300 casualties. At least some of these men came from the 98th Battalion, as they were referred to in David Waldron's diary entry for October 6. Among them was Private John Norman Carter. He had joined the 98th Battalion in St. Catharines in March 1916. His grandson later indicated that his marriage had broken down under the stress of a failed business and that he had been wandering the country looking for work for about three years. He entered the army out of a combination of patriotism and economic necessity. He and his wife reconciled before he left for England.[119] In the morning, the battalion practiced for its next attack and spent the afternoon reorganizing its depleted companies. One has to wonder how effective these new men would be in their first action. The weather turned showery after five clear, warm days. On the twenty-eighth, the unit began to move back to the front line, marching from Herisart to Vadencourt, where it proceeded to a bath parade and an issue of clean underwear. The next morning, a working party of 175 men and 3 officers was detailed to Courcelette for road building, and the battalion again moved closer to the front at the village of Bouzincourt. On the last day of the month, company attacks were practiced as the unit prepared for its next action. In what seems a surprising move for a unit somewhat reduced in strength, eighty men were ordered to report to the Royal Engineers' Supply Dump for two weeks. They may have been left out of battle (L.O.B.) in order to provide a cadre to rebuild the unit if it suffered heavy casualties in the next attack.

 The Human Balance Sheet

	September	Cumulative
Killed	48	154
Wounded	180	478
Shell Shock	18	76
Missing	19	71
Reinforcements	179	344

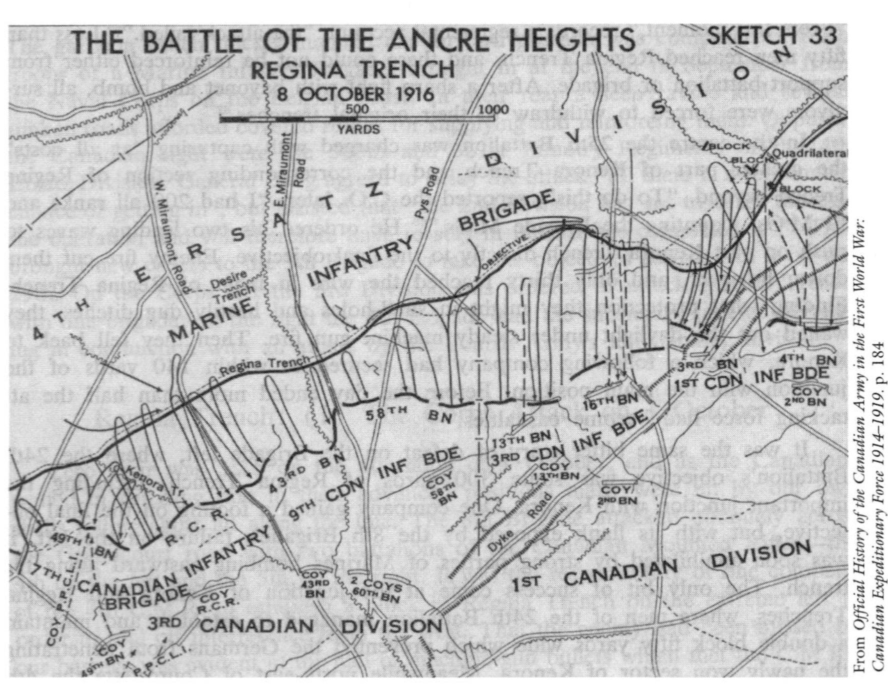

From *Official History of the Canadian Army in the First World War: Canadian Expeditionary Force 1914–1919*. p. 184

Chapter Eight

October 1916
Expendable

The weather for the first week of October was generally warm and dry, with the exception of the day the battalion spent in the Brickfields near Albert. The steady rain caused them to be issued tarpaulins for shelter before they were moved into Albert itself that night. The town was within range of German heavy guns and was largely in ruins by this time. Its basilica was famous for the statue of the Golden Virgin and Child, which artillery fire had moved from a vertical to a horizontal position. The next day, October 3, the unit was ordered to relieve the 16th Battalion on a line from the Dyke Road to East Miraumont Road. The marching was heavy, implying muddy conditions, but the men were in good spirits, and the relief was completed without casualties, as there was very little shelling that night. Shallow trenches made the new position a dangerous one. The next day enemy shelling was directed at the area around the dressing station and the unit's advanced headquarters. Two men were killed, and Captain Parsons and four soldiers were wounded. The stay in the front line was short, and a relief was carried out the following night. The day in the front line had been a rough one. There was heavy German shellfire all along the front, and the battalion reported enemy sniping activity from the area northeast of Destremont Wood. D Company on the left of the battalion position reported friendly artillery fire falling short around its position. This fire was in preparation for the battalion's major attack on Regina Trench on October 8.

A patrol of one officer and three men sent out to examine the enemy's front line reported back on the sixth that there was barbed wire all along the front they examined. While not stated directly in the Diary, it is clear that the artillery fire had not damaged the enemy wire. Part of the reason for this may have been that the heavy artillery was restricted in the number of high explosive shells it could fire each day, and it was these shells that were most effective in destroying wire obstacles. They were also the only way to destroy the deep dugouts used to shelter the German infantry during the bombardment by the more numerous field artillery pieces. These dugouts were excavated in the chalk subsoil to a depth of ten metres. There was no shell shortage at this time, and the restriction was one based on habits developed during the days when the shortage existed.[120] The eighteen-pounder field artillery guns that provided most of the preparatory barrage fired a shrapnel shell containing numerous small lead balls. These man-killing weapons were not effective at cutting wire, as it was difficult to have them explode on reaching the wire; this accounted for the wire in front of Regina Trench being intact.[121] The second problem was that the line of the trench was on a reverse slope and not visible to artillery observers, making it difficult for them to direct shells onto the trench.[122]

The battalion moved out of the line on the night of October 5 and took up a reserve position at Tara Hill. Even before the move, three men were killed and thirteen wounded. One of the dead was Private John Carter, killed by a direct hit from an artillery shell. He was buried behind the trench, but the grave soon disappeared. Despite the generally dry weather of the previous week, the ground was very muddy, and the men came out of the line tired from the heavy marching. Lieutenant Colonel Harry Genet injured his foot while coming out of the front line and missed the attack on the eighth. The unit only spent one day in reserve before receiving a warning order to prepare for a return to the front. Casualties were almost as heavy in reserve as they had been in the front line: two men were killed and seven were wounded. In addition, three men were reported missing, possibly lost during the frequent changes of position over the prior six days. The men would have been better off in the front lines rather than exhausting themselves changing position every day.

On October 7, led by Major Cassels, the battalion went back into the front line to occupy trenches extending about 450 metres east of East Miraumont Road. A, C, and D Companies occupied the forward trenches, with B Company in support in "Death Valley," just north of Courcelette. There is no mention of artillery fire by either side in the diary entry for this day. The next day, the battalion participated in the Canadian Corps attack on Regina Trench, one of the longest trenches constructed by the Germans on the Western Front.[123]

The Diary records that the weather on the day of the attack was fair and warm, with a southeasterly wind. The attack went in at 4:50

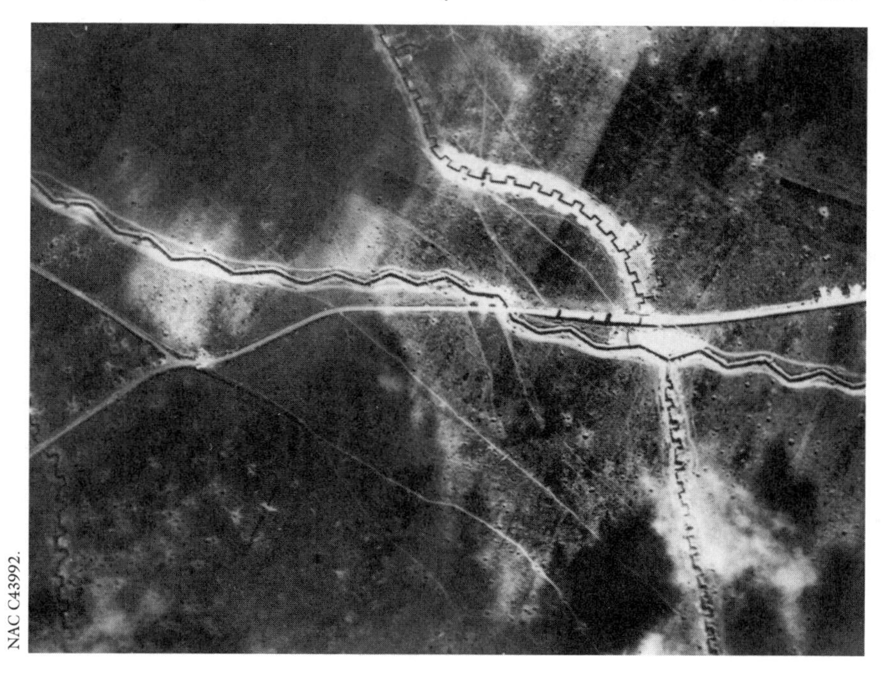

NAC C43992.

Air Photo by 7 Sqn. RFC Regina Trench, the Somme battlefield.

in the morning; again, there is no mention of artillery fire prior to or during the attack, although the official history indicates that the troops followed a creeping barrage across No Man's Land.[124] The creeping barrage would be fired mainly by eighteen-pounders, and the plan was for it to move over the battlefield in front of the attacking soldiers one hundred metres every few minutes. The heavy casualties among the officers in September meant that lieutenants, who normally commanded platoons, led several of the companies. D Company was on the left under the command of Major G.A. Reid. On its left was the 43rd Battalion of the 3rd Division. On its right was C Company, led by Lieutenant Jensen. A Company, led by Lieutenant Howard, was on the right flank of the attack adjacent to the 13th Battalion of the 1st Division. B Company of the 58th, under the command of Major McCrimmon, and B Company of the 60th Battalion were in support about 275 metres south of the attacking companies. Each company had one section of bombers (about eight men) and two Lewis guns with crews of nine each. The battalion's other machine gun, the Colt, was classified as a medium machine gun. In earlier attacks it was found to be too heavy to move forward with attacking troops.[125]

The attacking force of the battalion was roughly five hundred strong. Its first objective was to cover about over 350 metres of No Man's Land. The soldiers would then try to enter the enemy's defences and hold about 450 metres of enemy trench in conjunction with the units attacking on their right and left. Imagine a fit man running about 350 metres along a level piece of ground or around a racetrack. It would take about one minute to complete the effort. Running would seem to be the sensible way to get to the enemy trench line, for the longer it took to cross No Man's Land, the more time the enemy had to leave their deep dugouts, man their positions, and prepare to fire at the attacking troops. Now think of five hundred reasonably fit men trying to do this over wet, broken ground in the early morning light. Consider that each of them carried about forty-five kilograms of weapons, ammunition, and clothing made heavy by wet mud and that they would be tired from moving into and out of the line several times in the previous seven days. Think how long it would take these men to move ahead 350 metres at the steady walking pace recommended by the tacticians. What energy would they have left to break through several metres of enemy barbed wire placed in front of Regina Trench to halt their advance and make them easy targets for riflemen and machine gunners?

As the attacking companies left the shelter of their own forward trenches in waves of platoon strength, they faced machine gun and rifle fire that was later described by one wounded Canadian as "like walking through a sheet of flame."[126] Quite likely, the creeping barrage had lifted over the German front line too long before the Canadians reached a point where they could enter it, giving the Germans time to get out of their deep shelters after the barrage passed and prepare to meet the attack. Certainly the muddy ground and heavily burdened condition of the men prevented them from keeping up with the barrage. D Company on the left flank and the left half of C Company suffered many casualties even before they reached the wire in front of Regina Trench. Those who arrived at the wire found it to be four feet wide and four feet high with additional rolls of concertina wire about five feet high piled on top, all held in place securely by metal screw pickets. No one from D Company was able to enter the enemy trench. Major Reid tried to encourage his men to break through the wire despite being shot through the stomach while still seventy metres from the wire. Acting Company Sergeant Major Dick Ineson took control of the company after the death of Major Reid and continued to urge on his men until it became obvious that the attack could not continue. He then moved wounded men to shell holes and dressed their wounds. He also gathered a few men to him in an old gun pit and held off an enemy bombing attack, inflicting casualties on them by sniping. He received the Military Medal for his actions that morning.

Things went a little better for A Company on the right. The wire there was not as thick and was secured only by wooden stakes. Private Lawrence M. Simmonds, a teacher from Saskatchewan, found a gap left in the wire so that enemy patrols could leave their front line, and Lieutenant Wallace led the surviving members of his platoon through the gap into Regina Trench. They worked along it about ninety metres to the right, where a strong enemy bombing post stopped them. This was roughly where the 13th Battalion should have been if its attack had been successful. Men from the other half of A Company found another way into Regina Trench a little farther to the left, and, led by Lieutenants Howard and MacKendrick and joined by some of the survivors of C Company, they too entered the trench. They cleared it as far as a communication trench on the left and linked up with the rest of A Company on their right. This section of trench was held for twenty to thirty minutes before the inevitable German counterattack began. The enemy saw that the Canadians were isolated in the section of captured trench and began to bomb them from the bomb block on the right and the communication trench on the left. A Company's Lewis guns were knocked out, and the unit's supply of hand grenades had been exhausted during the clearing of the section of the trench they now held. This denied the men a way to deal with the Germans bombing them from the shelter of uncaptured trenches. Lieutenants Howard and MacKendrick suffered the fate of so many junior officers on the Western Front when they were killed trying to rally their men in the defence of the captured trench. MacKendrick, already wounded in the leg, was ordered to withdraw to the Canadian lines, but was killed by an exploding shell. Howard, who had won the Military Cross for his role in the battalion's attack at Sanctuary Wood in June, was seen going down fighting while surrounded by the enemy. Casualties were heavy among the members of A Company still in the captured trench. However, a few did manage to get out, joining with the survivors of C and D Companies in shell holes in No Man's Land and working their way back to their own lines after dark, about twelve hours later. Enemy shelling, sniping, and machine gun fire prevented them from getting back during the day and meant the wounded could not expect much help until dark. Initially, the battalion was not sure of its total casualties. Only one officer of the twelve who went into the attack returned unwounded. The diarist's sentence concluding the account of the action speaks volumes: "No praise can be too high for the splendid manner in which the men fought and continued to fight until the situation was hopeless, and the leaders had all been killed or wounded."

The concerns of the battalion the next day were to reorganize after the heavy losses incurred during the attack and to try to rescue the wounded. Enemy shelling and sniper fire made it difficult, if not impossible, to reach the men in No Man's Land. Runners carried messages and ammunition to the troops. Stretcher bearers carried the wounded who had returned to the battalion's trenches out to dressing stations from which they could be evacuated to casualty clearing stations further behind the lines. That night, the 5th Canadian Mounted Rifles of the 8th Brigade relieved the battalion, and it proceeded back to bivouacs at Tara Hill. Here the battalion was able to assess the cost of its actions over the preceding six days. The initial tally came to 4 officers and 26 other ranks killed, 5 officers and 106 other ranks missing, 3 officers and 135 other ranks wounded, and 3 other ranks suffering from shell shock. A separate entry was made for one officer and two men who were lightly wounded and remained on duty.[127] Private Waldron made several diary entries about the attack. On October 5, he mentions the draft from the 98th Battalion, which brought the 58th up to a strength of 673 men and 16 officers, and on October 9, as the battalion was relieved, he puts its strength at 117 men. His entry for the eighth is short and to the point: "Went over the top. Our division used as Sacrifice division and badly cut up. Tiny [Harold E. Doughty] and [Chester] Baker wounded."

The 58th was just one of eight battalions from four brigades of two divisions of the Canadian Corps participating in the attack on Regina Trench. None of the other attacking battalions had fared much better than the 58th, as the sections of trench captured on the eighth were all given up on October 9. According to the official history of the C.E.F., the 9th Brigade suffered a total of 941 casualties on the day of the attack.[128] Despite the *Globe*'s description of the attack as a "great incident in the military history of Canada" that reaffirmed the military ascendancy in battle of the Canadian soldier,[129] its general failure resulted in two parallel inquiries into the reasons for the poor results. One was started by General Hubert Gough, commander of the British Fifth Army, of which the Canadian Corps was a formation. Major General Arthur Currie, commander of the 1st Division, with the support of General Byng, conducted the other. Currie, who would later become commander of the Canadian Corps, determined that the men had been given no time to train for or rehearse the attack. The War Diary of the 58th makes this abundantly clear: they spent most of the days prior to the attack moving into and out of the front line. Secondly, the men did not know their objectives and, when their leaders were killed or wounded, as happened so frequently, they did not press on with the attack. Currie also learned that, despite the failure of the artillery to break the enemy's wire barrier, some men did enter the enemy trench. There they fought fiercely until overwhelmed by superior enemy numbers, as was the case with Lieutenant Howard. Currie proposed a number of recommendations to try to avoid such problems in the future. First, the troops should be allowed time to train for the upcoming attack. Second, they should be trained to read maps and know their unit's objective so that they could press the attack to its conclusion even if their leaders were eliminated. Third, the attack should begin later in the day to allow for an earlier resupply, under cover of darkness, of the troops who did succeed in reaching their objective.[130] Lastly, the very formation used in the attack, the walk forward by waves of infantrymen, should be thoroughly assessed.[131]

On the evenings of October 10 and 11, the battalion began a move that would see it arrive in Montigny-les-Jongleurs on the sixteenth, where it would spend three days carrying out training according to the syllabus approved by the army. The Diary makes specific mention of bombing, Lewis gun, and first aid courses. The Diary also mentions that there was remarkably little crime among the men of the battalion, perhaps indicating that despite the stress of battle, the men maintained their discipline. General Lipsett, 3rd Division commander, observed the battalion during its march between Warloy-Baillon and Vicogne on the thirteenth and commented on their good condition after their recent ordeal in the Regina Trench attack. None of the men dropped out of any of the marches that brought them to Montigny. On the nineteenth, the unit received a draft of thirty-six reinforcements, and it was noted that they had not been well fed on their way to the unit and that they were in "a fatigued condition." There is a strong possibility that one officer joined that battalion with this draft. Lieutenant R.E. Smythe had served with the 98th before it was broken up to provide reinforcements for units in France. His notes on his military service indicate that on his arrival in the battalion he was cheered by men from the 98th who had been with the 58th since September. Smythe had refused to report to a Pioneer Camp at Crowborough in August, thinking it was full of old men not likely to be sent to France. On returning to the East Sandling Camp, to the disapproval of the camp commander, he was sent to France as a replacement for an officer stricken with appendicitis. In this way he avoided being charged with disobeying an order. Other administrative notes were made about missing soldiers now being accounted for as wounded and the return of some of the lightly wounded to the battalion. On the twentieth, the battalion began the march that would take it to Villers-Brulin by the twenty-third. On October 24, Lieutenant Colonel Genet, who returned to the unit after the attack, inspected the unit. On the twenty-fifth, it moved to Bray, a few kilometres northwest of Arras. Training continued there for the next three days. One officer and thirty-two men were selected as an honour guard for His Royal Highness, the Duke of Connaught, on the twenty-ninth. The duke had been governor general of Canada before the war. On October 30, the unit completed preparations for its return to the front. Thirteen men who had been wounded in the last attack returned from hospital, and one reinforcement joined the battalion. It relieved the 43rd Battalion in the front line trenches of the left sub-sector of the centre sector of the Vimy front on October 31.

In two months of offensive operations on the Somme, the battalion lost 576 men. This more than doubled its casualties during its six months of service in the Ypres Salient. Moreover, many of the missing would later be confirmed as killed in action. In less than a year, the battalion had suffered more casualties than the number of men it brought to France.

The Human Balance Sheet

	October	Cumulative
Killed	37	191
Wounded	165	643
Shell Shock	5	81
Missing	110	181
Reinforcements	43	387
Returned Men	16	16

Chapter Nine

November 1916
Recovery

The month of November was a relatively quiet one for the battalion and most of the Canadian Corps, until the 4th Division joined them from the Somme front. The 4th would capture Regina Trench in the middle of November before coming to the Arras sector. There were no major actions by the 58th or the other units of its brigade. It was now in the area where preparations would begin for the major assault on Vimy Ridge in April 1917. Winter was approaching, and the weather turned cool and wet. The battalion had returned to the front line on October 31 and remained there until relieved on November 6. During the first four days in the line, the enemy kept up a heavy trench mortar bombardment of the battalion's positions and this, coupled with the wet weather, meant the trenches were in poor condition. With their reduced numbers, it was difficult for the companies to keep up with the maintenance of their positions. On the first, patrols went out to inspect the wire along their front and reported it to be in poor shape. Two soldiers were wounded, possibly from the mortaring. On the second there were heavier casualties, with five soldiers wounded and one killed, another soldier dying of earlier wounds, and one being injured by accident. On the morning of November 3, the Germans continued their heavy shelling of the battalion's positions. Canadian artillery tried to retaliate, but this response was judged ineffective. One of the battalion's Colt machine guns was destroyed by enemy fire, and two soldiers were killed. Lieutenant Anderson was wounded along with five other ranks. There were two shell shock casualties and another man was wounded through accident. Men could be shot accidentally by their comrades while on patrol or by the accidental discharge of weapons or grenades. It was so common for officers to be wounded by the accidental discharge of their revolvers that a memo came down from the division that revolvers were not to be loaded while the officers were in billets or their dugouts. If an officer should be wounded in these circumstances, he would face disciplinary action.[132] The Germans mounted a small attack on the fourth, but they were driven back to their own lines. Despite this attack and heavy shelling, only one soldier was wounded. The fifth was relatively quiet, and the companies spent time repairing the trenches. One soldier was killed and another wounded. The 43rd Battalion relieved the unit on the sixth, but it stayed close to the line and was not able to rest. Casualties were light, one soldier suffering shell shock and another dying of wounds.

November 8 began a quiet period, which lasted until the unit went back into the line on the twelfth. In that time there was a meeting of company commanders to discuss ways to improve conditions in the trenches and to plan a trench raid. Two of its soldiers, who had been reported missing after the attack on Regina Trench, returned from hospital, and two others reported wounded and missing were now listed as killed in action. Lieutenant Ellis was now known to be wounded and a prisoner. The battalion went back into the same section of trench it had occupied earlier in the month in relief of the 43rd Battalion. The only casualty in this period was one self-inflicted wound. The diarist does not say whether it was an officer or enlisted man. This was the first such report in the Diary. Up until this point, the diarist had frequently commented on the strength of the battalion's morale. This event was a sign that some men in the unit were struggling with prospect of being in the trenches for another extended period. One soldier seemed to find this more than he could bear and he chose to wound himself rather than face the possibility of death in action. This case would have been similar to the soldier who was accidentally wounded. The preferred method of wounding was to shoot oneself in the foot, something that could be made to look like an accident while cleaning a rifle. Sometimes bad food was eaten to inflict a sickness, or a gas mask was taken off during a gas attack.[133] Because the medical services of the time, even without antibiotics, had a good record of saving the lives of wounded men, the soldier who wounded himself could expect to survive. He did face military justice if he was detected in his action and might receive Field Punishment No. 1 or a prison sentence.[134] Obtaining a wound that sent him out of the line back to "Blighty," as England was known in the slang of the trenches, was worth the risk of a prison sentence for a man whose nerves had been shattered by the strain of war. The records of the C.E.F. indicate that there were 582 known cases, including 4 officers, during the war.[135]

A letter from Archie MacKinnon to his younger brother summarizes what the men had gone through since their arrival in France. He writes in an effort to dissuade his sibling from enlisting.

> Cardiff Wales
> Nov. 8 1916
> Dear Brother
>
> Received your letter O K the other day & glad to receive it. You say you want to enlist when you become of age you are crazy kid there ain't many fellows go to France that don't get hit. Look I was hit not so bad and I have been laying on my back 8 weeks on Saturday. You never see any Germans of any account but you will see all kinds of shells exploding killing and wounding fellows. If you want to see something like a shell blow up some steam boiler seeing your [sic] in the business. You are very seldom fighting you are burying dead or carrying stretchers with fellows on them 2 or 3 miles at least and filling sandbags or digging mud or

> something else. You sleep with clothes on lousy as H____ and nothing to eat. If you seen 5 min of it that would be enough. You don't get a meal never in the morning the sergeant will throw a _ loaf and a tin of Bull Beef at you and that does for 24 hrs whether the rats eat it or not. You are foolish to join. I know cause I have been through the mill and this is straight. I wouldn't go back again if I can get out of it. The war will last for a good many years yet so don't be in a hurry. I will close
>
> Cpl MacK[136]

The rest of November was notable for the lack of activity on both sides. Only one soldier was wounded in the period from November 13 to November 30. The battalion took its turns in the front line, relieving the 43rd Battalion in the same sector after being in reserve at Bray. On November 21, the battalion received the new Small Box Respirators (SBR). These gas masks were more effective against high concentrations of gas and, if put on in time and worn properly, protected the wearer from being gassed. They consisted of a mask with two windows and a breathing tube connected to a canister containing a chemical to neutralize the gas. The canister was worn on the chest. The wearer also had to place a clip over his nose to prevent him from breathing through it instead of the tube. These new masks were more comfortable than the P Helmets, but the unnatural method of breathing made it difficult to carry out heavy physical tasks for any extended period of time.[137]

Efforts were made to improve the trenches while in the front and reserve lines. The Diary notes on the twenty-eighth that the unit's snipers claimed to have hit two enemy soldiers. On the twenty-ninth, an enemy raiding party captured one noncommissioned officer and three men in a forward post. These posts were placed in No Man's Land to listen for German bombing parties or raiders trying to sneak up on the Canadian lines. The raiders had come in under cover of a heavy mist just before dawn and were believed to have surprised the post from behind. No sounds of firing or struggle were heard. The post had served its purpose in that the raiders did not reach the Canadian trench, but it also provided the Germans with prisoners who would enable them to identify the unit holding that section of trench. A Court of Enquiry was held on December 3, and no blame was attached to any other officers or men for allowing this to happen. On November 30, the unit moved back into brigade relief at Bray.

The lot of Canadian prisoners of war was not a pleasant one. The enlisted men were usually transported in crowded and dirty cattle cars to camps in Germany. They often found themselves forced to work for the Germans in industry or in the construction of fortifications. Their rations were usually meager unless they could supplement them with parcels from home. This was partly because the Germans themselves were finding it difficult to feed their people while the Allies blockaded their sea commerce. Sadistic captors often subjected prisoners to beatings and mistreatment for the slightest infractions against camp rules. If they had been wounded before their capture, the prisoners were not likely to be offered prompt medical treatment. Officers were treated a little better, but it was no rest camp.

The Human Balance Sheet

	November	Cumulative
Killed	7	198
Wounded	15	658
Shell Shock	3	84
Missing	4	185
Reinforcements/ Returned men	0	403

Chapter Ten

December 1916
Anatomy of a Trench Raid

The month began with the battalion in reserve with its headquarters at Maison Blanche, a ruin from the fighting of 1915 on the road from Arras to Souchez. On December 4, word was received that 7 officers and 150 men would be arriving as reinforcements. These were likely men from the 161st Huron Battalion, who had arrived in England in early November.[138] The only casualty before the unit returned to the front line in relief of the 43rd was one soldier wounded on the fourth. This may have been Private Art Frost of D Company. He was the son of Arthur J. Frost, a Toronto florist, and had arranged to send flowers for Christmas to the mothers and girlfriends of the Toronto men of the battalion. He was to collect the two dollars per bouquet after pay parade, but was wounded and sent out of the lines before that happened. The flowers were delivered, but the Frosts did not receive payment. After the war, the Toronto men went to see old Mr. Frost to pay their overdue accounts. He told them to forget it, that it was on the house. From that day on, all flowers ordered by men of the 58th came from the Frosts.[139]

The relief of the 43rd Battalion took place on the sixth, with the battalion returning to the front line trenches partway up Vimy Ridge, almost due east of Neuville-St. Vaast, by 10:00 P.M. On the same day, a neighbouring battalion carried out a trench raid, which captured two prisoners and killed seven of the enemy. Even before it returned to the front on the sixth, the 58th received its own orders to carry out a raid on December 10. The next day, a raiding party was chosen from all companies, and they gathered in the cave in Zivy Redoubt. The next two days saw careful preparation for the raid that involved cooperation between all arms of the division and the use of the specially trained troops. There was sufficient time before the raid for the men to practice the attack. The attachments to the Diary, operation order 34 and the detailed after-action report filed by the acting commanding officer, Major George Cassels, show that the unit had learned much from its previous nine months in the trenches. Every effort was made to apply all that knowledge to make the raid a success in terms of achieving its objectives and keeping casualties among the raiding force low.

The raid was to be carried out on a section of the enemy front line known as Balloon Trench. Enemy prisoners were to be taken so that the unit opposite the Canadians could be identified. Casualties were to be inflicted, and the enemy trenches and dugouts were to be damaged. Lieutenant A. Shortt would lead the raiders, who were divided into six parties, E, F, G, H, I, and J, each under the command of a noncommissioned officer. A and B Companies were to provide covering parties of one officer, one NCO, and six men to carry extra hand grenades and assist with the removal of wounded and prisoners and, if necessary, to provide support allowing the raiders to retire from the enemy front line. Telephone communications were established in an observation post near Stafford Crater, where Lieutenant Shortt and four of the parties would assemble before the raid, and a flash signal station would be set up at Pulpit Crater with parties I and J. These signalers would be in contact with battalion headquarters, the divisional artillery, the Stokes mortar and Trench mortar crews, and the Lewis gunners in support of the raid.

Each of the parties had a specific task. Party I, for example, was to carry a length of pipe filled with explosives, which would be detonated under the enemy wire to create a gap that would allow it and Party J to enter the enemy trench. Party G was to carry a portable bridge to place over the top of the enemy trench once it was through the wire to allow it to move overland to a point in the enemy's communication trench. From there, it would set up a block to protect the raiders in E, F, and H parties while they bombed the enemy's dugouts and moved along the trench in search of prisoners. Once the raid had begun, the divisional artillery would lay down a barrage on the third enemy line at Grenadier Trench in order to isolate the section under attack from reinforcement by the enemy. The battalion's Stokes mortars, the Vickers medium machine guns of the brigade Machine Gun Company, and the battalion's Lewis gunners would begin firing along fixed lines to the rear and flanks of the enemy, forming a box barrage to keep enemy troops outside the area from intervening in the raid.

In the three days before the raid, the unit sent patrols into No Man's Land to learn more about the enemy's trenches and wire obstacles. Major Carmichael was credited with discovering weak points in the enemy wire that allowed the raiders to penetrate into the trenches. The artillery and trench mortar crews registered their weapons by firing on the targets they would bombard on the night of the raid. This involved repeatedly firing each weapon, eighteen-pound field gun or three-inch Stokes mortar, and observing the fall of its rounds until the observer was sure it was hitting its assigned target. On the day before the raid, a close watch was kept on Balloon Trench to see if anything there changed before the raid started at 6:00 P.M.

At 5:15 P.M., as daylight faded from the skies, Lieutenant Shortt led his forty men out into the area in front of the battalion's trenches without attracting the attention of the enemy. Shortt, a twenty-year-old American from New York State, had already received the Military Cross. His party included Acting Sergeant Raspberry, who had also established a reputation for boldness in the attack on Regina Trench. Shortt had parties E, G, H, and F with him in Stafford Crater on the left of the raid, and Sergeant Fitton was with Parties I and J on the right in Pulpit Crater. Fitton led these two parties through eight feet of enemy wire to the spot where just a few strands blocked their entry into the German trench. There his men placed the pipe filled with ammonal that they were to explode

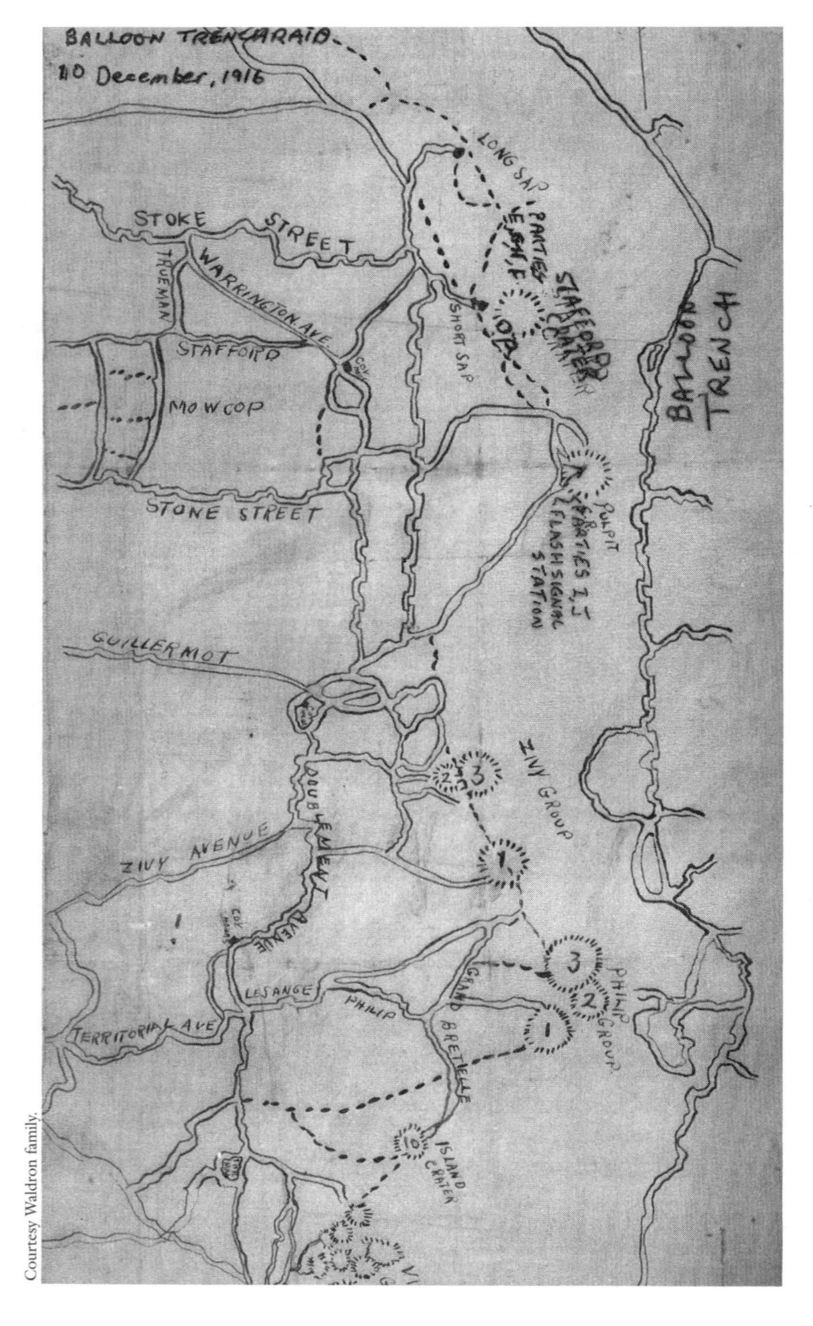

Courtesy Waldron family.

Balloon Trench raid, December 10, 1916. Map by David H. Waldron.

at 6:30 that night in order to cut the remaining strands of wire and signal the start of the raid. Lieutenant Shortt led his men to the gap in the wire where enemy patrols went out into No Man's Land. He and two of his riflemen from E Party cut the last strands of wire and waited for Fitton's party to explode their charge. This happened a few minutes behind schedule at 6:36 P.M., and then all parties rushed the enemy trench.

With the raid underway, the signalers back at Stafford Crater sent instructions to the supporting Stokes mortar crews to open fire on their preselected targets. The artillery opened fire two minutes later. The Stokes mortar knocked out an enemy machine gun firing from the area to the right of Parties I and J, which were on the right flank of the raiding force. This part of the plan had already produced good results.

The ammonal tube did what was expected of it, and the raiders in Parties I and J were able to penetrate into the enemy trench. Unfortunately, it turned out to be a section of trench that was closed by a thick wire obstacle where it connected to Balloon Trench. The two parties remained here for ten to fifteen minutes and threw hand grenades into the enemy positions, silencing an enemy machine gun firing on them from about eighteen metres to their left front and preventing German soldiers from converging on the other raiders. Not being able to move along the trench as planned, they made their way back to their own lines without waiting for Lieutenant Shortt's signal to withdraw after the time allotted for the raid ended.

Shortt led his four parties into Balloon Trench. In order to protect the rest of the raiders, Lance Corporal Simms was forced to kill rather than capture the enemy sentry stationed there. The Germans reacted to the raid and the artillery barrage by firing their red distress rockets to request the intervention of their own artillery. Several of the raiders in the trench were wounded when the enemy threw stick grenades in their direction, but they continued with their mission. The four parties went their separate ways and carried on bombing the dugouts lining both sides of the trench for about ten minutes. Imagine the scene during the time the raiders were in the enemy trench. Artillery fire from both sides was crashing about the area. Machine guns were chattering away, filling the air with bright tracer rounds. Men were popping out of and into dugouts and communication trenches, discharging pistols and throwing hand grenades while the raiders moved about unfamiliar terrain, throwing grenades and satchels full of explosive into enemy dugouts to wreak death and destruction. It would take bold men to carry out such a mission. When the men of Party J did not show up as expected to protect the right flank, Lieutenant Shortt and one of the sergeants moved in that direction to carry out that part of their mission. They met heavy enemy opposition and were killed. After spending the scheduled time in the trenches, Parties E, F, G, and H returned to their own lines without waiting for the signal to withdraw, a signal that would not come. Major Carmichael and Lance Corporal Webster returned to the enemy lines to try to rescue one of the wounded, but could not lift him out of the trench.

Three of the forty-one men were missing, including Shortt, and nine were wounded, two of them seriously. While no prisoners were brought back, the raiders were sure they had inflicted casualties on the enemy and severely damaged their trenches and dugouts. Major George Cassels felt that the raid had been very successful and that the supporting arms had played a significant role in its success. Sergeant Fitton was awarded the Military Medal for conspicuous gallantry in handling his men during the attack. The Germans seemed to be very nervous after the raid, but they did not retaliate by shelling the Canadian trenches the next day. As a result, the unit suffered no additional casualties.

Lieutenant Colonel Genet returned from leave on the twelfth, the same day on which the 43rd Battalion relieved the unit. It moved to Bray and went into divisional reserve. The next day, the men prepared for an inspection by Lieutenant Colonel Genet. Things were a bit more comfortable in reserve this time, as progress had been made on building huts for the men. With the return of Lieutenant Colonel Genet, Major Cassels was transferred to London to take up an appointment in the records section of the Adjutant General's Office. The battalion regretted losing him to this new assignment. While out of the line, the unit continued to be used for work parties, also known as "fatigues." On occasion, so many men were away on fatigues that it interfered with the training programs of the battalion. The battalion went on bath parade at Maroeuil and the next day marched to Aubigny for a Christmas party. Despite the stress of their time in the Arras area and the lack of rest while in reserve, no men went absent without leave, giving the impression that morale was still good. On December 17, the unit went on church parade in the morning and attended wiring competitions in the afternoon. Company B, which seemed to win everything that came its way, won this one too. There was a minor incident when six men of D Company were found drunk in their hut. The battalion went back into the front line in relief of the 43rd on the eighteenth. It left Bray at 3:00 in the afternoon, and the relief was completed at 11:00 P.M. During the period from the eleventh to the eighteenth, there were no casualties.

The battalion would spend its first Christmas in France in the trenches. On the nineteenth, there was a little snow. Byng, the corps commander, again paid them a visit, an action that would have endeared him to the men. Other than a little sniping, which left one man dead, the day was quiet. The next day, a neighbouring unit launched a trench raid near Ecurie, which resulted in a general shelling of the front line trenches, but which produced no casualties. One soldier wounded himself accidentally. Enemy trench mortars were more active the following day and did some damage to the trenches. Lieutenant J.H.G. (Harry) Strathy and one scout approached the enemy lines near Pulpit Crater and successfully bombed it, causing casualties among its occupants. The battalion suffered three wounded from the mortaring. On December 22, 143 other ranks joined the battalion as reinforcements.[140] The weather turned rainy and stormy for two days, and the rain and enemy mortaring caused several sections of trench and dugouts to collapse. The weather improved on the twenty-fourth as sixteen more reinforcements arrived. On Christmas Eve the unit was relieved by the 43rd and went into brigade reserve at Maison Blanche.

Christmas Day was clear and bright, with a light wind from the southwest. The men carried out their fatigues before receiving a Christmas dinner of extra rations, particularly of rum and a special issue of pudding. The Diary takes care to note that "there was no fraternizing" with the enemy as had happened at Christmas in the first two years of the war.[141] There may have been a fatal confrontation on that day. A German called tauntingly from his trench, challenging any "Britisher" to come out and fight a duel in No Man's Land. After some time Private Andrew Alston Anderson, possibly in the lines on a carrying party, took the challenge. Armed with their pistols, the men faced each other at close range. The German fired first and missed. Anderson took aim and shot, killing the German. He approached the fallen foe and took the man's Luger pistol and binoculars as trophies of war.[142]

On Boxing Day, Sergeants Fitton and Lamb were awarded Military Medals for their actions during the trench raid of December 10. The battalion remained in brigade reserve until December 30, when it returned to the front to relieve the 43rd Battalion. While in reserve, casualties had been light and frequently involved accidents such as the one on December 30, when two men were killed while cleaning hand grenades under the direction of the brigade bombing officer. Wet weather and enemy artillery caused the collapse of more trenches. Even the Germans, who generally had the better ground, were experiencing the same problems and were forced to go overland to move around their positions. This gave the battalion's snipers many targets, although they reported no hits.

The Human Balance Sheet

	December	Cumulative
Killed	3	201
Wounded	16	674
Shell Shock	0	84
Missing	3	188
Reinforcements	200	603

Chapter Eleven

January 1917
Winter Sets In

New Year's Day was not marked by any special celebration, as the battalion was in the front line. The trenches were in terrible disrepair. Many of the dugouts in this section of the line had caved in as a result of the prolonged wet weather and steady enemy shelling. The German trenches were likely in the same condition despite their tendency to pick the higher and drier ground for better observation of their enemy's line and stronger defensive value and despite their better efforts at trench construction. The poor conditions of the trenches forced men to leave their shelter in order to move about, and this may have led to the death of Lieutenant Empson, who was shot in the back by a German sniper. The Yorkshireman was regarded as a promising officer, and his loss was much regretted.[143] The battalion's snipers were also active and claimed several hits the next day. One battalion soldier was wounded on January 2.

A strong westerly wind, coupled with rain, made the weather on the third miserable. Enemy trench mortars shelled the right side of the battalion's sector, evidently trying to damage the top of a mine shaft in the area. No casualties were reported. Lieutenant Dashwood rejoined the unit, having returned from hospital. He had been wounded on August 20 the previous year. The commanding officer,

Lieutenant Colonel Harry Genet, was awarded the Distinguished Service Order.

The fourth was a better day in terms of weather, but the trenches were still in poor condition and very muddy. A large working party from another battalion was in the area helping to clean things up. Enemy trench mortars were very active, and the head of the mine shaft received two direct hits. Four men received wounds, and three were disabled through shell shock. The fifth was rainy again, and the enemy's continued use of trench mortars added to the misery. The battalion was relieved that night. The enemy must have suspected that something was happening, for they directed artillery fire to the right side of the sector during the relief. Fortunately, there were no casualties.

The battalion marched out to the hamlet of Bray, about six kilometres northwest of Arras, where it served as the brigade reserve battalion. During the next five days, it suffered little from enemy activity. The officers found their quarters more comfortable than on their last stay there. They even had occasion to establish an officers' mess, their first since the Ypres sector. The men spent the first day on bath parade, cleaning up from the mud of the front line trenches. The next day was Sunday, and there was a church parade followed by an inspection by Lieutenant Colonel Genet. The remainder of the day was a holiday, possibly in recognition of New Years. The area around Arras likely provided diversions for the troops, and they may have visited small shops and *estaminets* (cafés). Men with money to spend would always find a welcome in any inhabited town or village. The language was not a barrier as the Canadians learned to speak enough French to ask for "les oofs" (a bastardized version of "oeufs"), and the French could speak enough English to offer "chips." In the larger centres, the men could have their photographs taken and made into post cards to send home, or they could buy delicate silk cards as an alternative. There were many Canadian units in the area, and the men often took time to walk to neighbouring units to visit friends or relatives.

On the eighth of January, sixty-three replacements were assigned to the battalion, and new training began. Men spent time learning about the key weapons of trench warfare, the Mills bomb and the Lewis gun. There was no training mentioned on the tenth, perhaps because of the gas warning issued that day. There was a gas attack, but it affected units several kilometres north of the 58th. The next day, the battalion relieved the 43rd in the front line. There were no casualties during this time in reserve.

The battalion remained in the front line from the evening of January 11 until the evening of January 17. This spell in the front line seemed to be uneventful. Private Waldron recorded his participation in several night patrols, one with his good friend Lorne Craig, during which they were bombed by their own men.[144] The rain stopped, and this, coupled with the cold, made trench maintenance easier. The condition of the trenches improved, and time was spent repairing the wire in front of the right-hand company's sector and constructing strong points in the front line. Casualties were light: one man killed and five wounded. The unit was relieved on the seventeenth and went into reserve in the Maison Blanche area in support of the 43rd and 52nd Battalions. Winter took the trenches in its grip for the next few days; the Diary notes that the temperature was very cold and that a raid prepared by the 43rd was called off because of snow. The cold weather would likely freeze the mud and dry up the trenches. The men would try to find shelter from the cold in small rooms or dugouts, known as funk holes, carved into the sides of the trenches. If fires were used to provide warmth, the smoke would give away positions and draw enemy artillery and trench mortar fire. The men had to use their ingenuity to find clothes to retain body heat, as the standard issue battledress was meant for the more moderate English climate. Both sides used their artillery extensively while the unit was in the reserve area. Again casualties were light, and most occurred while men from the unit were involved in a working party on the twenty-third, the day the unit went back into the front lines.

The weather warmed up a little during this tour in the front line, but the ground was still too hard to allow much maintenance of the trenches. It was cold enough to freeze the water pipes and jeopardize the battalion's water supply.[145] Enemy activity increased midway through the tour. A working party was dispersed one night, and the enemy registered their artillery at several points along the battalion's sector of the front. Enemy artillery likely accounts for the unit's casualties on the twenty-eighth, one killed and four wounded. These were the only casualties on the tour. The 43rd relieved the battalion on the evening of the twenty-ninth, and this time it went into divisional reserve, returning to the hamlet of Bray, northwest of Arras. The cold weather of the severest winter in thirty years froze the pipes in the division baths, and the men were not able to clean up after their tour in the front lines. On the last day of the month, several cases of mumps appeared in C Company, and that unit was quarantined.

The Human Balance Sheet

	January	Cumulative
Killed	4	205
Wounded	15	689
Shell Shock	3	87
Missing	0	188
Reinforcements	63	666

Chapter Twelve

February 1917
Preparation for Something Big

In February, a new element was to be introduced to the battalion's weaponry. The appearance of aircraft over the front lines had been noted in the Diary soon after the unit arrived in France in 1916.[146] Their purpose was to scout out enemy positions and note all movement and activity on the ground. Aircraft could take photographs of the enemy lines and drop bombs or strafe the lines with their machine guns. This month saw the first attempt to have the battalion work in concert with aircraft. At this time, wireless or radio communication was in its very early stages of development, and communication between air and ground was entirely visual. Flares would be fired to attract the attention of the pilot, and then various combinations of two-letter Morse code would be flashed at him to signify the unit or the problem facing it and the help requested. Headquarters would place large wooden panels on the ground to indicate their location.[147] The battalion's initial efforts on February 2 were unsuccessful, for the aircraft assigned to the exercise did not arrive over the rendezvous. However, the experience did show that innovative minds were at work, trying to solve the problem of how to follow the progress of attacking units and provide them with needed support in the form of artillery fire or reinforcements. Every effort was being directed towards breaking the deadlock that was trench warfare in 1917.

February 2 also saw the presentations of medals to at least two men from the battalion. Waldron's diary mentions his friend Lorne Craig receiving the Military Medal and Sergeant Raspberry receiving the Distinguished Conduct Medal.[148] The cases of mumps, which first affected C Company on January 31, spread to A and B Companies, and the whole battalion was placed in quarantine. There were sixteen cases in total, and when the unit returned to the front, C Company was left in reserve. Training continued in the cold weather without any further mention of attempts to work on aircraft support schemes. Three companies relieved the 43rd Battalion on the fourth of February. One company of the 52nd took the place of C Company as support company, and one company of the 43rd remained in reserve at Rhine Shelters. The battalion did not have the manpower to do much trench repair work, as the other units' companies were not available for working parties. Fortunately, not much work was required; the trenches were reported to be in excellent condition. This may account for the low casualty figure for this tour: one killed and three wounded. On February 9, Major Dougall Carmichael, Lieutenants J.H.G. Strathy, A.T. Field, and J.G. Gauld, and seven other ranks carried out a small attack on an enemy position known as the Letter Box. This position on the east side of Sheba's Breast Crater had been attacked by artillery fire the previous month, but it had been rebuilt.[149] The decision was made to blow it up with an explosive charge prepared by Private Waldron. Lieutenant Field and two scouts remained near the Canadian lines as a close-covering party. Lieutenant Gauld and three privates remained in the middle of No Man's Land as a covering party. Major Carmichael, Lieutenant Strathy, and Private Lue Bishop placed the charge of seven kilograms of gun cotton in the Letter Box despite being challenged by two enemy sentries. The charge exploded, and the next day it was noted that the Letter Box had ceased to exist.[150] This raid was successful, and there were no casualties. Carmichael and Strathy were each awarded the Military Cross for their actions, and Bishop was awarded the Military Medal.[151] On the tenth, German storm troops raided the positions of the Royal Canadian Regiment on the 58th's right after the explosion of a small mine. Artillery fire from the Canadian lines drove the Germans back to their own lines. The same night, the 9th Brigade was relieved by the 4th Brigade, and the 58th moved into divisional reserve. The battalion acted as brigade reserve until the fourteenth. The front was relatively quiet during these three days, and casualties were light. One soldier was killed, and Lieutenant F.E. Gray and three soldiers were wounded. By the fifteenth, the unit was in billets at Houdain, about fourteen kilometres northwest of Mont-St. Eloi. The next day it marched another eight kilometres further north to Marles-les-Mines near the Bois des Dames, where it was to remain during the period of training from February 15 to March 11. This was the longest stretch out of the front line since the battalion had arrived in France almost a year earlier.

Major General Louis Lipsett addressed the officers at the beginning of the training period and was present twice in February to check the battalion's progress. A number of new techniques, developed out of the Canadian Expeditionary Force's experience during the attacks at Mount Sorrel and the Somme and Major General Currie's studies of French tactics at Verdun, were introduced. The Diary does not record the training syllabus in detail, but it does provide some hints about the changes that would be evident in the next attack. On February 22, the battalion witnessed a demonstration of the new platoon drill and a mock attack by the Divisional Demonstration Platoon. Noted particularly in the Diary was the demonstration to the Lewis gunners of the technique for firing their weapons from the hip while on the move. The platoon of roughly thirty men now had a variety of means to deal with enemy strong points. The Lewis gunners would provide covering fire while the riflemen and grenadiers would work in close to rush a strong point or wipe it out with Mills bombs. At this point in the war, the bombers were put back in the platoons, and not handled as a separate unit in their battalions.[152] By the end of the month, the battalion was carrying out practice attacks on a two-company front. This probably meant two platoons from each company leading the attack and one or two coming up behind in support or reserve.

This period was not devoted only to combat training. There were the usual Sunday church parades and inspections. Route marches were incorporated into the training to keep the men fit. A schedule of inter-unit football games fostered morale and gave the men an outlet for their aggressive energies. The battalion defeated the 60th Battalion one to nothing, but lost to the 9th Field Ambulance. Toward the end of the month there was a brigade boxing championship. The period away from the front line was being used to restore the spirits of men. They had time to go for meals of eggs and chips at local estaminets, wander through the villages, take in the latest Charlie Chaplin film, and make the close acquaintance of the French girls.

In February, another batch of reinforcements was received into the unit. In the 12 months since the battalion had come to France, 725 men had arrived to fill its depleted ranks, and there is no doubt that this changed the character of the unit, which had arrived in France with 970 all ranks. The unit supplying the reinforcements was the 8th Reserve Battalion, a composite unit made up of the 110th, 147th, and 159th Battalions.

The Human Balance Sheet

	February	Cumulative
Killed	2	207
Wounded	7	696
Shell Shocked	0	87
Missing	0	188
Reinforcements	59	725

Chapter Thirteen

March 1917
Keeping the Enemy Off Balance

The training in the new techniques of attack continued into March. The demonstration of the new attack tactics was again done by the divisional platoon. While artillery was very important to the success of an attack, the infantry had to be able to deal directly with enemy defences and not simply call for more artillery fire. Early in the war, the infantry platoon had been armed only with the rifle and bayonet, and the enemy was to be driven from his trenches by close-quarter fighting. With the increased firepower of light machine guns and grenades of various types, the infantry platoon now had more ways of capturing its objectives than in 1915 and 1916. Private Waldron noted the practice attack in his personal diary: "Assault on tape trenches in huge field near Auchel turned out very good. Trenches represented German lines on our front. Attack near at hand."[153]

On March 4, members of the 116th Battalion joined the 58th for training purposes.[154] On the sixth, the unit received fifty reinforcements from the entrenching battalion. On the seventh, the men went for baths. The same day, a warning order came down to prepare the battalion for a return to the support trenches on the ninth. A party, composed of the second in command and officers from the four companies, made a reconnaissance visit to the front line on the eighth. The same day, the unit participated in a brigade tactical scheme that was likely the culmination of three weeks of training in the new platoon-centred tactics. Also on the eighth, Major MacKay returned to the battalion, and Lieutenant McCord was struck off strength.

From March 9 to March 11, the battalion was on the march to La Targette to take up its role in brigade support. The three companies, which arrived at La Targette on the eleventh, appear to have been over-strength, as they totaled 556 men instead of 300 to 360. Possibly there were some support troops from the battalion with them. The unit remained in support at Neuville-St. Vaast from the twelfth to the seventeenth. The village was only a pile of rubble, and the men found shelter in dank cellars smelling of slime and decay. Throughout this period, there was only one casualty. Private John A. White of Gloucester, Ontario, died after being wounded by an enemy sniper on the morning of March 16.

The battalion moved back into the front line on March 17. The Diary comments twice on the aerial activity, which was greater than usual. No doubt the Canadian and British commanders were using aircraft to learn more about the German defences in order to plan a successful attack. The Germans would send up their planes to drive away the Allied machines and to see what preparations their enemies were making for the attack to come. The first few days in the front lines were quiet. On the twentieth, Lieutenant Colonel Genet issued an operations order for a trench raid that night. It was British army policy that each division conduct two raids a week in its sector of the line. With twelve battalions in a division, each of them would need to carry out a raid every six weeks. Because the raid was ordered for that evening, there was little time to rehearse the men in their specific tasks. However, the battalion had been training in platoon tactics for three weeks, and it had men with experience from previous raids, so the lack of immediate rehearsal did not emerge as a weakness in the plan. During the day, friendly artillery registered the targets necessary to help the raiders.

Lieutenant Dashwood, the A Company commander who had been wounded on August 20, 1916, and who had returned to the

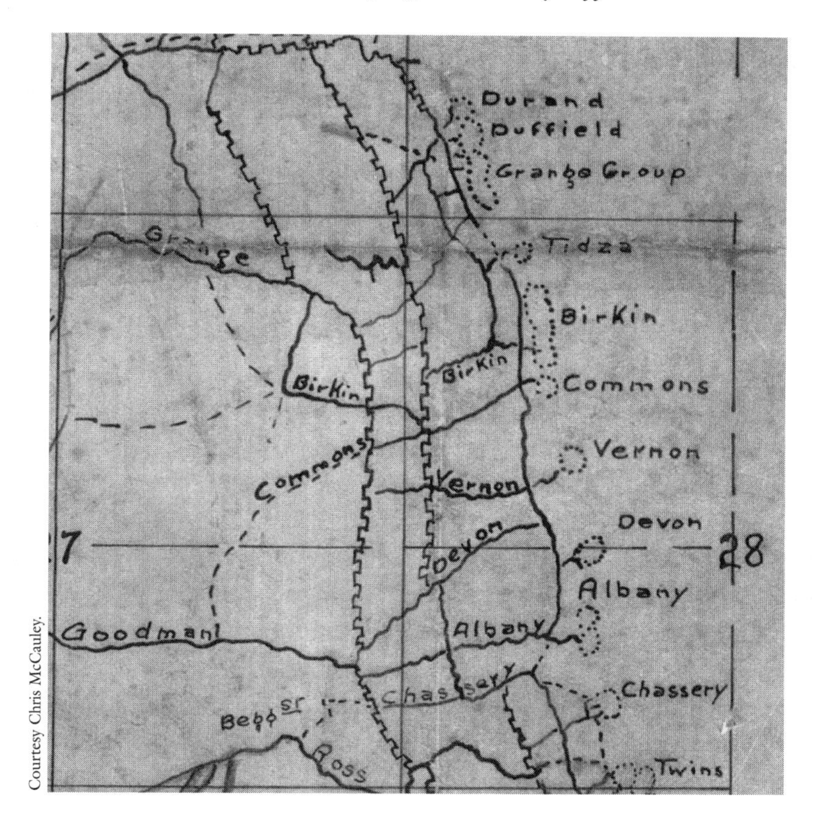

Courtesy Chris McCauley.

Birkins/Commons Craters raid, March 21, 1917.

battalion on January 3, 1917, led the raiding party. Lieutenant R.E. Smythe was to be second-in-command of the thirty raiders and led the six men in Group B, including Corporal Yates and Private Henry Thorold. Sergeant Fitton, a leading participant in the raid on Balloon Trench in December, was in charge of Group C. In total, there were five groups of six men, including the noncommissioned officers, to carry out specific tasks during the raid. There were no instructions about specific weapons as in the Balloon Trench raid, and one can assume that the men carried Mills bombs, revolvers, and clubs, the favourite weapons of Canadian raiders. B Company was to supply a section of eight rifle grenadiers and a Lewis gun crew to cover the raiders as they advanced on Commons and Birkin Craters. A Company would have a section standing by to cover the withdrawal of the parties from the enemy positions. A flash signal station was established in the observation line to communicate with A Company headquarters. One Stokes mortar would bombard a key point in the enemy line at the beginning of the raid.

Unfortunately, the raid was not a complete success. All parties entered the enemy trenches shortly after zero hour at 2:30 A.M. on the twenty-first. Party A encountered resistance at the enemy bombing post in Birkin Crater. The German sentry there threw stick grenades at them before being driven off by the raiders. Party B was unable to clear the bombing post on the north side of Commons Crater, as it was strongly held. They did manage to throw bombs into it, but four of Smythe's men were wounded at this stage. Before all the raiders could reach their objectives, they heard a series of whistle blasts, which most of the men took to be the signal for withdrawal. These blasts were given by the enemy and were likely the signal for stretcher-bearers. All but four of the raiders withdrew immediately, three of them, including Lieutenant Smythe, wounded. Captain Dashwood came over to give the Smythe party the order to withdraw just before they were overwhelmed by German reinforcements. Two more men were wounded by the enemy's retaliatory artillery fire. While the raiders were sure they had caused casualties among the enemy, they were unable to take any prisoners or identify the unit occupying the enemy trenches.

While the wounded were under the care of the battalion medical officer, they were approached by an officer from brigade headquarters and the adjutant. They proceeded to ask the men from Smythe's party questions about the enemy, since his men were the only ones who entered the German trenches. The officer from headquarters prefaced each question with, "The General wants to know...." One of the wounded regained consciousness long enough to hear, "The General wants to know what the general attitude of the enemy was," and blurted out, "Tell the damned old fool it's hostile," before lapsing back into unconsciousness.[155] Dashwood was awarded the Military Cross. Corporal Yates received the Distinguished Conduct Medal and Private Thorpe the Military Medal. Smythe was sent to hospital in England for four months.

The day after the raid, the unit was relieved by several units of the 7th Brigade. It moved first to camps near Mont-St. Eloi. The men were billeted in huts spread over the hillside below the shattered towers of the old church. On the twenty-third, the battalion moved another twenty kilometres northeast to Divion, where they found very comfortable billets. They were given the next day to clean up and rest. On March 25, they attended a church parade. The next day, three companies attended bath parade, and specialist training resumed. The rest of the battalion bathed on the twenty-seventh, and training continued. On the twenty-eighth, Lieutenant Colonel Genet commanded a ceremonial parade for the distribution of awards by the commander of the First Army. Training continued over the next two days. The men tested their gas respirators in the gas hut by being exposed to non-lethal tear gas. There had been a gas alert on March 19, but no casualties were recorded. On March 31, the unit began the series of marches that would take it back to the front lines. There had been rain off and on for eight days, and the diarist, Captain Rose, mentions that the roads were very bad. One can only imagine what the trenches must have been like.

The Human Balance Sheet

	March	**Cumulative**
Killed	1	208
Wounded	5	701
Shell Shocked	0	87
Missing	0	188
Reinforcements	50	775

Chapter Fourteen

April 1917
The Battle for Vimy Ridge

The 58th Battalion was to be a reserve battalion in the coming assault on Vimy Ridge. This was a very fortunate development for the men of the unit. The Germans had held this six-kilometre-long ridge of high ground north of the city of Arras for over two years, and it gave them excellent views of the Allied positions to the west of the ridge. It was said to be the most heavily fortified portion of their front. The British and French armies had tried to take this commanding feature twice without success, and they had suffered combined casualties of about 160,000 men. German casualties incurred while defending the Ridge were estimated at about one hundred thousand men. Together, these figures made this one of the bloodiest spots in France.

The area behind the Canadian front lines was a beehive of activity as roads were prepared for the movement of vast quantities of stores and munitions necessary for the attack. Trenches and tunnels were dug to allow the men to move, unmolested by enemy fire, to the point where they would launch their attack. Telephone cable was buried to keep it safe from enemy shelling. General Byng and the commanders of the four Canadian divisions applied every lesson learned in the previous two years of their involvement in the war to ensure that the attack achieved its objectives.

The 58th Battalion was heavily involved in these preparations. For the first six days of the month, large portions of the battalion were assigned to working parties. The wet weather of a typical spring meant that the roads and trenches were very muddy, making the work of the men difficult, but Captain Rose indicates that morale was still high. Lieutenant Colonel Genet went on leave on April 2. Again he was to be away from the battalion as it was about to participate in a major action. Major R.A. Macfarlane, who had risen from the rank of lieutenant when the battalion arrived in France, took his place. On the fourth, twenty-four reinforcements came to the unit. There is no further mention of artillery preparations until the sixth, when Rose indicates that the bombardment of enemy positions was growing more intense. The same day, three men were killed while on working parties.

There was an innovation at work in the Vimy plan as the Canadians developed methods to locate German artillery batteries in order to silence them with counter-battery fire once the attack went in. They used aerial photographs to spot the digging of enemy gun positions or changes in the enemy lines. Observers were stationed at posts behind the Canadian lines and equipped with high quality surveying instruments to plot the muzzle flashes of enemy artillery when it fired. A system was devised to track the observations from a number of the posts to confirm that all posts were observing the same gun. If they were, its position could be plotted with a high degree of accuracy. Lastly, the Canadians developed a system of sound ranging, which utilized a series of microphones to record the sound of guns firing and the explosion of their shells on their targets, again to determine the location of enemy batteries. All these methods were combined to locate as many enemy batteries as possible before the Canadian infantry went over the top. These enemy batteries became the targets of specific Canadian batteries, which fired on them to destroy them before they could harass the second and third waves of the Canadian attack or support their own counterattack.[156]

On April 7, Private Young was tried for desertion and found guilty. Trials of this nature were usually held near the front and carried on with a minimum of legal wrangling. The soldier usually had an officer to act on his behalf, but this officer was almost never a qualified lawyer. Young's sentence is not recorded in the Diary, but no men from the 58th were executed during the war. In most such trials, the officers in charge recognized that the soldier had simply cracked under the constant strain of the front line life and recommended clemency. During the war, twenty-five Canadian soldiers were executed by firing squad for a variety of offences.

The attack on Vimy Ridge was originally slated to begin on April 8. The battalion discontinued its working parties and prepared to move into the line. The attack was postponed by one day, and the battalion moved up to Assembly Trench B at a point almost 150 metres west of the Bethune-Arras Road. They were at their new position shortly before one o'clock on the morning of the ninth and dug new trenches to shelter from the expected enemy bombardment. One man died of wounds and two went missing at this stage of the battle. At 5:30 A.M., the final bombardment began. The artillery preparation for the Canadian attack had already spread fifty thousand tons of shells over the German front line.[157] Behind the whole front of the British Third Army, of which the Canadian Corps held only one part, there were 2,879 guns, one for each 9 metres of front. They had been allocated 2,687,000 shells for a bombardment, which would be shorter in time, but heavier in weight of shells, than that which preceded the attack on the Somme in 1916.[158] The new No.106 fuse allowed artillery shells to detonate on impact and explode *in* the enemy wire rather than *under* it, thus helping to clear away the obstacle that had made German machine guns such a deadly weapon during previous attacks.[159] The sister brigades of the 9th left the shelter of the Grange Tunnel and entered the snowy air, beginning the attack and achieving their objectives on schedule. Within two hours they had advanced about a kilometre to the Bois de la Folie on the far side of the ridge. Enemy artillery fire was relatively light, thanks to the counter-battery technology developed by the Canadians. The Germans did fire some gas shells at the Canadian rear areas, but they had little effect. Only one man was gassed. At 8:30 P.M., the battalion was placed under the orders of the 7th

Brigade. D Company was attached to the Royal Canadian Regiment and moved to its sector of the new front line near the Bois de la Folie at 9:30 P.M. The battalion suffered only two casualties on this momentous day for Canada. For the first time in the war, a formation in the British Expeditionary Force had captured nearly all of its objectives and had driven the Germans over six kilometres.[160] This was a tremendous achievement when gains were usually measured in hundreds of metres.

The rest of the battalion remained in reserve on the tenth and only moved into the line to relieve the Royal Canadian Regiment and part of the Princess Patricia's Canadian Light Infantry, also of the 7th Brigade, on the eleventh. On moving into the front line, D Company rejoined the battalion and was ordered to take three enemy trenches in Bois de la Folie in front of the battalion position. Lieutenant Allen's platoon was assigned to the attack, but it seems that the force was too small to accomplish the objectives set for it. The right section, under Sergeant John Bennett, attacked up Phillip Trench, but it met strong resistance. Bennett was killed, and four men were wounded as the party was forced to retreat to avoid being outflanked by the enemy. The centre party, under the command of Lance Corporal Alexander, had more success as it moved along the trench known as Artillerie Weg, bombing enemy dugouts and inflicting heavy casualties on the enemy before being forced to retire in the face of German attackers coming up from their support lines in large numbers. Acting Corporal Leslie Sadler of Mossley, Ontario, led the left party. Its advance up Staubwasser Weg helped the centre party in its mission, and it too had some success, able to establish two trench blocks from which it could bomb the enemy positions. An enemy attempt to outflank this party was beaten off by rifle and machine gun fire, and the party was able to retire successfully to the battalion's lines. Unfortunately, Sadler was killed. Lieutenant Pitts, commander of D Company, felt the enemy trenches could have been taken if there had been a general attack. His report states that snipers, using the cover of the woods to their advantage, inflicted most of the casualties on his unit. In addition to the casualties among this force, the acting commanding officer,

Major Macfarlane, and Lieutenant Scott were wounded. Macfarlane was the type of officer who led from the front. He had been wounded during the attack on Fabeck Graben Trench on the Somme in September 1916 and had done reconnaissance during the raid on Balloon Trench in December 1916.

Another of the casualties was Private Clarence Martin. Martin had originally joined the 110th Battalion from Perth County, Ontario, with his older brother, Norman. Reverting from the rank of acting sergeant in order to go to France, he had arrived with the twenty-four reinforcements on April 4 and been issued a new rifle that day. His son passed on an oral account of the incident in which Clarence was wounded:

> About 9 o'clock one morning, 13 of us were sent over the top to draw enemy fire while the rest were engaged in other things. One man turned back almost immediately. I got out the farthest before being hit in the right leg with an explosive bullet [compound fracture of the right femur]. Nine others were killed and two others wounded beside myself. I lay on the field all day. Because the machine gun fire was so murderous, no one could get to me and, by 5 o'clock, I came to the conclusion I was not going to bleed to death and that I could not stay there. I lengthened the sling on my brand new rifle, that had never fired a shot, put my broken leg on it and, with the sling over my shoulder, started to crawl to our own trenches. I did all right till I came to our own people, and that's when I fainted. They carried me to the aid post. The doctor said put him in that tent over there. I was supposed to be dead in the morning.[161] When they checked in the morning, I was still alive, so they threw me on a mattress on the back of a truck and took off. They didn't even wait to tie the broken leg to the other one. It was a bad trip, with the broken leg flying in the air at every bump.[162]

Having enlisted on March 4, 1916, Martin's actual service in action had been less than a week. He would not be discharged from the army until March 9, 1920, almost three years after being wounded.

One mother received inaccurate notice of her younger son's death at Vimy Ridge. Mrs. Duncan Ross of Waldegrave, Nova Scotia was notified of the death of two of her sons in the Vimy attack. While the death of Major Arthur Ross was accurately reported, that of Lieutenant William G. Ross was an error. A letter written by him after his supposed date of death arrived in Nova Scotia before official notification of the mistake. Later in the war, he would be invalided back to England with trench fever, a disease transmitted by lice, and survive the Great War to serve as a training officer in the Second World War. Death would finally claim him in 1965.

Captain Eager took over as acting commanding officer the next day and ordered another attack on Staubwasser Weg and Artillerie Weg. Two parties from A Company made the attack and, against light opposition, were able to move about halfway through Bois de la Folie and establish trench blocks. Three Canadian soldiers, wounded and captured the previous day, were found in the trenches and sent back to the Canadian lines. While the men from A Company occupied the trenches, Lieutenants Dashwood and Dempsey, accompanied by a corporal, moved farther east to examine Buck Trench. There the enemy surprised them, and Dashwood and the corporal were killed. Dempsey killed two of the enemy before he was wounded and taken prisoner. Dempsey would die of his wounds on April 14. Lieutenant Dashwood had been wounded in August 1916 and had returned to the battalion late that year. The parties from A Company had to return to their own lines at dark. The day's casualty total seemed quite high, given that the Diary reported no resistance to the initial move into the first two trenches. In addition to Dashwood, six other ranks were killed. Three more other ranks, along with Dempsey, were missing, and twenty-one men were wounded.

In the aftermath of small actions like these, there was time for the survivors to visit the scene to look for casualties. In a number of cases, family members would go out looking for relatives who might have been killed or wounded. Private Fred Campbell told his nephew of one such occasion near Vimy Ridge when he met his brother, Lewis, as they turned over bodies looking for each other. One can only try to imagine their relief at finding each other unharmed.[163]

On the night of April 12 and 13, the Germans staged a tactical withdrawal from the area and moved east another five to eight kilometres. They were able to accomplish this as their portion of the area had not been fought over and was thus more easily traversed than the recent battlefield. The rain of the previous three days had turned the churned-up soil into heavy mud, making the tracks forward to the new Canadian front line almost impassable. When advance scouts reported that the enemy was retreating, the battalion was ordered to move forward to take the enemy trenches and relieve the 60th Battalion during the night. The 43rd Battalion moved eighteen hundred metres in front of the 58th to set up outpost lines and prevent the enemy from returning to his old positions. During the fighting, four men were killed in action, thirteen were wounded, and three went missing. Among the dead was twenty-year-old Sergeant George Fitton, who had won the Military Medal after the Balloon Trench raid and who had participated in several of the battalion's other raids.

Two companies of the 58th took over the 60th Battalion's positions around La Chaudiere to the north of Vimy while two companies maintained the battalion's original positions around Vimy. The men were beginning to show signs of strain from being on the move and in action for an extended period. Casualties were lighter than the two previous days, with a total of only one officer and six men being wounded. On the fifteenth, the unit moved further east to take a position on the railway line. The newly captured territory yielded a substantial haul of booty. Captain Rose mentions ammunition and engineers' stores lying all about. Eight artillery pieces and one trench mortar were included in the total. The enemy dugouts had electric lighting, something unheard of in the Allied front line trenches.

Enemy activity increased the following day. There was a small attack on the 43rd Battalion's frontage, but it was quickly turned back. Enemy artillery was more active and bombarded the Canadian positions, particularly at night. The 52nd Battalion moved up to relieve the 43rd and suffered heavy casualties during the relief. On the night of the seventeenth, the 1st Canadian Mounted Rifles of the 8th Brigade relieved the 58th. They had just about reached the end of their endurance after nine days in the line. They marched nine kilometres west back to billets at Villers-au-Bois. The last three days in the line had cost the unit another six men killed, thirty wounded, and two missing. Even on the relief there were casualties: a new officer, Lieutenant W. A. Allen, and one other man were killed, and three men were wounded. The route out of the line had taken them over the crest of the ridge near the village of Thelus, and it was under continuous enemy shellfire.

April 19 saw the unit begin to pull itself together. The men spent the day cleaning up for company inspections. On the twentieth they were addressed by Major General Lipsett and inspected by the commanding officer. They were not subjected to any working parties while in reserve at Villers-au-Bois until the twenty-fourth. There were no casualties.

On April 24, the unit moved into reserve at the Quarry Line and was put to work on road repair. Two officers were added to the battalion on the twenty-sixth: Lieutenants Piper and Jucksch. Arnold Jucksch joined the battalion from the 147th Battalion of Grey County. He possessed a great deal of artistic talent. As he was fluent in German, he had been trained as his previous unit's intelligence officer. The British army had adopted some of his ideas on patrolling and sniping before he came to France.[164] A sad comment was entered in the diary on April 28, when the 60th Battalion was broken up to provide replacements to other units. It had been part of the 9th Brigade since its arrival in France. Captain Rose lamented that the 58th would be sorry to lose so many good friends. A Quebec battalion, the 60th was disbanded because it had been unable to draw enough men from its home province to meet its manpower requirements.[165] On the last day of the month, the 9th Brigade replaced the 7th in the line, and the 58th replaced the Royal Canadian Regiment in brigade reserve at La Folie Ridge. There were only two casualties in the period from April 19 to the end of the month.

The Human Balance Sheet

	April	Cumulative
Killed	23	231
Wounded	81	782
Shell Shocked	0	87
Gassed	1	1
Missing	11	199
Reinforcements	26	801

Chapter Fifteen

May 1917
Keeping the Pressure On

The month began with the unit in a reserve position on Vimy Ridge. The weather improved, and Captain Rose comments that the men were "having a great time." The trenches were in poor condition, but there were plenty of enemy dugouts and the Prinz Arnulf Tunnel in which to find shelter. Out of the line, Sergeant George T. Bell took the opportunity to write a twenty-seven-page letter to the woman he had married a week before leaving for overseas. Less than a month after the capture of Vimy Ridge, he gave his wife a taste of what had gone on since then:

> . . . am writing this letter in one of Fritzie's dugouts, he having been kind enough to leave the vicinity recently. . . . No doubt you have read about the great doings over here lately and were also worried to know how I was. I did not see everything, but I have seen quite a lot, enough to make me proud to be a Canadian. . . . I do not believe any men can best those who are out here with us. They go up the line and can take a lot from Fritz but generally give him more in return. They come out completely tired out but after a night's sleep they are

> around as cheerful as ever. I guess this war talk is tiresome to you, Dear, but I just wanted you to know that we are on top and will stay there.[166]

The 58th was occupied with working and salvage parties on the Ridge. The enemy left them pretty much alone, except for a heavy shelling attack on the sixth while the 4th Canadian Mounted Rifles were relieving them. The unit suffered only two wounded that day, while the 4th C.M.R. had three killed and four wounded. On the third, the battalion's position on the Ridge gave them grandstand seats to observe an attack by the 1st and 2nd Canadian Divisions on the town of Fresnoy. The Canadians took their objectives, but the British unit to their right was unable to capture Oppy.

On the seventh, the unit was relieved by the Princess Patricia's and moved well behind the front lines and out of enemy observation to Villers-au-Bois. Five men were wounded during the move, but all remained with the battalion. On the eighth, Lieutenant Colonel Genet replaced Brigadier General Hill while he was on leave, and Major Carmichael stepped in as acting commanding officer for the balance of the month. The battalion held a muster parade and then let the men rest. Lieutenant Cusler wrote home that he had borrowed a tent and slept on the green grass rather than indoors in a billet.[167] In mild spring conditions, the unit carried out three days of training in open warfare techniques. While this seemed a little premature in light of the fact that there had been no breakthrough, there was a focus on small unit tactics that could be used in any attack. On the third day of training, three new officers, Lieutenants Hooper, Ross, and Smith, joined the battalion. Captain Jack Affleck of the 9th Field Ambulance had joined the battalion on May 2. On the day before returning to the trenches, the unit attended church parade and had a half-day holiday.

May 13 saw the unit assume the role of support battalion. For five days it sent out men to various working parties for road maintenance and trench cleanup. There were no casualties during this period, and the unit returned to the front with 26 officers and 771 men.

The front was now about five kilometres east of the town of Vimy and extended in a line through Méricourt, Acheville, and Oppy. The front was still active, but the men knew how to keep out of harm's way, and casualties were light. The officers took time to mete out punishments for various minor infractions. Private Charles E. Knight was given two days of Field Punishment No. 1 for the destruction of government property while on active service. This involved being tied spread-eagle to the wheel of a general service wagon for two hours a day and was colloquially referred to as "crucifixion." It was fairly common to see men trussed up in this fashion for a variety of minor offences.

On the first day back in the front, Major J.D. MacKay was accidentally gassed. There was no mention of a gas alert or use of gas by the enemy, but it is possible he was affected by gas lingering from an attack before the 58th moved back into the front line. The Germans used gas against the Canadians every day in May.[168] On the twentieth there was a short, but heavy, bombardment of the battalion's front. There were no casualties. The men were able to watch considerable air activity each day as the opposing sides continued to look for weaknesses in each other's lines. On the twenty-second, the unit carried out a small raid on Blue Trench. Lieutenant Charles Burrows led four parties of bombers and rifle grenadiers to the enemy forward line and found Blue Trench in such poor condition that it could not be occupied as a forward listening post. The men returned to their own lines, leaving a bombing party in the nearby Bluenose Trench, which was connected to the front line by a communication trench. There were no casualties in the action. Elsewhere, enemy artillery accounted for one death and the wounding of two men. During the relief of the battalion on the twenty-third, enemy artillery caused six casualties.

While in the support line, the battalion was involved in the usual working parties. Casualties were light. A new occupation was assisting the Canadian engineers in tunneling operations on the twenty-fifth and twenty-sixth. The chalk soil of the Vimy area lent itself to this activity, and tunnels in the chalk had played a significant role in the success of the Vimy Ridge assault, for they had allowed the men to assemble safe from the enemy's artillery fire.

Mines had also been dug under the enemy's front line and exploded as the final barrage began on April 9, 1917.

The battalion was relieved on May 27 and moved back to Winnipeg Camp. One soldier was accidentally wounded during the relief. The first day out of the support lines was spent cleaning up and resting. Working parties resumed the next day. The men were employed cleaning up the camp. They were given their pay and offered baths. One soldier was wounded on the twenty-eighth, the last casualty for the month.

The Human Balance Sheet

	May	Cumulative
Killed	1	232
Wounded	29	811
Shell Shock	1	88
Gassed	1	2
Missing	0	199
Reinforcements	3	804

Chapter Sixteen

June 1917
Leading the Way

The battalion started the month of June in reserve at Winnipeg Camp. From there, the men were sent on working party duties for the first five days of the month. The weather was fine and dry. There were no casualties. On the sixth there were four casualties before the unit was relieved by the 42nd Battalion for the march back to Villers-au-Bois. One of the wounded stayed with the battalion.

On the seventh, one small working party of an NCO and thirty-five men was sent out before dawn. It was noticed by an enemy pilot observer and subjected to about forty-five minutes of artillery fire. Most of the fire went over the party, for the German observer seemed to be giving the wrong map coordinates to his gunners. Just as the fire came to an end, one shell fell short, causing casualties among the group. Private James H. Rawlinson was struck in the head by a small shell splinter and rendered blind in both eyes. He would later write about his recovery and rehabilitation at St. Dunstan's School for the Blind in a slim volume that was published shortly after the war.[169]

Training began again on June 8 with company drills. There was only one casualty on the ninth, when the battalion trained for half a day and had a half-day holiday. Lieutenant Ernest Porter joined the battalion that night. On Sunday, June 10, there was a brigade church parade, followed by a march in front of Major General Lipsett, commander of the 3rd Division. Rain arrived on the eleventh and stayed all morning. In the evening, a night training exercise was carried out by all companies and scouts. The next day, the unit relieved the 4th Canadian Mounted Rifles in the Winnipeg Camp area. The day in camp was spent preparing for the return to the front lines. The relief of the 42nd Battalion was carried out that night and completed at 1:40 A.M. on the fourteenth. There were no casualties. The following day, the support company, D Company, moved up to the left flank of the battalion to take over a portion of the trench occupied by the 12th Brigade, and one company of the 43rd Battalion moved into support the 58th. The Diary describes the day as quiet, with normal aircraft activity. Enemy trench mortars bombarded the position that night, and there was one casualty. The casualty bill was heavier the next day, with three soldiers killed and five wounded. They may have been hit as they worked at improving the battalion's trenches or by the trench mortar attack that evening. There were no casualties on the sixteenth, possibly because the nightly shelling by the enemy trench mortars and artillery was met with an effective response from the Canadian gunners. There is no mention in the Diary of artillery attacks the last day of the tour in the line. One soldier died of wounds, and two others were wounded before the battalion moved back to the transport lines that night. Another soldier died of wounds, and two more were wounded the next day, on the return to Villers-au-Bois.

For the next six days, the unit remained in the Villers-au-Bois area and made the diarist's task an easy one by doing much the same activity each day. Here it trained for an upcoming attack. On June 6, Major General Arthur Currie, commander of the 1st Canadian Division, now considered one of the elite divisions in the British army, was promoted to lieutenant general and appointed commander of the Canadian Corps of four divisions. One of the hallmarks of Currie's command and that of his predecessor Byng was careful preparation. His men trained over ground made to resemble their attack objectives, and each man was given a map so that he could continue to the objective even if his officers and NCOs were killed or wounded. Each morning during this period the battalion trained over ground that had the enemy trenches marked out in white tape.

In the afternoon there was time for sports, an activity that improved fitness and built team spirit. Undoubtedly, the platoons also practiced their tactics with the various specialists working in concert. Under Currie's direction, the platoon held up to fifty men and had scouts, a stretcher-bearer, six Lewis gunners, eleven rifle grenadiers, eleven bombers, and fifteen riflemen. The men would no longer advance in waves in open order march. They would advance as small groups, mutually supporting each other in fire and movement tactics. Part of the platoon would advance while another part of the platoon would provide covering fire. On June 22, Lieutenants Thomson, Kress, McLeish, and Montgomery joined the battalion. Lieutenant Thomson was returning after being wounded while the battalion was in the Ypres sector in May 1916. On the twenty-third, the Diary notes the second anniversary of the battalion's birth. On the morning of the twenty-sixth, the unit left the Villers-au-Bois area and moved up to the transport lines. In the evening it moved up to the front line to relieve the 2nd Canadian Mounted Rifles. The relief was accomplished with difficulty in the darkness.

All the training of the previous week would be put to good use immediately. The 4th Division had advanced toward Lens on the battalion's left, and word came down that the battalion was to attack that morning. Lens was a French mining town that had fallen to the Germans in 1914 and remained in their hands despite repeated British attempts to retake it. At 8:30 A.M. on June 26, Major Orr called an orders group for his platoon commanders. His C Company was to advance from Partridge Trench north to capture Ace and Adept trenches in an area between the Lens-Arras Road on the west and the Railway Trench on the east. The advance would be in concert with the 43rd Battalion on the battalion's left. At 9:05 A.M., word was received that the 4th Division had reached their objective, and the officers of C Company joined their platoons at 9:15 A.M. The attack went in at 9:30 on a fine summer's morning. No. 11 Platoon made the first bound of about 140 metres from Partridge Trench to Ace Trench on the left of the Railway Trench. No. 9 Platoon moved up the right flank along Railway Trench to Amble Trench and Alcove Trench, where it established two trench blocks. No. 12 Platoon held

Partridge Trench. The leading platoons pushed patrols north to determine if the enemy strong point at the junction of the Railway Trench and Avion Road was held. By 10:30, the first objectives were achieved, and the leading platoons were ready to move on to Adept Trench, another 450 metres further north. Major Orr asked Captain Torrance to move elements of B Company up on his right flank, freeing No. 9 Platoon and allowing it to advance up Railway Trench to the junction with the Avion Road. Still having a gap in his right flank, Major Orr moved a platoon from A Company in between B Company and No. 9 Platoon. No. 11 Platoon moved up on the left flank and captured Adept Trench from Beaver to Railway Trench. No.12 Platoon moved from Partridge to Ace Trench at noon. The advance was accomplished with only three men wounded.

This set the stage for the next attack. At 3:45 in the afternoon of the same day, Lieutenant J.H.G. Strathy and two men from A Company left on a reconnaissance patrol to determine the enemy's situation at Avion Trench. They moved about 450 metres north to Avion Switch Trench and observed an enemy sentry there before reporting back to headquarters. Additional patrols were sent out that night, two by D Company on the left flank and two by B Company on the right. They were to gather information about the unit holding the German line and, if possible, hold the trench until morning. The D Company patrols failed to reach Avion Trench before returning to their own lines at Adept Trench. Lieutenant Field led the third patrol north along Railway Trench in the centre of the battalion's frontage, but it too failed to reach its objective. The last patrol, led by Lieutenants Gauld and Jucksch, was either luckier or more aggressive. It succeeded in entering Avion Trench. Jucksch had laid a tape on the ground before dark to guide his patrol toward its objective. At 11:00 P.M., Jucksch led his section of twelve men along Amble Trench while Gauld moved his along the roughly parallel Alcove Trench. As they progressed along these trenches, they found that the trenches converged and they proceeded together to the junction with Avion Trench. They found no Germans in Amble or Alcove trenches, although there were signs that the enemy was retreating as the patrol advanced. Imagine the tension as the soldiers moved further into enemy territory, knowing that at any moment they could encounter a superior force waiting to ambush them. They could see the evidence of a hasty retreat as stick grenades lay along the trench walls and candles continued to burn in the dugouts. They could smell the freshly dug earth where the Germans had tried to erect a trench block to impede their advance. The enemy finally put in an appearance when the patrol reached Avion Trench. Jucksch and a bombing party moved along Avion for about ninety metres to the east and found large quantities of German equipment in the trench, indicating that the unit holding it was about to be relieved. Jucksch returned to let Lieutenant Gauld know what he had learned, and Gauld returned to the bombers to lead them in a bombing attack further along the trench. They had gone only a little over thirty metres when they encountered a large group of enemy soldiers. They immediately used their favourite trench-clearing weapon, the Mills bomb, and cleared out about one hundred metres of trench. The Germans retreated rapidly from this assault and then sent up an illuminating flare that turned night into day. Another party of Germans tried to outflank the Canadians by coming in behind them from No Man's Land. Each side threw grenades at the other. The Canadians used rifle fire to cover their orderly withdrawal from Avion Trench. The only casualties were five men lightly wounded. They were back in their own lines by 2:45 the next morning. They reported that Amble Trench and Alcove Trench were lightly held and that Avion Trench, in front of the village of Avion, was strongly held by the 165th Regiment.[170] It appeared the patrol had interrupted the relief of the unit in the line.

During the day on the twenty-seventh, the platoons of the 58th shifted to the right in preparation for their next attack to capture Avion Trench that night. Their position in Adept Trench was consolidated, and the 43rd Battalion moved up to Adept Trench at the point where it joined Railway Trench. The 52nd Battalion covered the battalion's right flank east of Alcove Trench. During the attack, the enemy shelled its old line, now the Canadian front line, and caused significant casualties. This was a common event in trench warfare, for artillery on both sides usually knew the location of their own trenches and could quickly bring heavy fire down on them to drive off an enemy attack. Three men were killed and twenty-two wounded along with Lieutenants Anderson, Wallace, and Gauld, the leader of the successful patrol of the previous night.

War correspondents described this southern suburb of Lens as a "labyrinth of ruined houses" that was "crawling with machine guns as thick as black beetles in a dirty London basement."[171] There had been no mention of artillery support in the previous day's operation, but this attack would begin with a rolling barrage near daybreak on the twenty-eighth. The 43rd Battalion would move strong patrols forward on the 58th's left flank while the 52nd Battalion would move up on the right flank and participate in the capture of Avion Trench. B Company was responsible for Amble Trench on the right of the battalion front, and A Company would move north along the left with Railway Trench as its left-hand boundary. It would be prepared to defend its left flank when it reached the objective until the 43rd Battalion moved up to join it. Each company would attack with two platoons forward and one in support. Each man was to carry a pick or a shovel to be used to dig in on the objective. Lieutenant Hooper was to bring a Signals Section forward to A Company's headquarters to maintain communication with the battalion. Capture of Avion Trench was to be signaled by a combination of flares that were to be observed by friendly aircraft.

The attack began as planned at 2:30 in the morning, and the two companies were on their objectives by 3:05 A.M., reporting their positions at the southern edge of the village of Avion by flares. The enemy did not put up much of a fight. A Company started off slowly after the barrage began. They soon gained confidence and "were quite cool in the face of M.G. fire encountered on [their] left flank and front." The platoon on the extreme left flank lost two killed and one wounded as it established a trench block. The right-hand platoon found the enemy had evacuated Avion Trench, and they reported that fact to the 43rd Battalion. Major Carmichael's B Company on the right was fired upon by a machine gun. He moved to within fifteen or twenty feet of it before shooting two of its crew. Carmichael personally led his men into the trench and bombed the dugouts before consolidating the new position. Three Germans were taken prisoner, and many were killed. Major Carmichael was awarded a bar to his Military Cross, equivalent to a second Military Cross. Both companies sent strong patrols forward to see how far the enemy had retreated. The Germans responded to the attack by shelling their old trenches with a large quantity of shrapnel. B Company's patrol, under Lieutenant Jucksch, was in Avion, south of Lens, when the next phase of the attack began that evening. Spotting an enemy soldier in a trench ahead of him, he called out in German ordering the man to come to him, which he did. Jucksch then shot him with his pistol.[172] Casualties in this stage of the advance were relatively light.

At 1:30 in the afternoon, still on June 28, Operation Order 77 gave C Company the task of penetrating the built-up area of Avion, establishing an outpost line in the centre of town, and then placing an advanced post north of the outpost line on Slag Heap. Again, the two flanking battalions were to move forward at the same time. An artillery barrage would begin at exactly 6:56 P.M. to assist in the move by the platoon to establish the forward post. It would move forward at 7:10 P.M. Flares were to be used to indicate that the final objective had been reached. Communications were to be by wire from a forward signaling station in Avion Trench.

The first part of the operation went smoothly. No. 11 and No. 12 Platoons each established three outposts in the centre of Avion by 5:35 P.M. C Company headquarters moved forward at 5:50 P.M. No. 9 Platoon was ready to jump off at 6:30 P.M. and waited for the barrage to commence. The platoon reached Slag Heap by 7:40 P.M. and sent up the required flare. Lieutenant Cusler sent back word that his platoon had captured thirty-five prisoners and two machine guns. Soon after, the enemy counterattacked, and Cusler sent back word by runner that he needed reinforcements. Major Orr instructed No. 12 Platoon to move forward. Orr filled the gap in the outpost line by moving up a platoon from B Company. The enemy also attacked the outpost line, wounding Lieutenant Bertram of B Company. The counterattack was strong enough to drive the two advanced platoons from Slag Heap back to the outpost line and force Major Orr to place all available men from company headquarters, including the officers' batmen, in the outpost line. The withdrawal from Slag Heap was conducted in orderly fashion, despite enemy pressure from three sides. All the wounded men and German prisoners were brought back, along with the two captured machine guns. Lieutenant Cusler and Lieutenant Piper, the commander of No. 12 Platoon, were wounded, along with eleven other men, and two men were killed. The last stage of the operation had failed because the party of the 43rd Battalion on the left flank had not matched the advance of Lieutenant Cusler's platoon. Cusler would be awarded the Military Cross for his leadership in this action.

Cusler sent off two letters in July. One was to Dorothy Frier, a nursing sister with the C.E.F. whom he had met while in hospital in London the previous June:

> Dot my Dear, so you think I have forgotten you because I do not write. Well dear far be it for I have thought of you ever & if I could only tell you all you could quite understand. I have certainly had some mighty heavy fighting, went over the top 4 times in 3 days & all very successful. The last trip was the best. I had 26 men to attack 300 Huns. We killed about 100, took 35 prisoners & two machine guns & only had one killed and three wounded, being one of the wounded myself. We were completely surrounded but fought our way out taking our whole party. It was great fun, but there are a few other points far more interesting. All I can say is that at one time I was reported dead & in German hands. All is well & I only have a slight bullet wound in the head, went through my tin Hat & down the inside out the front. They sent me down to H.Q. to give some information as to the knowledge I had gathered & they sent me out to [?] the A. [?.] S. Saw Billy & he wanted to send me through but I pleaded with him to let me go back to my unit & he consented, but after a day more I couldn't stick it. I was dizzy & it got dirty so here I am at Corps for a rest. But I go back in a day or so for

> 4 officers have been put out in my Company alone & I am needed. I did want so to go through & get some leave & get down to see you, but really old Dear I am needed with the battalion for I am just so Chesty that I do not want to leave the men to an inexperienced officer. The battalion now can decide if I deserve promotion. I have done my part if they are not satisfied all I can say is I did but my best. Yours ever with Love, do write old Dear even if I can't always, Elmo.[173]

His letter home to his family on July 4 told them that he was well and was returning to the battalion that day.

The next two days were spent consolidating the gains of the previous forty-eight hours. The enemy retained control of the northern portion of the suburb and, between it and Lens, they created a flooded area criss-crossed with belts of barbed wire that made further advances difficult.[174] They shelled the new Canadian position heavily, causing numerous casualties. Lieutenant Kress was wounded on June 29, and Lieutenant Dixon was wounded on the thirtieth. There appeared to be another fatal casualty on the twenty-eighth or twenty-ninth, as well as nine more wounded men. On June 30, the enemy shelling accounted for ten killed, seven missing, and twenty-nine wounded before the battalion was relieved by the 116th Battalion late that night. The stage was being set for the attack on Hill 70, north of Lens.

The Human Balance Sheet

	June	**Cumulative**
Killed	22	254
Wounded	113	924
Shell Shock	0	88
Gassed	0	2
Missing	8	207
Reinforcements	4	808

Chapter Seventeen

July 1917
Relative Calm

On Dominion Day, 1917, the men were out of the line but still in reserve and within reach of enemy artillery. One man was killed and thirteen were wounded. July 2 was a brighter day. Three men were killed and ten were wounded, one man staying with the battalion as it was relieved by the Royal Canadian Regiment and moved to the Quarries. The unit rested there on the third and suffered only one casualty that day. The battalion moved again to Canada Camp near the Château de la Haie, west of the Arras-Bully road, on the fourth and suffered five casualties. There were three casualties on the fifth. The day was taken up with company and unit inspections and muster and pay parades as the battalion sorted itself out after the Vimy operation and subsequent actions.

While the events from April 9 on had gone well for the Canadian Corps, the same could not be said for the offensives of the French and the British. The capture of Vimy Ridge had not been a key part of the plans of the senior partners in the Entente. It had been more a diversion to draw German attention and reserves from the coming French offensive in the Champagne region. This offensive, as planned by General Nivelle, was designed to break through the German lines and lead to the end of the war. As of April 4, the German command had captured a copy of the plan and upset the attack by withdrawing to a line further east and leaving a swath of desolated territory in front of the French. As a result, they were ready for the main French attack when it was launched on April 16. The slaughter of the French infantry in another futile frontal assault brought about the near collapse of the French Army. Its men mutinied in large numbers, vowing to defend their own trenches, but declining to advance against uncut German barbed wire. The British offensive, begun on April 9 with the capture of Vimy Ridge, was continued in the direction of Lens in order to prevent the Germans from moving more troops to the French sector and giving France a blow that would knock it out of the war. Revolution was sweeping Russia at this time, and the Russian summer offensive collapsed as the soldiers deserted and went home, looting as they left the front.[175] The Western Allies were concerned that something similar could happen in France if the French troops were pressed too hard.

The battalion began a short period out of the line with the usual activities. Mornings were spent in some sort of training exercise, and the afternoons were given over to leisure pastimes. On the tenth, the battalion went into divisional reserve, replacing the 4th Canadian Mounted Rifles. It remained in reserve until the eighteenth, supplying working parties for the 8th Brigade. Captain Frank Vipond joined the battalion on July 12, replacing Canon Hedley as chaplain. There were no casualties from the sixth to the sixteenth, but on July 17, five men were wounded. The battalion went back into the line in relief of the 2nd Canadian Mounted Rifles on July 18. It returned to the area of its previous action in June, south of Avion in Adept Trench.

The first day back in the line was a quiet one. The enemy bombarded the trenches under cloudy skies, killing two men. The next day the weather improved, and it remained fine for the rest of the tour. Canadian artillery was noticeably active from the nineteenth to the twenty-first. This was part of the preparation for an attack by the 116th Battalion on July 22. This attack was successful and drew an enemy counterattack (that was beaten off) and enemy shelling that extended to the 58th's sector. The Diary reports little damage to the trenches and only light casualties. Calm returned to the front after the attack by the neighbouring battalion, and only one more man was killed before the relief on the night of July 25. Lance Corporal Thomas A. McComb, a theology student from Victoria College, was ordained on the battlefield by the Reverend Dr. Chown, general superintendent of the Methodist Church, with the sound of gunfire in the distance.[176] Chown, an honourary colonel, was visiting the troops in France. Fourteen men were wounded, but four of them remained with the battalion until the 78th Battalion relieved it.

On July 26, the unit moved from the transport lines to the billets at Gouy-Servins, about ten kilometres west of Avion. A draft of seventy-three other ranks joined the battalion that day. The draft was made up of men who had joined other units and then volunteered to be sent to France as reinforcements. Among this draft was Private Norman Martin. He had joined the 110th Battalion from Perth County, Ontario in February 1916, after a year of teaching. He rose quickly to the rank of sergeant, but, like his brother Clarence, he had reverted to private to get to France. Training resumed for the balance of the month as the battalion restored itself and integrated the new men into their units. The weather was quite variable, with thunderstorms one day and clear skies the next.

Private Harry Miner missed one of the frequent parades during this period out of the line, and his absence was noted. Miner had enlisted with the 142nd Battalion, but transferred to the 161st Huron Battalion in order to go overseas more rapidly. He had reverted from the rank of lance corporal to reach France. He joined the 58th in late December 1916. Missing the parade caused him to receive a sentence of seven days of Field Punishment No. 1. Miner's action seems not to have affected the generally good opinion formed of him as he was sent on a noncommissioned officers course in August and promoted to lance corporal in February 1918.[177]

The men would have a chance to relax in the hours when they were not actively training. They might spend time trying to rid their clothes of lice by passing the seams over a lit candle. This was a bit of an art, as moving the garment too slowly could set it on fire. They might also visit the Red Cross or Salvation Army canteens set up in the reserve areas. Private Lewis G. Campbell, one of three brothers to serve with the 58th, told his son of an occasion when the unit came out of the line after an extended period. Tired and hungry, just glad to be alive, they were charged for their refreshments by the Red Cross. The Salvation Army gave them away for free, a practice appreciated by Lew and remembered long after the war. Time away from the front lines also provided time to settle old scores. Lew also told a story about the theft of an unpopular officer's horse. One night, it was stolen and sold to a French butcher for slaughter. (Then, as now, horsemeat was much more popular in Europe than in Canada.) No one ever discovered who did the deed.[178]

The Human Balance Sheet

	July	Cumulative
Killed	6	260
Wounded	51	975
Shell Shocked	0	88
Gassed	0	2
Missing	0	207
Reinforcements	73	881

Chapter Eighteen

August 1917
Hill 70 and Lens

The capture of the French city of Lens had been assigned to the Canadian Corps in July. It had been under German occupation since the opening days of the war and had been fought over at irregular intervals since then. It was now a heavily fortified ruin, key to German control of one of France's coal mining areas. General Currie objected to the idea of attacking the city itself and proposed to the British High Command that Hill 70, north of the city, be the Corps' objective. His appreciation of the situation was that the city would be dominated by the hill if it were recaptured first. He would rather have Hill 70 under Canadian control in order to dominate the German positions. The weather turned very wet before the attack and forced its postponement until August 15. The Germans expected the attack, but Currie's preparations and his massing of powerful artillery and machine gun fire allowed it to succeed. By August 18, Hill 70 was firmly under Canadian control.[179]

On August 23, the assault on the city of Lens began. Fighting in a built-up area was an unfamiliar experience for the Canadians. Despite their valiant efforts to capture the city, its many fortified cellars and mining tunnels filled with enemy soldiers kept the Canadians from totally liberating their objective. General Horne, commander of the First Army, called off the attack, and the front stabilized until the

 Canadians moved north to participate in the Passchendaele offensive. The 58th Battalion played only a minor role in these operations. It was in rest billets at Gouy-Servins at the beginning of the month and remained there until August 15. A 1st Division officer billeted in the area in November described it as the worst billet of his experience, with muddy streets, ruined houses for shelter, and no creature comforts.[180] As with the major assault at Vimy Ridge on April 9, the battalion would be in reserve. Four days of rain hampered the planned training. The weather improved after the fourth, and the training program was implemented. The companies took turns on the rifle ranges on alternate days. Platoon and specialist training was conducted. During this time, an illness began to haunt the unit. While there were no casualties from enemy action, seven men were evacuated between the second and the seventh. Perhaps the mumps epidemic had returned, but the disease is not identified in the Diary. The rain began again on the tenth, forcing the 9th Brigade to cancel the training maneuvers planned for the eleventh. Five new officers were taken on strength on the sixth. One of them was Albert Thomas Skill. He had been in the 97th Regiment for nine years, and in February 1916, he joined the 158th Battalion for overseas service with the rank of captain. In order to reach France, he voluntarily reverted to the rank of lieutenant. Major R.G. Geary was removed from the battalion roll while he was in Paris on special duty. Geary had transferred to the 58th from the 35th Battalion. He had been mayor of Toronto for three one-year terms, beginning in 1910. The rain ceased again on the thirteenth, and the maneuvers were completed. On the fourteenth, the operation order directing the battalion to move away from the front was received. The battalion's guardian angel must have been working overtime, for this move allowed the battalion to avoid some of the heaviest fighting the Canadian Corps had experienced to this point in the war. The unit arrived at Raimbert on the fifteenth, when the attack for Hill 70 was in full swing. There, it was involved in training exercises and "dumbell contests" (talent shows) until the twentieth, when it moved toward the front in several stages. There was a brigade sports day during this period, and again the battalion did well. Private Findlay Settle of Thornloe, Ontario received a medal for a first place finish in football.[181] Lieutenant Jucksch captained the lacrosse team, which won a silver cup as brigade champions.[182] On August 17, Major Orr, C Company commander, was granted compassionate leave for a return to Canada. At about this time, at least one reinforcement arrived with the battalion. Private Percy Bayley came to the unit from the 110th Battalion. Initially considered unfit because of hammer-toes on his left foot, he was re-examined as the reinforcement supply situation worsened and declared fit.[183] Prior to moving back into reserve behind the attacking units, four more men were evacuated with the unidentified illness. Just as the attack on Lens was about to begin, the 58th was in brigade reserve at Cité St. Pierre, a suburb on the northwest side of Lens.

The battalion spent the period from August 23 to 27 providing working parties to assist the units in the line with trench construction and ammunition supply. While enemy shelling was fairly heavy, casualties to the battalion were relatively light. Only four men were killed and another four wounded before the unit moved into the front line in relief of the 52nd Battalion. These light casualties were in contrast to those suffered by the 44th Battalion of the 4th Division, which lost one company of roughly two hundred men when they ran out of ammunition and grenades after capturing a slag heap known as the Green Crassier.[184]

On August 28, the battalion was in a suburb of Lens, with B and C Company forward, A in support, and D in reserve. A collapsing wall struck the ration party from C Company. This caused eight of the fifteen casualties suffered that day. While there is no specific comment about artillery fire on this day, the Diary is not sure if the wall collapsed of its own accord or was knocked down by a dud shell. The battalion began work on an advanced trench. Enemy artillery struck again on the twenty-ninth, and this time it mixed in gas shells with the usual high explosive and shrapnel shells. Lieutenant Helwig was wounded, and two men were gassed.

On August 30, the officers and men of C Company applied the skills learned in weeks of practicing the tactics of platoon attacks that had been introduced almost a year earlier, after the Somme offensive. Although the Diary contains no operation order, there was a

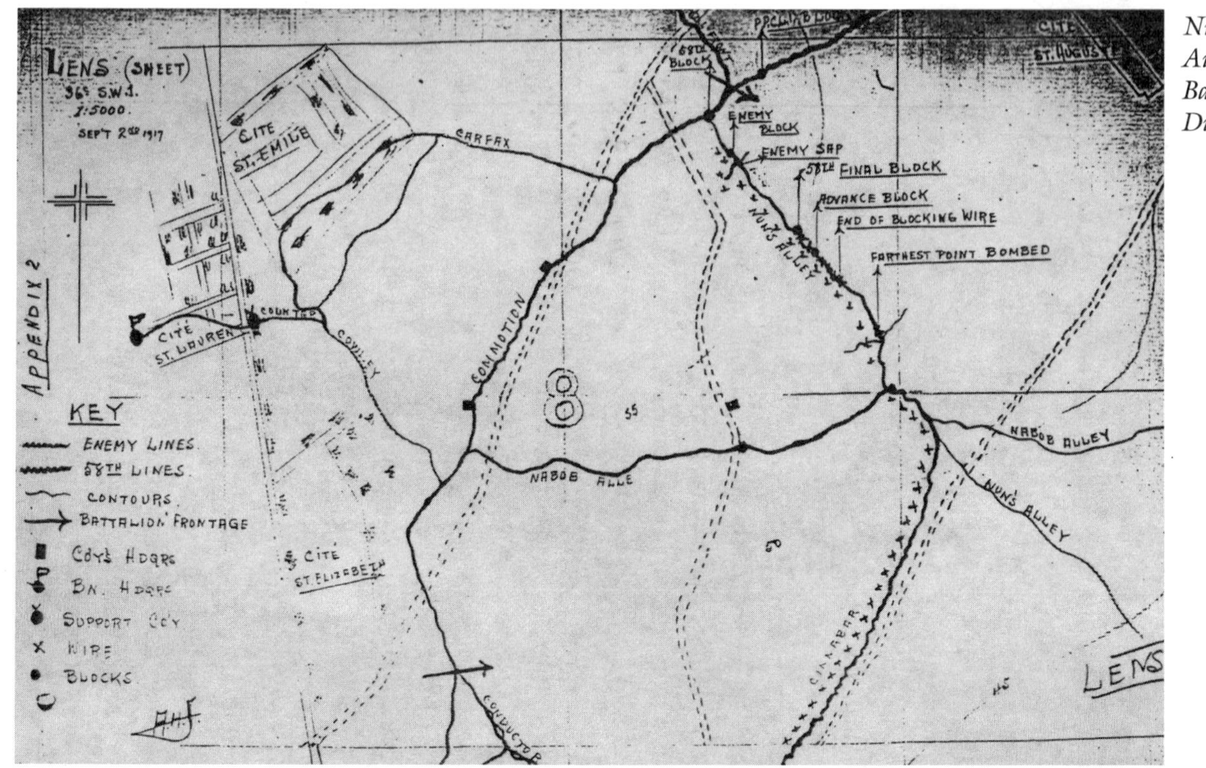

Nun's Alley raid, August 30, 1917. Battalion War Diary, August 1917.

NAC PA7348.

Lieutenant Frank E. Gray won the Military Cross at Nun's Alley.

small raid on a German position known as Nun's Alley. This trench ran at a right angle between the Canadian front and the German lines in the area between Cité Ste. Elizabeth and Cité St. Auguste. About eighty kilometres from the enemy's Cinnabar Trench it crossed a small rise in the ground that allowed unobstructed observation into the Canadian or German trenches, depending upon who held it. Led by Lieutenant Frank E. Gray, a mixed force of bombers and rifle grenadiers attacked the enemy post at the head of Nun's Alley, in broad daylight at 1:30 P.M., without artillery support. The rifle grenadiers and a three-inch trench mortar provided covering fire as the bayonet men and the bombers moved south along the trench. Gray was wounded in the head and shoulder during the first rush and fell to the ground before rising again and attacking the German machine gun nest.[185] The eight men in the enemy machine gun post were killed, and the gun was captured. Lieutenant Gray was evacuated from the lines. The twice-wounded Lieutenant Cusler took his place and the advance along Nun's Alley continued. Two more enemy posts were dealt with in the same way. By now, the raiders were approaching the rise, and the enemy realized

Courtesy Jane Cusler.

Lieutenant Warner E. Cusler on his way to Buckingham Palace to receive the Military Cross for his actions during the attack at Avion in June 1917.

Courtesy Jane Cusler.

Photo taken from German prisoner after Nun's Alley raid. Lieutenant Cusler thought most of the men in it were killed trying to retake the post. Note the stick grenade in the left hand of the soldier in the foreground.

that it was the Canadians' intention to seize this high point. About thirty Germans counterattacked overland, as there was a barbed wire obstacle in the trench. The raiders had recaptured a Lewis gun and used it to good effect. Few of the German attackers returned to Cinnabar Trench. The bombers cleared the dugouts in the sides of Nun's Alley, and three prisoners were captured. Private Norman Martin had come forward to help build a bombing block in the section of captured trench. He joined the bombing party after casualties reduced its numbers and helped to bomb the dugouts and capture one of the machine guns. The enemy then tried several more counterattacks, including two supported by artillery fire, in an effort to force the Canadians out of the trench. They were driven off each time and suffered heavy casualties estimated at 150 men. As the enemy reaction intensified, Major Macfarlane took control of C Company and supported the attackers. He was very experienced in this sort of operation, as was Lieutenant Cusler, and they held onto the gains. The Princess Patricia's on the battalion's left flank took over a portion of the 58th's line to allow more men to support the advanced party and retain the captured portion of the trench. The raiders suffered few casualties in the attack. Cusler was wounded, but remained in the line, and four men were evacuated with wounds. Cusler recommended Lieutenant Gray for the Military Cross and was himself recommended for a bar to his Military Cross by Major Macfarlane. Cusler sent home a brief account of the action in a letter to his family: "I carried on where he [Gray] left off & believe me we did slaughter those brutes. I am so glad we did as well & that I was able to hang on until relief came. It was good sport & a joyous victory even if only a petty scrap."[186] Cusler sent home two photographs of a group of Germans taken from one of the prisoners. The men were part of the 365th Regiment and were likely killed during the counterattacks on Cusler's position.

Most of the 58th's casualties came when the enemy shelled the whole divisional front to disrupt the Canadian defence and support their own counterattacks. The totals reported on the thirty-first included nine men killed, two dead of wounds, thirty-nine wounded, and two gassed. Six more men who were slightly wounded remained with the unit. One of the dead was Captain Lewis B. Henry, killed by enemy shellfire. Henry had joined the unit in late July after spending a number of months in England training men in the skill of rifle shooting. He was a graduate of the University of Toronto, and his yearbook photograph carried the caption, "His sole goal was to be a colonel." Sadly this fine shot and dedicated soldier would not achieve it. Another of the dead was the recently ordained Thomas McComb. Their peers and the higher command recognized the skill of the attackers. Lieutenant Colonel Genet received congratulations from Lieutenant Colonel Agar Adamson of the Princess Patricia's, Brigadier General Hill, and Major General Lipsett. Here was an operation carried out primarily with the resources of the battalion. Since raids were usually staged at night and attacks usually came early in the morning and were announced by artillery fire, the Canadians had the element of surprise in their favour. They brought a local superiority of numbers to bear on three enemy posts and defeated them in detail, with weapons under their own control. When it became clear that the enemy was caught off guard, the men had exploited their success and retained control of their gains. The Princess Patricia's was able to respond to the request for help, and this support allowed the battalion to reinforce its attackers. It was one of the unit's most successful operations to this point in the war. Lieutenant Gray received the Military Cross. Lance Corporal E.C. Dexter was awarded the Distinguished Conduct Medal, and four other men, besides Private Martin, received Military Medals.[187]

The Human Balance Sheet

	August	**Cumulative**
Killed	19	279
Wounded	71	1046
Shell Shocked	0	88
Gassed	2	4
Missing	0	207
Sick	16	16
Reinforcements	5	886

Chapter Nineteen

September 1917
A Temporary Reprieve

The battalion began the month in the lines north of Lens. Enemy shelling continued to inflict casualties, and one soldier was killed and nine were wounded on September 1. Before the unit was relieved the next night, Lieutenant S. McLeish was killed, and two soldiers were wounded. It moved to Cité St. Pierre in brigade reserve. The following day, it moved into billets in the area of Bouvigny, about five kilometres west of Lens. Four men were wounded before the relief was completed.

The Diary comments that the men were "rather played out with hard trip in the line." They were paid and went for a bath parade on the fourth. The next day, they moved again to billets at Mont-St. Eloi, west of Vimy Ridge. The battalion moved again on the sixth to Neuville-St. Vaast. They were headed back to the front and, on the seventh, they relieved British units in the Acheville section, southeast of Lens. Here, they served as brigade reserve and were called on for working parties. Casualties were light and came from gas rather than shellfire. The specific gas is not noted in the Diary, but it could have been mustard gas. The battalion files contain a report dated July 19, 1917, that describes the delivery of this new gas by the enemy and the symptoms among those affected by it. In the first use against British troops on July 12 and 13 in the Ypres area, there had been a

Courtesy Bernard Quigley.

Private 681246 John L. Quigley, buried alive by a shell while manning a machine gun post at Nun's Alley, September 1, 1917.

smell of garlic or mustard in the air, leading to the common use of the term mustard gas. Many of the casualties caused in the first attack occurred because proper precautions had not been taken once the gas shells started to land. The German tactic was to mix gas shells among the shells of a normal artillery bombardment. When they discharged their noxious contents, they made a "plop" noise that identified them as gas shells. The smell of gas had not been strong and, since it was unfamiliar, the alarm was not sounded. Men

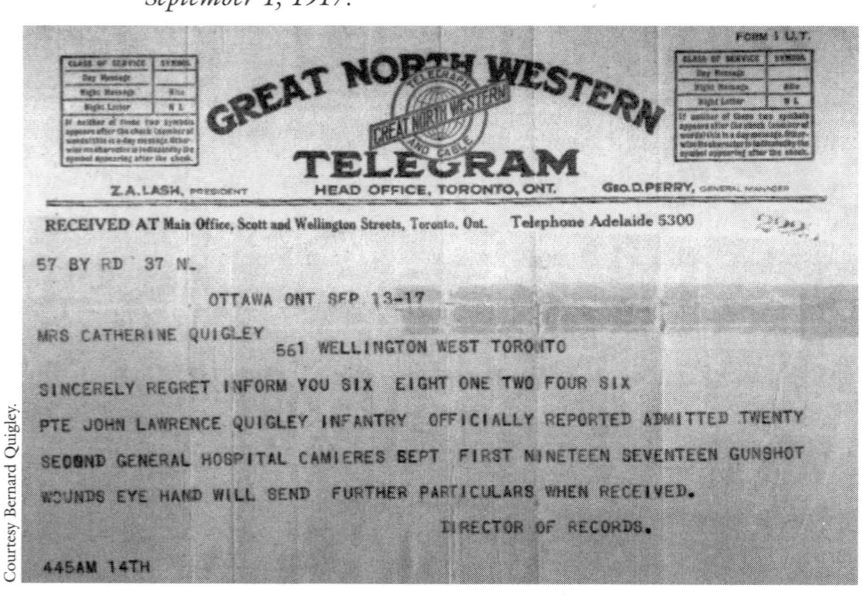

FORM 1 U.T.

GREAT NORTH WESTERN TELEGRAM

GREAT NORTH WESTERN TELEGRAPH AND CABLE

Z.A. LASH, PRESIDENT — HEAD OFFICE, TORONTO, ONT. — GEO. D. PERRY, GENERAL MANAGER

RECEIVED AT Main Office, Scott and Wellington Streets, Toronto, Ont. Telephone Adelaide 5300

57 BY RD 37 NL

OTTAWA ONT SEP 13-17

MRS CATHERINE QUIGLEY
561 WELLINGTON WEST TORONTO

SINCERELY REGRET INFORM YOU SIX EIGHT ONE TWO FOUR SIX PTE JOHN LAWRENCE QUIGLEY INFANTRY OFFICIALLY REPORTED ADMITTED TWENTY SECOND GENERAL HOSPITAL CAMIERES SEPT FIRST NINETEEN SEVENTEEN GUNSHOT WOUNDS EYE HAND WILL SEND FURTHER PARTICULARS WHEN RECEIVED.

DIRECTOR OF RECORDS.

445AM 14TH

Courtesy Bernard Quigley.

Casualty telegram detailing Private Quigley's wounds.

sleeping in dugouts were affected because, like all gases, mustard gas was heavier than air and tended to seep into low-lying areas. Gas blankets designed to seal the entrance to the dugouts and keep the gas from seeping in had not been used. In some cases men thought the danger had ended, removed their respirators before the gas had dissipated, and were seriously harmed by the gas. Where the recommended actions had been taken, there were no casualties. Mustard gas could accumulate on clothing and blister the skin. The initial symptoms were irritation of the eyes and breathing passages. Later, there would be a free discharge of mucous from the nostrils and occasional fits of vomiting. Severe cases of poisoning could lead to bronchitis. The gas could also cause serious damage to eyes and lungs.[188] It was a persistent gas that poisoned the water and mud of the trenches for days and weeks, making it very difficult for the men holding the trenches to continue to function.[189] After the introduction of mustard gas, the Canadian Gas Service adopted new methods to train the Canadian soldier in how to deal with it and the other gases encountered in the war. As with infantry tactics, the soldier would have to be aware of his surrounding and use his initiative while being on the alert for the slightest sign of mustard gas in his environment.[190]

On September 11, the battalion returned to the front line in relief of the 43rd Battalion. The sector was described as quiet during the four days the battalion was in the line. On two nights during that tour of the front line, the Royal Engineers projected gas at the enemy lines. It was likely released from large cylinders and would have relied on the wind to carry it across to the enemy trenches. On the first night it was released, the wind was from the northwest at a little over six kilometres per hour. Two days later, it was released when the wind was blowing from the southwest at almost ten kilometres per hour. It was probably released at night to prevent the enemy from seeing the gas or to catch him off guard while he slept. In cases where the troops were well rehearsed in anti-gas measures, the casualties would be light. However, the wearing of gas masks was not something the men enjoyed, and their use reduced the effectiveness of the troops. No longer a breakthrough weapon, gas was used to harass and wear down the enemy.

Casualties were light during the four days in the line, with three men being killed and eight wounded, one of whom remained in the lines. On the fifteenth, the battalion was relieved by the 116th Battalion and moved to Thelus Cave, south of Vimy Ridge. An interesting incident at this point was the transfer of forty-six men considered surplus to the battalion's requirements to the Canadian Corps Reinforcement Camp. On the twenty-third, the unit would receive forty-one new men from the C.C.R.C. and another thirty-nine from the 9th Brigade Training Battalion, along with three officers: Lieutenants F. Clinchett, L.E. Douglas, and G.A. Ewens. It may have been that the battalion was unloading some poor quality soldiers, or perhaps these were men who had served a long time in the ranks and needed an extended rest to restore their spirits.

While in reserve the first day, they were able to rest before providing working parties that night. They moved to Le Pendu Camp by light railway on the eighteenth and took over the billets of the Royal Canadian Regiment. They spent the day resting and again received their pay and bathed. On the twentieth, they trained by companies. On the twenty-first, they practiced attacks over mock enemy trenches in the morning and participated in a division football tournament in the afternoon. The battalion football team won the division championship over the 123rd Canadian Pioneer Battalion by a score of six to zero. They trained again the next morning and then went to see the football team play in the corps semi-final, where it lost to the Royal Garrison Artillery (the men who served the very heavy guns in the artillery arsenal). Training continued on the twenty-third, and that night, the football team was treated to a dinner with the officers of the battalion. Training continued on the twenty-fourth.

Some of the men had a break from the training routine on September 25. While the rest of the battalion continued with ordinary training, ten officers and several men were able to take in a demonstration of air power presented by No. 16 Squadron of the Royal Flying Corps. Five officers and one soldier were able to go aloft for twenty-minute flights. Training continued for the next two days as the companies carried out mock attacks on enemy trenches signified by lines of white tape. On the twenty-eighth, eight officers and forty men were taken to the tank centre at Wailly for a demonstration. While tanks had been used in the Canadian action at the Sugar Refinery near Courcelette on the Somme in September 1916, the battalion had not worked with them in any of its attacks. It is interesting to see the battalion being exposed to the two weapons that had been developed in this war and that would have such a great impact on the Allied victories in 1918. The lessons learned by the Germans during their defeat in the final one hundred days would be developed into their blitzkrieg tactics of the opening battles of the next war.

In the same week, one member of the battalion was sentenced to death for desertion. Private Leo Emil LeDoux had been charged with desertion and escaping confinement. General Plumer of the British 2nd Army commuted the sentence to ten years of penal servitude. LeDoux was fortunate to be serving in Lipsett's 3rd Division, as only two of its men were executed by firing squad for desertion.[191] There would be at least one other similar case in the battalion before the end of hostilities. Lieutenant James Pedley of the 4th Battalion indicated that often the man was expected to serve his time with his old unit. In such a case, he served without pay and carried out his duties just as any other man would. At the end of the war, Pedley described the scene of three men being called out from the ranks and their sentence of death being mentioned. They were then told that since the sentence had been commuted to life imprisonment, subsequently reduced to two years for good conduct, their time had been served in the ranks and they were free men.[192]

The last two days of the month were spent in a more relaxed fashion. On Saturday, the battalion participated in a sports day with the corps at Villers-au-Bois. In the evening, the men attended a concert staged by the YMCA. There was a church parade on Sunday morning. This was followed by a decoration parade during which three officers and nine other ranks received decorations for bravery and good service. Unfortunately, the War Diary does not contain a list of those who were awarded decorations.

 The Human Balance Sheet

	September	Cumulative
Killed	4	283
Wounded	23	1069
Shell Shocked	2	90
Gassed	0	4
Missing	0	207
Sick	0	16
Reinforcements	37	923

This marks the last time the War Diary refers to shell shock casualties. They are likely included in the wounded total from this point on.

Chapter Twenty

October 1917
Passchendaele: The Third Battle of Ypres

The Third Battle of Ypres, or Passchendaele, was entering its final stages in October. It had been conceived of as an offensive designed to break through the German lines at the Ypres salient and push on to the Belgian coast to eliminate the German submarine bases located there. By this time, almost every division available to the British General Staff had played a role in the offensive, and it was now the turn of the four divisions in the Canadian Corps. After months of fighting and heavy casualties, the British had managed to advance about five and a half kilometres from the start line. The attack had literally bogged down in the Flanders mud, and the objectives were scaled back from the ports on the English Channel to the village of Passchendaele and the ridge on which it sat overlooking Ypres.

The military reputation of Field Marshal Sir Douglas Haig, commander of all of the Imperial troops on the Western Front, was seriously impaired by his decision to continue attacking after the late summer rains began. The constant shelling by both armies over the previous three years had resulted in the destruction of the drainage system of this low-lying area of Europe. The usual late summer rains fell onto this boggy soil and turned it into a sea of yellow mud, waist deep in places. Haig seemed to be fixated on the idea that one more effort here would break the German lines. He continually sent orders for the next attack without realizing what the conditions were like at the front and how difficult it was for the men to attack in them. The British, Australian, and New Zealand Divisions had already lost 250,000 men in almost 3 months of fighting for the meagre gains they had achieved. The result of their efforts was to push the salient deeper into the German lines and expose the Allied troops to more German artillery fire. Haig seems not to have had any concept that his plan was wasting the lifeblood of his nation and its dominions and that he was squandering its human capital for no purpose. It is seen as the low point in the war for British generalship. As the war entered its fourth year, it seemed reasonable to expect that more could have been done with the resources available than to order futile attacks in horrible conditions.

The strain of the war and its previously unheard-of casualty figures were beginning to eliminate the combatants. Russia had gone through a revolution in the spring at about the time the Nivelle offensive was forcing the French Army into mutiny. By October, the Bolsheviks were about to take control of the Provisional Government and make peace with the Germans, taking Russia out of the war. The Italians seemed to be on the verge of elimination from the war after they lost the Battle of Caporetto. Austria, Germany's ally, had advanced a staggering seventy-five kilometres into Italy and inflicted six hundred thousand casualties on the Italian army.[193] The British government transferred five of Haig's divisions to Italy in order to support the Italian efforts to stabilize the front.

The battalion began the month at Le Pendu Camp in the Arras area. For the next ten days, its major activity would be training over ground made to resemble enemy positions. Sometime during this period, Major Macfarlane assumed temporary command of the battalion. On October 1, six new officers joined the unit. The tactics being developed for cooperation with tanks were explored the next day with four officers from C Battalion of No. 9 Section Tanks. Because there is no mention of tanks in the Diary after the second, it is questionable how much use they were to be in the coming attack, but it was another sign of things to come. The weather changed on the third. The wind was constantly above thirteen kilometres per hour, and it rained for six days straight. Bad weather forced cancellation of training on two of the six days. On the fifth, twenty reinforcements arrived. They were mostly men returning to the battalion after recovering from wounds.[194] Major Macfarlane and the medical officer, Captain Jack Affleck, made the rounds of the battalion's positions during a storm on the seventh and then played bridge after dinner that night. Affleck's diary indicates that the bridge continued the next two nights. The unit had received forty-one reinforcements from the Canadian Corps Reinforcement Camp on September 23, but it turned out that this draft had not been authorized. These men were returned to the C.C.R.C on the ninth. There was no training on the tenth as bad weather again forced its cancellation. The battalion received the operation order warning it that it would move to Ourton the following day as the first stage of the relocation to the Ypres front.

When the move took place on October 11, the weather was a little better. The battalion had to split into two unequal sections, as there were insufficient billets for the entire unit at Ourton. A Company was billeted at nearby Dieval. These villages were west of Le Pendu Camp. The battalion joined A Company in Dieval for an inspection the following day, but it was cancelled when the weather deteriorated. Three men left the unit to join the 9th Machine Gun Company. On the thirteenth, the company commanders inspected their men, and on the same day the warning order for the next stage in the journey to Ypres was received. On the fourteenth, the battalion held a church parade with the 116th Battalion from the 9th Brigade. The remainder of the day was spent preparing for the march to Tincques, where the battalion would entrain for the trip to Caestre on the approach to the Salient.

On October 15, the battalion, without A Company, moved south through La Comte, Mazincourt (present day Magnicourt-en-Comte), and Cjelers (present day Chelers) to Tincques. The march took over three hours, and there were no marching casualties. It took from 7:00 A.M. to 8:00 A.M. to load the train, which left Tincques station for Godewaersvelde, sixteen kilometres east of Ypres, at 8:40 A.M. A Company followed twelve hours later. The battalion marched south to Caestre, and A Company took up billets at St. Sylvestre-Cappel, about three kilometres away. The battalion had begun its service here in Belgium in February 1916. The next day was spent resting after the journey. The unit carried out company parades the following day. On October 18, the unit received thirteen reinforcements and went on a route march in the afternoon. On the nineteenth, a party of twelve officers and twelve NCOs went to the area the battalion would be occupying when it moved to the front lines. It is possible that Lieutenant Smythe was with this party, as he had rejoined the battalion in September after recovering from his wounds.

That day, Private Norman Martin of Science Hill, Ontario wrote to his mother:

> Well this is Sunday, so I had better write a few lines again, to let you know that everything is OK. We have not had any Canadian mail, for over 2 weeks now, so we are waiting very patiently, or impatiently, I should say, each day. I have been looking for that box you were sending, but I guess it was delayed too. Probably a boat has gone down. [German submarines were sinking over three hundred thousand tons of Allied shipping each month in 1917, and this was reducing the flow of food to Great Britain and the Western Front.][195] I have received a couple of St. Mary's Journals lately though, and I read them from beginning to end, and then I pass them on to the other boys from St. Mary's. We are having a very uncomfortable spell of wet weather now. [It had rained during previous attacks in the Passchendaele area, but October 18 to 21 were fine days. The rain resumed on the twenty-second as the Canadians prepared for their first attack.] The fine days seem to have gone and the rain and cold have come again. The mud has begun to get quite thick and deep again. I don't know, but hope, and have an idea, it [the war] may quit about Christmas time which is only about two months away now. But likely we will have lots of cold

> trips this winter. I don't know if I will be able to stand the winter or not, as I am bothered a lot with rheumatism lately. I got a letter from Clarence [his brother, also from the 58th, who was wounded in the fighting east of Vimy] and he was around, but his leg is not completely healed yet. He was waiting for his medical board and then he will do what he has to do. I hope he can make Canada on it, as I don't see that he can do much out here for quite a while yet. I see Ivan Doupe and Cecil Fulcher every day and most of the other St. Mary's boys, but they are not as fat as they were in Canada. I think I have lost [weight] myself too. We are on very limited rations now, three men on loaf of bread for a day for quite a while, and when you just get a small piece of fried pork besides your bread for breakfast, and a piece of cheese and a spoonful of jam for supper, and still cut off a third of a loaf, it isn't much. But nevertheless it is better than the poor horses that have to stand out all day and night — days like these — and they have no shelter but are tied along the roadsides in the winter. I guess I had better close now, hoping to hear from you soon. Your dear son, Norman Martin.[196]

The operation order to move to the Wieltje area east of Ypres came on October 20, and the move took place in two stages on the twenty-first. The battalion reunited at Caestre and proceeded by train to Ypres, from whence it marched about six kilometres to the Wieltje area where it bivouacked at Camp C.

As already described, the conditions in the expanded Ypres salient were going to make the coming attack by the Canadian Corps very difficult. General Currie insisted that he be given time to prepare for the attack. These preparations involved the rebuilding of shell-cratered and muddy roads, the creation of artillery positions that would support the guns and not allow them to sink in the mud, and the movement of the troops who were going to participate in the attacks with sufficient time for them to rest before going forward in the mud. The reputation of the Canadian Corps also allowed him to demand that the Corps be used in its entirety and that it be placed under the command of General Plumer rather than General Gough. It was Gough who had commanded the Canadians at the Somme, where costly frontal attacks had been made with insufficient artillery preparation. The first stage of the attack would start on October 26. There was no mention of rain in the Diary during the thirteen days prior to the attack, and the ground was drier than it had been before the previous attacks by the Australian and New Zealand divisions, making the tasks of repairing roads and preparing gun positions easier.

The German defences were different this time for two reasons. First, the waterlogged soil did not allow the creation of deep trenches and dugouts to shelter the defenders. In addition, the successful attack by the Canadians at Vimy had confirmed for the Germans that it was a mistake to hold the forward positions with large numbers of troops, which would be killed off by the British artillery barrage. Instead, the forward positions should be held lightly, leaving the bulk of the forces available for a rapid counterattack. For these reasons, the Germans created long, low, reinforced-concrete bunkers, known as pillboxes, with walls and roofs five feet thick to provide shelter from artillery fire. It would take a direct hit from a fifteen-inch shell to destroy one of these bunkers. Roughly two thousand of these structures were spread out, checkerboard fashion, over the area.[197] The German defenders would be highly trained machine gunners, and each of the bunkers would be placed so that it could protect its neighbours from frontal attack. The Canadians would have to eliminate each one of these strong points individually in order to capture their objective.

The 58th was in the reserve area on October 22, and the men participated in working parties that day. The next day, it moved a step closer to the front line by traversing the muddy ground on narrow wooden duck-walks, or "bath mats," and entered the support trenches in relief of the Auckland Battalion, a unit from New

Zealand. In his autobiography, Lieutenant Jucksch gives a vivid description of the conditions:

> It was mud-mud-mud; a sea of mud; churned and churned by shellfire; over and over again. I remember going up to what we thought were trenches & all we had to walk on was what we called a bath mat; two strips [of wood] with crosspieces. On the way up I saw near this walk a hand partially sticking out of the mud & it seemed at times to be moving, so I quickly crawled & waded through the mud & discovered there was a man almost completely buried under this hand! I scraped the mud away from him & washed his face and sent him out, just in time to save the poor fellow.[198]

The mud was so deep and so soft that, when artillery shells landed in it, they exploded well below the surface, throwing up a shower of mud and doing little damage unless they made a direct hit on men or equipment. Lieutenant Ewens, who had joined the battalion exactly one month before, and another soldier were killed, and eight soldiers were wounded during the move.

NAC PA4432.

Bellevue Spur pillbox, Passchendaele.

Courtesy Geoff Stead.

"Laying duck-boards in the mud," Passchendaele.

On October 24, the battalion moved into the front line, with headquarters located at a captured German pillbox known as Waterloo Farm, about 450 metres northeast of Gravenstafel. The line was held on a one-company front, with D Company in the forward position and A, B, and C in support. Currie's plan would give the battalion a day to rest before going into the attack. The battalion would go forward on the morning of the twenty-sixth with part of the Bellevue Spur, about eleven hundred metres in front of it, as its final objective. The men would start in the flooded valley of the Ravebeek, known as the Marsh Bottom, and move parallel to the Gravenstafel-Mosselmarkt Road up the Bellevue Spur, which ran out of the Passchendaele Ridge and past the hamlet of Bellevue itself.

One of the hallmarks of General Currie's leadership was the continual demand for information about the enemy, right up to the time of the attack. This required observation of the enemy lines and usually involved sending out patrols. Lieutenant R.E. Smythe and two scouts carried out a reconnaissance at 10:00 P.M. on the night before the attack. He and the scouts also had the task of laying tapes in the area in front of the battalion's trenches to mark the point at which the attack would begin. While in No Man's Land, Smythe had noticed the glow of a cigarette coming in their direction. It turned out to be a party of nine Germans. Smythe had studied German while in hospital and challenged them before they could see the tapes. He learned they had come to relieve another unit. He ordered them to advance and placed himself and the scouts behind them. When Smythe cut off their avenue of retreat, the Germans moved into the field of fire of a Lewis gun that had been set up in No Man's Land to cover Smythe's patrol. Smythe called on the Germans to surrender, which they refused to do. Instead, they scrambled for cover in a nearby shell hole. Smythe shot their leader and, in the melee that followed, two more Germans were killed and five captured. The prisoners, members of the 464th Hanover Regiment, were taken back to battalion headquarters, where they gave up valuable information about enemy positions. Smythe was awarded the Military Cross for his action that night. At midnight, the attackers moved into the area selected by Lieutenant Smythe as the jumping off trench. D Company held the left flank on a two-platoon frontage, with its other two platoons in reserve and B Company in support. A Company was on the right flank, with one platoon forward and the rest behind, and C Company was in support. The 43rd Battalion was on its left, and the 46th Battalion of the 4th Division was on the unit's right. The 52nd was in support. The assembly in the jumping off trench was completed by 4:00 A.M. without any casualties. At 5:40 A.M., on a misty, overcast morning after a night of rain, the covering barrage began, supplied by 210 eighteen-pounders of the field artillery, 190 howitzers, and 26 heavy guns.[199] The barrage was to be over six hundred metres in depth across the Canadian front and advance at a rate of ninety metres every eight minutes.[200] Indirect machine gun fire, a Canadian specialty, was used to thicken up the barrage.

The battalion's leading platoons followed the artillery attack as closely as they dared over open ground devoid of any cover. The soil had turned to slime through the combination of artillery fire and drizzle. At some points along the front, the mud was hip-deep. The men had to cover 450 metres of ground before they reached the main enemy line. They found the wire in front of them well cut by the preliminary barrage.[201] However, the enemy immediately replied with his own artillery fire and shelled the area between the

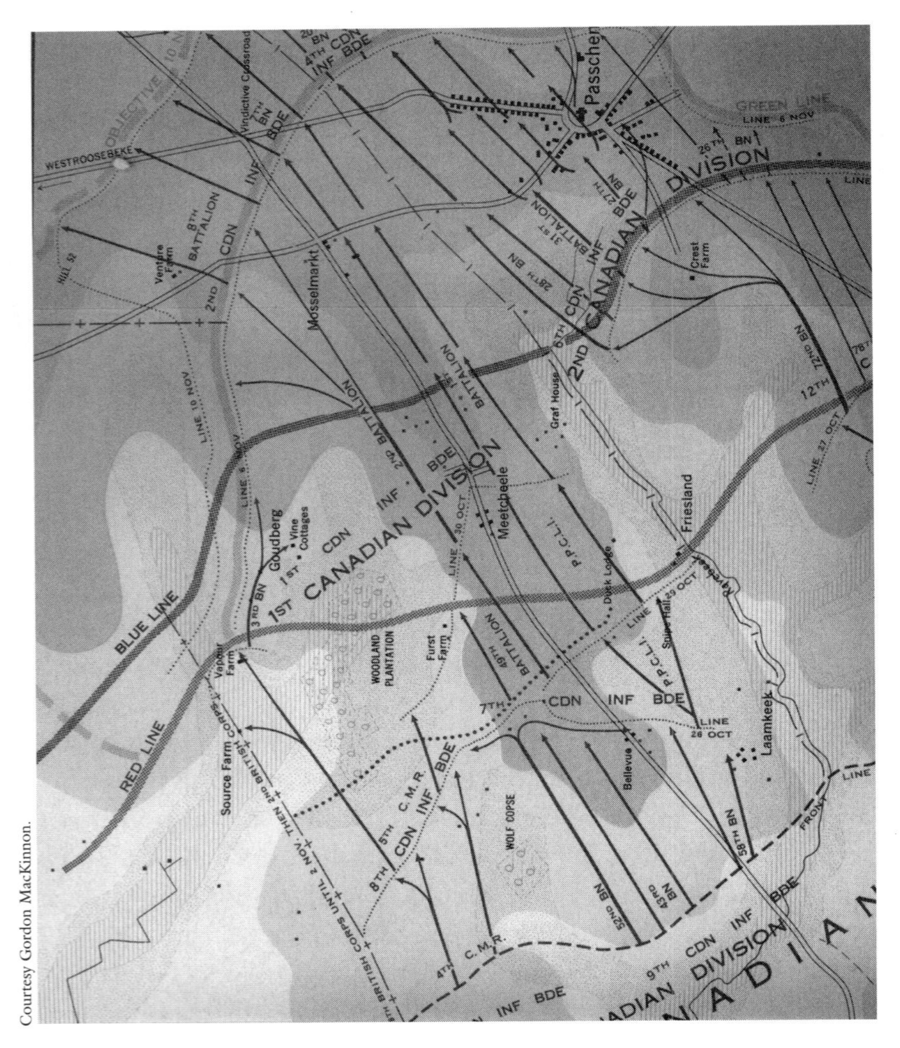

Courtesy Gordon MacKinnon.

58th Battalion's sector of the first stage of the Passchendaele attack, October 26, 1917.

Gravenstafel Road and the swollen Ravebeek water course, causing casualties among the troops assembled there for the next phase of the attack. When the barrage lifted and moved on to the next enemy line, it was apparent that the shells were unevenly distributed over a depth of about 275 metres. This dispersal caused some casualties among the attackers, but they proceeded with the assault. The men had to deal with heavy machine gun fire coming from the enemy troops who had sheltered in the bunkers during the barrage and those from the hamlet of Bellevue. Rather than walking toward the enemy trenches in open order waves, as they had done on the Somme a year earlier, the troops used the much-practiced platoon tactics of mutual support and worked around behind the machine gun positions. Published accounts of the capture of these strong points usually describe actions by one or two men crawling forward to get behind the enemy machine gun and using hand grenades to kill the crew or making a desperate rush into their midst with rifle and bayonet. Certainly, it took great courage to work through the clinging mud in the face of heavy enemy fire to eliminate these obstacles to the advance. Several Victoria Crosses, the British Empire's highest decoration for valour, were won in this way by men of other units involved in the attack. Such feats of valour had to be witnessed by an officer, and most of the platoon commanders were killed or wounded, which may account for why none were awarded to men of the 58th. It was likely in this fashion that the men of the battalion captured three pillboxes and Dad Trench, a position that curved from the remains of the road in front of Lamkeek Farm toward the Gravenstafel-Meetcheele Road. In addition, Acting Company Sergeant Major Andrew A. Anderson killed five machine gunners with his rifle to help his company advance. The attack continued as fresh platoons came forward and established positions ahead of Dad Trench. They moved another five hundred yards along the road toward Contour Trench. The German artillery shifted its fire to the trenches captured by the Canadians and forced them to withdraw temporarily.[202] Major Macfarlane learned that about one hundred members of the battalion returning from being wounded had arrived at the transport lines under command of Lieutenant Arthur Field. He had Field and

Lieutenant Smythe bring them into action in a second phase of the attack.[203] Smythe describes the men as moving forward like bands of Indians and infiltrating behind the German lines to take a key pillbox from the rear and facilitating the capture of several others. The German defenders continued the struggle for this position until about 2:30 in the afternoon, when four officers and sixty men surrendered.[204] The captured trench also contained another officer and eleven men who had been wounded and were then taken prisoner. Another five machine guns were captured at the same time. Canadian newspapers reported after the battle that the enemy had been ordered to fight until killed or captured, since the positions here were considered by the German commanders to be crucial to their whole line.[205] Other accounts of the battle indicate that the battalion initially captured part of Bellevue Ridge, but that it was driven back by enemy artillery and machine gun fire.[206] The Diary gives no indication of an advance beyond Contour Trench or of any retreat. Lieutenant Don Cameron sent a letter to Edgar "Pat" Patten's family, care of a Miss Gissing, to let them know how Pat had died. After assuring the family that their son was a noble officer, well loved by his men, he gave a detailed account of the action:

> The bare details of his death are as follows: - We left our "jumping off" trench in front of Bellevue Spur, Passchendaele, on the morning of the 26th, October last at 5:40 A.M. I had the Platoon immediately on "Pat's" right and Mr. [William Ambrose] Moore had the Platoon on his left. We got well away but almost immediately encountered heavy machine gun fire from both our flanks and our men began to drop quite fast. I got a few men together and rushed the enemy strong point on the right flank, which finished them. I then noted that our left flank was being held up by the excessive machine gun fire, and as Mr. Moore was killed, I knew that both Pat and I would have to go for that "Pill-box" ourselves. I ran across to Pat and found him encouraging his men as calmly

> and quietly as if he had been on parade. We both decided we should have to open machine gun fire to finish off the Bosch, but as both our machine-gun crews had all been killed or wounded, we had to go back, find the gun, dig it out of the mud, carry it up on our back and open fire. Well, we did this but I found my gun much closer at hand than Pat found his and I had fired quite a number of rounds before I saw Pat coming up carrying his gun on his shoulder. I remember saying to myself "Good old Pat, now Fritzie will get it" but from what his men told me a little while later, he didn't have an opportunity to fire a shot. As he got into position, a German sniper got him with a rifle bullet directly through the forehead and he must have died instantaneously. I did not know about this until about an hour afterwards. So far as I can make out, he was killed at about 8 A.M. Just at this time, I discovered that I was the only officer left out of the 16 of us who went over the top and as you may imagine, I had my hands pretty full until about 2 P.M. when I had my arm broken by a shell. After that I have only a confused idea of what happened as I had to stay with the men and encourage them to hold the ground we had won until I was relieved about 4 P.M. On my way to the dressing station, I tried to find his body, but was unsuccessful owing to the mud and darkness.[207]

Patten's body was never located, but he is commemorated on the Menin Gate. Lieutenant Cameron was awarded the Military Cross for his actions in the attack, including the capture of an enemy pillbox after five hours of fighting. Acting Company Sergeant Major Andrew Anderson took over one company, possibly Cameron's, after all the officers were killed and wounded and held the position until relieved, despite being wounded himself. He received the Distinguished Conduct Medal for his gallantry.

On the night of October 26, the battalion consolidated its position in the captured trench. Lieutenant Jucksch established contact with the units on the flanks and maintained communications with battalion headquarters. The wounded were moved into the shelter of the pillboxes around Lamkeek Farm. German dead were stacked like cordwood around the pillboxes until their own artillery fire blew their bodies away.[208] Eight machine gun posts were established in shell holes on an arc from Lamkeek Farm to Bellevue, including three with captured guns. The enemy made no serious attempt to recapture the 350 to 450 metres of lost ground and contented himself with directing heavy shellfire on the Canadian positions. The 116th Battalion relieved the battalion on the evening of the twenty-seventh.

The whole operation had cost the unit 303 casualties out of roughly 500 attackers, its heaviest losses in one action to this point in the war. Four officers and twenty-one other ranks, including four stretcher-bearers, were decorated for bravery. The final objective had not been gained, but the advance had moved the Canadian lines out of the swampy ground known as Marsh Bottom onto the Bellevue Spur and would ease the next stage of the attack toward Passchendaele.[209]

The following day, Canadian newspapers carried extensive accounts of the fighting without identifying the specific battalions involved. The *Globe* described the conditions under which the men advanced to attack the German strong points. It also mentioned that these attacks were launched from virtually the same trenches the Canadians had defended in April 1915. Part of the account seems to describe the actions of the 58th near Lamkeek. "There was sharp hand-to-hand fighting at Lamkeek-Bellevue, but an attack of our battalions on the southern ridge, to the right of the Marsh Bottom, found the enemy largely demoralized."[210]

On relief by the 116th Battalion, the unit moved back to Abraham Heights, south of Gravenstafel. The enemy shelled the field artillery battery near the battalion's position, but the situation was described as normal. That night the unit was relieved by the Princess Patricia's and moved to Wieltje. The final casualty bill was prepared on the twenty-eighth. Captain Affleck's diary entry records that only seventy men answered the roll call that day. Five officers and fifty-four men had been killed in action. Lieutenant Skill had died leading a platoon from D Company in the first assault. One officer, Lieutenant H.R. Thomson, and three men died of their wounds. Thomson had been wounded in May 1916 in the Ypres Salient and had returned to the battalion in June 1917. He was being sent out of the line on the night before the attack when he was struck by a shell fragment and killed. Also among the dead was Private Norman Martin. Another twenty-seven men were missing and likely killed. Nine officers and 204 men were wounded. The battalion rested on the twenty-ninth. During the night, enemy planes bombed the camp. On October 30, the men were taken by bus to Esk Camp in the Watou area, about sixteen kilometres west of Ypres, to continue their richly deserved and essential rest to the end of the month. The unit reported no additional casualties after the twenty-eighth. The month had cost the 58th Battalion almost three hundred men and they had captured half of a farm field.

The Human Balance Sheet

	October	**Cumulative**
Killed	65	348
Wounded	222	1291
Shell Shocked	0	90
Gassed	0	4
Missing	27	234
Sick	0	16
Reinforcements	-1	922

Chapter Twenty-one

November 1917
Passchendaele Retained

The new month found the battalion in a rest camp at Watou, about five kilometres west of Poperinghe. The first day saw a muster parade, to take a count of the men with the battalion, and a pay parade, as well as the arrival of two new officers, Lieutenants Walter W. Johnson and Elliot G. Strathy, the younger brother of Lieutenant J.H.G. Strathy, along with 117 other ranks. The younger Strathy came from the depot battalion of the Canadian Mounted Rifles, having arrived in England before his unit. He kept a diary of his experiences during the war, including his time with the 58th. The process of rebuilding the fighting strength of the battalion began the next day. Company training took place the next two mornings. One of the missing men from the attack at Bellevue Spur was reported safe on the third. On the same day, Brigadier General Hill, commander of the 9th Brigade, addressed the unit and complimented it on the attack of October 26. The men attended church on the fourth and, no doubt, a few words were spoken in memory of their fallen comrades. The battalion marched to Poperinghe for baths on the fifth. Training resumed on the morning of the sixth and continued until the eighth. Major General Lipsett, commander of the 3rd Division, addressed the men on the afternoon of November 6. One has to believe that he too would have been full of praise for the achievements of the battalion. Another thirty-five reinforcements bolstered the battalion's fighting strength the next day.

In the course of day-to-day activities in the battalion, the officers had to censor the letters the enlisted men sent home. They were allowed to self-censor their own mail. Lieutenant Strathy used the task, assigned as part of his duties as orderly officer, to meet the spiritual needs of one of the men.

> 6/11/17 Tuesday
>
> I was orderly officer today for the first time since I joined the Army. We had a good work out this morning. This afternoon I was censoring staff letters when I came across one from a lad named Powell who apparently had written his people for a Bible which hadn't come so I went to the padre & got one for him, in return for which I got a very nice note. Had a cup of hot chocolate before going to bed.[211]

Elliot Strathy's diary also indicates that Lieutenant Colonel Genet returned from leave on the seventh. That night the officers held a special dinner, and Strathy records the menu in his diary.

> 7/11/17 Wednesday Rain
>
> We started work but rain called it off for the morning. In the afternoon the Bn parades to Pop. to the Theatre. Tonight we put on a special dinner. Col. Genet returned from leave today.
>
> Menu
> Sardines on Toast
> Mock turtle Soup
> Roast Chicken Stuffing & Bacon
> French Peas Mashed Potatoes
> Raspberries & Custard
> Apples Pears
> Coffee – Wine[212]

Jucksch also mentions a dinner at about this time in his autobiography. The colonel was in attendance and found the bill rather steep, so he suggested that Jucksch do something to redress it by liberating a case of champagne from a large stack near the restaurant door. Positioning himself in front of a taller officer as they headed for the door, he was able to have the other man slide a case on his shoulder as he went through the door. He shared the spoils with the other officers.

On November 9, the unit began the move back to the front lines. The first step was to march to L'Abeele and then entrain for the ride to Ypres. Lieutenant Elliot Strathy described the train as very "ramshackle rather battered by shrapnel."[213] From there, the men marched to the Wieltje area, east of Ypres. Strathy was disappointed that they didn't march through Ypres, but he did see the ruins of the Cloth Hall in the centre of the city from the line of march. The night was spent at Camp C. The next day, the battalion moved into brigade reserve at Capricorn Keep. Lieutenant Colonel Genet was admitted to hospital in Etaples with rheumatism and acute articular myalgia. It is not surprising that a man in his fifties would be affected by these ailments in the wet and cold conditions of trench warfare. Perhaps the dinner was a farewell celebration for him. Major R. A. Macfarlane now assumed permanent command of the battalion. Before it moved into the front line in relief of the 10th Battalion, eleven men were evacuated sick. Elliot Strathy's diary gives a graphic description of the condition of the area the battalion moved through:

> We were camped very close to the Main Road along which there was a continuous stream of waggons, trucks, horses & mules loaded with all sorts of supplies. Our transport lines were the other side of Ypres where we entrained. The broad gauge R.R. came up this far but a narrow gauge line runs several miles farther up. The shelling does not bother me as much as the air raids in Poperinghe.

Saturday 10/11/17

We moved about a mile farther up, under shell fire all the way some of which came uncomfortably close. Our destination was several old German pill-boxes, rather cramped quarters but fairly safe except from a direct hit. I met Craig of 12th [???] he is in 127th Ry Troops & they are extending the narrow gauge railway toward the front. The pill-boxes have very thick walls & would, I imagine, be a nasty thing to attack. There was an old tank stranded near here & Johnson & I inspected it. It had been hit by a shell & rather badly messed up inside. One of the crew was still in it crushed under the water. I should think he had been dead for several weeks. The tank was about 20'x 8'x 8' – not as large as I thought they come. I got a letter from Miss Tyrwhitt today asking for Raymond's address. Yesterday's camp was close to the Duck Walk but today's is a short distance away from any road & we have not had as much shelling, though we can hear & see lots of shells falling all around us. There is the same continuous stream of shells going up to the guns & ambulances coming back loaded. Rained nearly all day.

Sunday 11/11/17

Busy all morning making preparations for the move forward, getting the ammunition distributed & the new Lewis Guns in shape. We moved off at 3:30 as we had a long march, probably 6 miles to our destination. We had no packs but all the men carried 220 rounds of ammunition so we moved slowly. The other 3 platoons went up the duck walk but we went up the road. The mud in some places was only up to the knees. We passed countless batteries of our guns banging away & Fritz was replying. We found the balance of the Company at the end of the duck walk when we picked up our guides, & then on we went. It was pitch dark & the road or rather the path was very narrow & there was a continuous stream of men coming down & there were shell holes in the road into which we kept slipping so that it was a most cheerful trip. At the side of the road lying in the mud were the bodies of men who had been killed going up or coming out who had not yet been buried – not very cheerful for the first trip in. We reached what the guide said was our destination at about 8 o'clock & then he left us. As it turned out it was the right Bn but the wrong Company. However finally got settled into our place which was a comparatively comfortable "Hasty Fire Trench." I had about 100 yds on the left (N) of the main road, divided into 3 sections which we afterwards connected up. We were in front line with C Co. on our left & A & D Cos in support. There was a fair amount of shell fire but nearly all in the support trenches though one of our guns which was firing short bothered us a good deal as it almost blew us in several times. During the [?] a Boshe came over & gave himself up. He was a well set up man. Some others came over too but they were fired on by our men before they were close enough to get away. Every hour or so I made a tour from one end of the trench to the other to see that everything was in shape. My first night in the front line was not bad. I had 20 men with me. Sergeant Douglas did not come in this trip so Priaulx [Probably Reginald Priaulx 453217 of the Channel Islands] acts as Platoon Sergeant On the way up Murphy my batman disappeared with my rations, but I got another one "Stucky" – a very good chap. It moved into the front line

> north of Passchendaele near Vindictive Crossroads at 11:30 on the night of the 11th, with B and C Companies in the front line northeast of the intersection.and the other two in support.[214]

The final stage of the Canadian Corps' attack to capture Passchendaele had been completed on the tenth, but the enemy would not let the Canadians keep it without a fight.

The twelfth was a fine day, with a light breeze blowing from the southwest. Enemy shelling was very heavy; Lieutenant Condie and fifteen men were wounded, and one man was killed. The next day started in a similar fashion, with heavy enemy artillery fire in the morning and early afternoon. At 4:30 P.M. the enemy barrage intensified, and soon afterward an attack was launched to drive the battalion from its positions. Captain Affleck obtained a pistol with which to defend the regimental aid post, as the enemy seemed poised to break through behind a heavy barrage.[215] Lieutenant R.E. Smythe, the commander of C Company on the left front, observed enemy infantry gathering for the assault and fired a flare to alert the brigade artillery. The barrage arrived on target almost immediately and caught the assembled waves of attackers in the open, inflicting heavy casualties on them. Company Sergeant Major James Farr brought up his Lewis guns from D Company to assist the forward platoons. The surviving attackers were subjected to a withering hail of rifle and machine gun bullets as the men responded to the leadership of Lieutenant Smythe and platoon commanders Lieutenants Johnson and Field. The report by Major Macfarlane noted the cool way they handled their men under heavy machine gun fire from the enemy. Lieutenant Walter Johnson, who had gone to England with the battalion in 1915 as a lance corporal and had only joined the battalion at the beginning of the month, was praised for his ability to direct the fire of his men on the enemy and was given much of the credit for defeating the attack. He then led a patrol into No Man's Land and captured seven Germans without suffering any losses to his party. The defence was so successful that the support companies of the battalion and the 43rd in reserve were not required.[216]

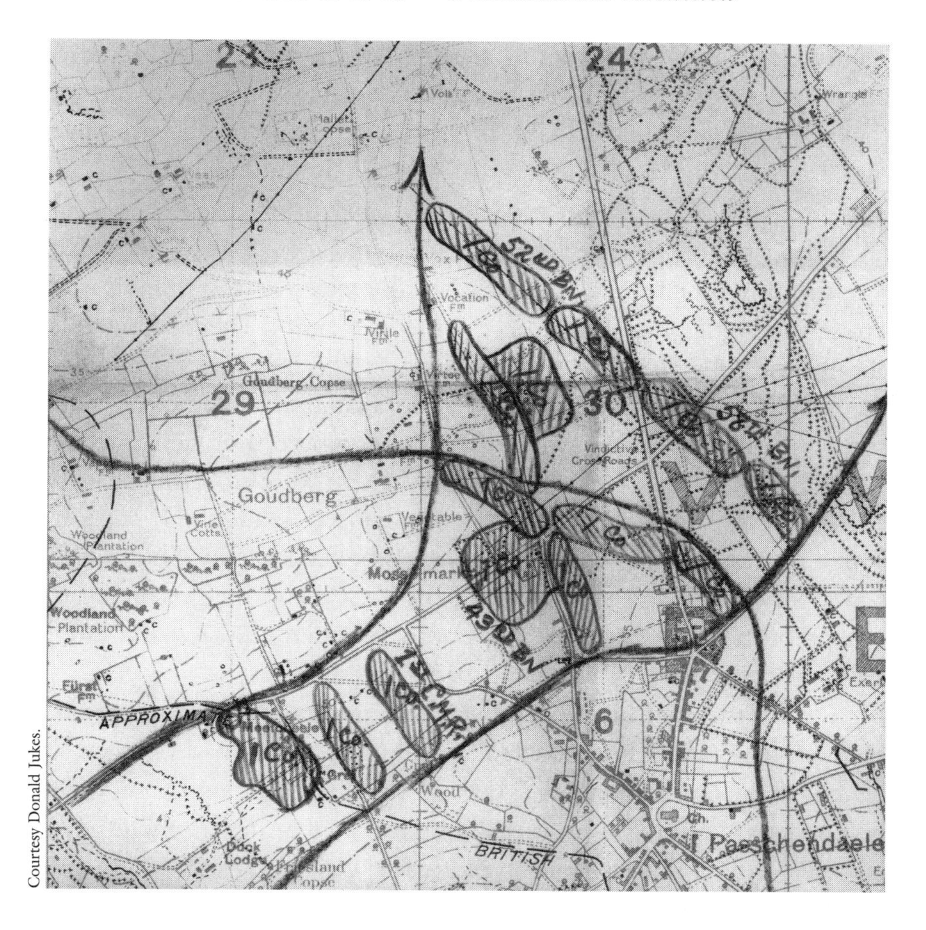

Courtesy Donald Jukes.

58th Battalion's sector at the defence of Vindictive Crossroads, November 13–14, 1917.

The enemy barrage did claim some lives. Captain Samuel Greenshields Torrance of B Company and one soldier were killed, and another nine soldiers were wounded.[217] Enemy artillery was less active on the fourteenth, but it inflicted more casualties than on the previous two days. Lieutenant Elliot Strathy, whose service with the battalion had begun only on the first of the month, and fourteen other men were wounded. Strathy had expected his relief at about 7:00 P.M. and left his shelter to look for it when he was hit by a shell burst. He said later he heard it coming and tried to dodge, but that he didn't dodge far enough. He was brought out of the lines by

Lieutenant Johnson, with the remains of his platoon, when the relief was completed.[218] The casualty toll among the officers meant that Company Sergeant Major James Farr had to take over command of D Company. The Royal Canadian Regiment relieved the battalion that night, and it moved back to Outskirt Farm.

The battalion marched into the shattered city of Ypres the next morning and then traveled by train five kilometres west to Brandhoek. From there, the men marched to Derby Camp. They proceeded about thirty-eight kilometres southwest to Haverskerque by bus on the sixteenth. The next day, they made a nineteen-kilometre route march to Auchy-au-Bois, west of Bethune, where they remained in billets for the remainder of the month. There were no casualties on the march to Auchy. The next three days passed in a leisurely fashion with a clothing inspection on the eighteenth, baths on the nineteenth, and a pay parade on the twentieth. The NCOs and men received an extra month's pay as a Christmas bonus. Six men reported sick after arriving at the billets in Auchy-au-Bois.

On the twentieth of November, the largest tank attack of the war to this point was launched on the Cambrai sector. It had been conceived of as a large trench raid, but the British High Command, desperate for a success after the limited advance at Passchendaele, changed it to a major assault designed to capture and hold enemy trenches. It went in without a preparatory artillery barrage and caught the enemy by surprise. The German commanders believed that the British had shot their bolt at Passchendaele and would have nothing left for another attack before the winter set in. All 381 tanks available to the British were used in the initial attack, and there were no infantry reserves, as all but nine of the sixty British divisions on the Western Front had had their offensive strength exhausted in the swamps before Passchendaele. The initial rupture in the German lines was eight kilometres deep on a nine-and-a-half-kilometre frontage. The results were very impressive, given the fact that it had taken 3 months and over 250,000 casualties to achieve a similar change in the front at Passchendaele. One is tempted to think what the result might have been if the Canadians, Australians, and New Zealanders had been available to exploit the initial success instead of recuperating after the bloodletting east of Ypres. In fact, the Canadians had been assigned to General Byng's Third Army for thirty-six hours in early October 1917, before being transferred to the Passchendaele front.[219] Within ten days of the initial attack, the Germans had staged a massive counterattack and restored their lines. Nevertheless, the British generals did learn from their early successes, and these lessons were incorporated into the final offensives of 1918.

Training resumed on the twenty-first and continued the next day. On the twenty-third, the battalion marched nine and a half kilometres east to Lillers to purchase Christmas presents. One wonders if the presents were for a gift exchange or for family at home in Canada. There is no mention of anything like this the previous year. That same day, the battalion received a draft of officers and ninety-nine other ranks. At the beginning of the list of names was Captain Warner E. Cusler. He had been in London to receive the Military Cross for his role in the attack at Avion in an investiture ceremony conducted by King George V at Buckingham Palace. He was returning to the battalion after recovering from being wounded during the attack at Nun's Alley. Returning with him were three men promoted from the ranks, who came back to the battalion as lieutenants: Thomas F. Lamb, a sergeant during the Balloon Trench raid and a holder of the Military Medal; Dick Ineson, winner of the Military Medal at the attack on Regina Trench; and Lorne B. Craig, lance sergeant on the Balloon Trench raid and also a holder of the Military Medal. Lieutenants R. Pollock and J.F.W. Anderson, who had been wounded previously, and four new lieutenants — W.R. Smith, G.M. Dallyn, R.W. Kerr, and P. N. Horton — also arrived with them. The battalion's morale must have been lifted by the return to its ranks of these wounded and decorated veterans. These men knew the score and had proven their ability and courage in more than one action. The efficiency of the unit would no doubt be even higher now that Major Macfarlane was in command. Lieutenant Colonel Genet, by a set of coincidences, had been ill, injured, or on leave for all of the battalion's major actions after the attack at Mount Sorrel. The team that would lead during the bitter battles of the coming year was in place.

Training resumed on the twenty-fourth and continued through the remainder of the month. It focused on anti-gas measures, rifle firing, and specialist skills in order to bring the new men up to the same proficiency as the veterans. Six soldiers had been evacuated with an unspecified illness on the twenty-third, and another three were evacuated on the twenty-eighth. Five reported back from hospital on the twenty-sixth. On the twenty-fifth, the casualty figures from the Passchendaele operations were revised. Four men who had been listed as wounded were now listed as killed in action. Seven who had been listed as wounded were now listed as wounded and missing. One listed as missing was now listed as wounded. These revisions did not change the total casualties from the operation, but they did set the record straight. On the twenty-ninth, the battalion received another twenty reinforcements to replace some of its losses.

On November 30, the battalion received its ballots for the upcoming general election in Canada. One of the big issues in the election was the proposal to introduce conscription for overseas service. Up to this time all soldiers in France were volunteers. The high casualty rates were using up the pool of men willing to volunteer for the war, and the number of volunteers had been in decline since the Somme battles of the fall of 1916. For political reasons, there was a large group of men in England in the 5th Division. Major General Garnet Hughes, son of Sir Sam Hughes, the ex-Minister of Militia, was hoping to bring this division to France. He fought any proposal to break it up and send it to France to relieve the shortage of trained infantrymen. Despite his efforts to keep it intact, many of its men volunteered for service in France and gave up a grade in rank to serve with the fighting units.[220] Garnet's father still had much influence and was able to keep his son in command of the 5th Division until the situation became critical in the spring of 1918. Sir Robert Borden's Conservatives and many English-speaking Liberals formed the Union Party to promote the proposal, but it was rejected in Quebec.

In order to improve the chances of being re-elected, and on the assumption that they would likely vote in favour of conscription, the Borden government gave the vote to nurses with the C.E.F.

and to women who had relatives serving overseas. This was the first time that women in Canada had the federal franchise.[221] The Union government won re-election. Part of the reason for the victory may have been the ability of the government to send the vote of the soldiers to any riding it chose, not necessarily the ones in which they had lived, and thus to turn what would have been marginal losses into wins for the party. While the Union government won the vote, it effectively alienated French-speaking Quebec from the English-speaking majority and ended the long association of the province with the Conservative Party. For most of the remainder of the twentieth century, it would be a Liberal stronghold.

The Human Balance Sheet

	November	Cumulative
Killed	3	351
Wounded	40	1331
Shell Shocked	0	90
Gassed	0	4
Missing	0	234
Sick	23	39
Reinforcements	249	1171

Chapter Twenty-two

December 1917
Restoring the Edge

The battalion began the month at Auchy-au-Bois, a small village about thirty kilometres northwest of Lens. The weather for the first nine days of the month seemed to be good: there was no mention in the Diary of rain or snow, and four days are described as fine. The mornings were spent in training sessions. The syllabus was likely much the same as on previous occasions. An undated memo in the battalion files refers to lessons learned from the attacks around Lens the previous August. The memo urges riflemen to pay more attention to snap shooting and rapid aiming. Highly trained snipers had been very useful in picking off enemy machine gunners at long ranges. The Lewis gunners are also encouraged to practice rapid aiming and observation of targets. There are several recommendations for the use of bombs or grenades. One is that bombers be schooled in the use of smoke grenades. The second is that the rifle grenadiers concentrate on the use of the No. 23 rifle grenade that out-ranged the German stick and hand grenades. The grenadiers are cautioned not to rely on the rifle grenade in an assault where ranges could exceed the ability of grenadiers to observe the effect of the grenade on the target. Lewis gun fire and rifle fire from snipers are identified as better ways to deal with enemy machine gun posts. Light trench mortars had not been used at Lens, but the memo writer recommends that they be attached to infantry units for attacks. Passing mention is made of the need to improve the visual signals and find a signal flare that would not be confused with enemy flares.[222]

There are also recommendations on the organization of the infantry platoons. These would usually average thirty-five to thirty-eight men. Each platoon would be under the command of a lieutenant, with two runners for his platoon headquarters. The two halves of the platoon would each be under the direction of a senior noncommissioned officer, a sergeant or full corporal. Each half would be divided again into a Lewis gun section of six men and one lance corporal and a composite section of three rifle grenadiers, six riflemen, and one lance corporal. Depending on the tactical situation, each of the sections could lead or support the other. Two of the riflemen were to be scouts or snipers, and they were to lead the way, making sure the platoon was going in the right direction. If they were snipers, they would be expected to deal with enemy machine gun posts.[223]

The month began slowly for the battalion. Captain Affleck was preparing to return to the 9th Field Ambulance. He made the rounds of the companies with other officers in the battalion. On the sixth, a farewell dinner was held for him after Captain Hessian arrived to replace him.[224] On the seventh, the unit carried out its usual training in the morning and then conducted a night exercise after dark. The next day, it trained in the morning and attended a concert at nearby Westrehem that night. It had Sunday off and attended church parade. On the tenth, training resumed, with half the unit on the rifle ranges and the other half carrying out the usual training. Training was curtailed as the four companies took turns on bath parades before attending a battalion concert that night, again at Westrehem. The next day saw regular training in the morning and a first-time event in the afternoon: lectures were held at Westrehem on the subject of returning to civilian life. There is no suggestion about the topics of the lectures. A hint of what might have been covered comes from a memo written in April, just as the Germans commenced their last major offensive of the war. It was from somewhere in France and announced the start of a vacation from Vimy University. The memo mentions that classes have been going on for four months, covering such topics as Agriculture, Business Efficiency, and Elementary Practical Science. There is also a reference to thirty libraries that lent out thousands of books. Captain Edmund H. Oliver, who was returning to the Chaplains' Service but hoped to return to the university as circumstances permitted, signed the memo. With almost a year of hard fighting to come, it was a remarkably optimistic and forward-looking project to initiate under war conditions.[225]

Battalion training continued in similar fashion from the twelfth to the nineteenth, when the unit moved to Gonnehem. The next day it moved southeast about seventeen kilometres to Vaudricourt, and Major R.A. Macfarlane rejoined the battalion briefly and took over command from Major Carmichael. On the twenty-first, the battalion moved to the Bully-Grenay area on the northwestern edge of Lens. The next day, it relieved two British units and moved into the support lines at Cité St. Pierre, a suburb of Lens. For the next five days, the unit provided working parties. The tactical situation was quiet and there were no casualties. Christmas dinner was held at battalion headquarters, and the officers of the transport lines were invited to join in the festivities. Major Macfarlane went on leave on the twenty-sixth, and Major Carmichael resumed command of the battalion.

On December 28, the battalion went back into the front line in the Cité St. Emile sector. This was near where it had staged the very successful raid on Nun's Alley in late August. A Company occupied the right front at Nabob Trench. D Company held the left front in Nestor Trench. C Company was in support at Congress and Catapult Trenches, and B Company was in reserve at Counter Trench. There were no casualties during the relief. The next day, there was a small attack by the enemy. It began with a brief, but heavy, trench mortar barrage at 9:45 A.M. The shelling did considerable damage to the trenches, and a direct hit killed Captain William A.P. Durie, Company Sergeant Major David Embree, and Private Henry Gordon of A Company when they went to inspect the damage. At 10:15 A.M., a force of twenty Germans with two scouts in the lead was seen to leave their lines and proceed toward Mason House. The battalion's lines were weakly held in front of Mason House, but the platoon's leadership soon routed the enemy. Sergeant J.C. Hardy shot the two scouts with his revolver, and Lieutenant P.N. Horton dispersed the rest by firing a Lewis gun at them. There were two other casualties from this short action. One footnote to this action occurred after the war. It was the immutable policy of the Imperial War Graves Commission that all the dead of the war were to buried near where they fell. Durie's mother wanted her only son's body returned to Canada, but her request for the repatriation of her son's remains was denied. When her son's body was moved from its initial resting place for reburial in the British Cemetery at Loos, she saw her chance and spirited it back to Canada, where it was reburied in St. James Cemetery, Toronto, with full military honours.[226]

Early on the morning of December 30, the battalion was subjected to a gas attack. It began before dawn when the enemy fired about six hundred gas shells toward the Canadian lines. About two hundred of them landed in the area of the 58th, and the rest landed on the 52nd Battalion area. The men in the trenches noticed the flash of the gas projectors and recognized them for what they were from the gas lectures.[227] They put on their gas masks before the gas spread, and it was mainly men in the dugouts who had not seen the flashes who were affected by the gas. The total gas casualties were Lieutenant W. H. Smith, who had joined the unit at Vimy in April 1917, and six men. The attack lasted about twenty minutes and was combined with a high explosive bombardment of the support areas.[228] The accidental explosion of a hand grenade wounded another five. That night, Captain Warner Cusler conducted a wiring party in front of Mason House to improve the defences of this vulnerable section of the line that was only fifty yards from the German trenches. Despite the moon's glow on the fallen snow, Cusler was able to control his working party successfully for seven hours. He was recommended for a bar to his Military Cross, but it was not awarded. Private Harry Miner was awarded the Croix de

Guerre for keeping his men together during the seven hours they were erecting the wire, all the while under sporadic enemy machine gun fire.[229] The work resumed the next night. Altogether, about 380 metres of wire were strung without casualties.

The Human Balance Sheet

	December	Cumulative
Killed	3	354
Wounded	7	1338
Shell Shocked	0	90
Gassed	7	11
Missing	0	234
Sick	0	39
Reinforcements	0	1171

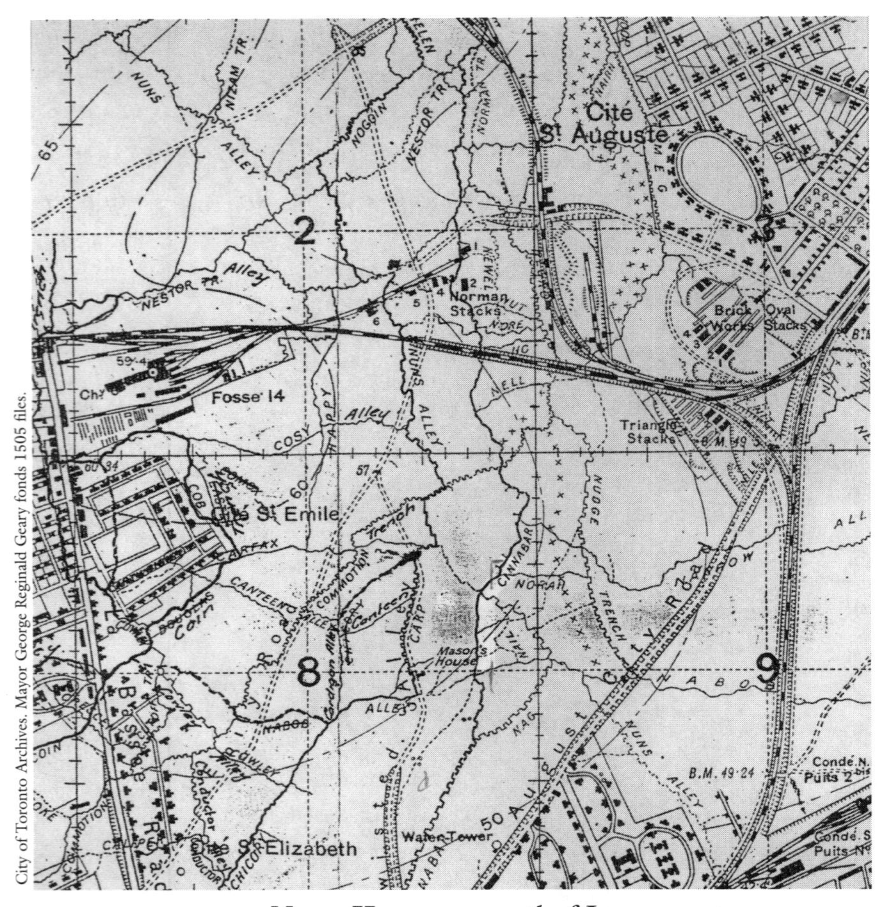

Mason House area south of Lens.

Chapter Twenty-three

January 1918
The Perfect Raid

The battalion was in the front lines for New Year's Day. The Diary makes no mention of any celebration to mark the passing of the second New Year in France. The weather was cold, and the enemy was quiet. The major activity was increasing the wire obstacles along the section of front line allocated to the battalion. On the third, the battalion was relieved by the 116th Battalion and moved out of the Cité St. Pierre area to billets in Les Brebis. C Company went back to the St. Pierre area to relieve a company of the 43rd Battalion and provide working parties.

On the first day out of the line, the balance of the battalion spent its time resting and cleaning up. Despite the cold weather, training resumed on the morning of the fifth, and the men were paid in the afternoon. Training continued the next morning, and D Company relieved C Company in Cité St. Pierre. The weather was a little warmer for the next morning's training session. In the afternoon, Dr. Oliver lectured the battalion on "Civil Training" in the Brebis cinema. After a week in the line and several days of training in the cold, it is doubtful that many men would have been able to stay awake in the warmth of the cinema. The colder weather returned the next day for the training session. That night, the men attended a performance by the Princess Patricia's Concert Company in the cinema.

The ninth of January saw the unit move back to the Cité St. Emile sector to relieve the 116th Battalion. Battalion headquarters was at Counter Trench, C Company was in the right section of the line, and B Company was in the left section. D Company was in support, sheltering in dugouts in the Catapult and Congress trenches, and A Company was in reserve at Counter Trench. The battalion re-entered the front lines with 24 officers and 407 other ranks. It is possible that men were away on specialist training or on leave, but the battalion was effectively below half strength. It had arrived in France in February 1916 with 970 all ranks.[230] There had not been any reinforcements for a number of weeks. The supply of volunteers back in Canada was drying up, and the Military Service Act, passed in August 1917, had not yet filled the reinforcement pipeline.

On January 10, the battalion's original commanding officer was transferred back to England to assume a training command. He had been away from the battalion prior to the action at Passchendaele. Major R. A. Macfarlane had assumed command of the battalion then, but his promotion to lieutenant colonel had not yet come through. After almost two years on the Western Front, the 58th was made up of a mix of seasoned professionals, well schooled in the art of war as practiced at the time, and volunteers eager to learn from them. Macfarlane and Carmichael had risen in rank as the original senior officers were killed, wounded, or transferred away. Many of the lieutenants had been promoted from the ranks of the noncommissioned officers. The area was a quiet one, but not for long. Lieutenant Jucksch, already the holder of the Military Cross for his actions at Avion in June 1917, took a raiding party of forty-two men back to Les Brebis to train for a raid on the enemy position known as Commotion Sap. This was very close to the area captured in the raid at the end of August. This time, the attack was designed simply to capture prisoners, always a sought-after objective of any raid,[231] and to inflict casualties and damage on the enemy in the Cinnabar Trench and Commotion Sap area. It would show the Germans the calibre of opposition they faced and establish that the Canadians controlled No Man's Land. On the day of the raid, three new officers joined the unit: Lieutenants H.M. Bell, M.G. Duffett, and J.R. Hanning.

Lieutenant Jucksch had volunteered to lead the raiders in December, and for five weeks he spent every night in No Man's Land, listening to enemy activity in a portion of their line known as "the Sheep's Nose." On one or two occasions he made some noise and was fired on, but his luck held, and he was not injured. He supplemented his listening program with aerial photographs and captured maps in order to build up a picture of the enemy position and then build a replica in which to train the raiders. He put them through the replica trench several times in daylight and once at night and even used the explosion of an ammonal tube to add realism to the exercise. When it was detonated, it blew out most of the windows in the village.[232] At 5:00 P.M. on January 13, Jucksch led forty-one heavily armed men out into No Man's Land to within nine metres of Commotion Sap. Initially Jucksch placed three sections, each under the command of an NCO, in the area just behind him in No Man's Land, while he and Scout F.W. Cormack went forward with an ammonal tube to cut the enemy wire in the area of the sap. They started out with two of these three-metre-long pipes, but found it too difficult to move them silently and sent one back. Although the enemy wire was only forty-five metres in front of the battalion's trenches, the ground was so cut up from shelling and the tube so awkward to handle that it took forty-five minutes to reach the wire. As it was, the enemy heard something and threw one stick grenade that landed between Jucksch's legs and then failed to explode and another that landed between the two men but again did not go off. Jucksch believed that the Hun sentry must have been nervous and had forgotten to pull the detonator on the grenades before he threw them. On reaching their first objective, a mass of wire Jucksch had observed on scouting the area two nights previous, he and Cormack began to shove the tube under the wire. On the first attempt the tube did not go straight under the wire. They withdrew it and tried again. This time the tube was pushed in the right direction, but it scraped against the wire and seemed to alert the defenders to their presence. Jucksch and Cormack saw three men look in their direction, but there was no other reaction from the enemy. They waited half an hour before sliding the tube

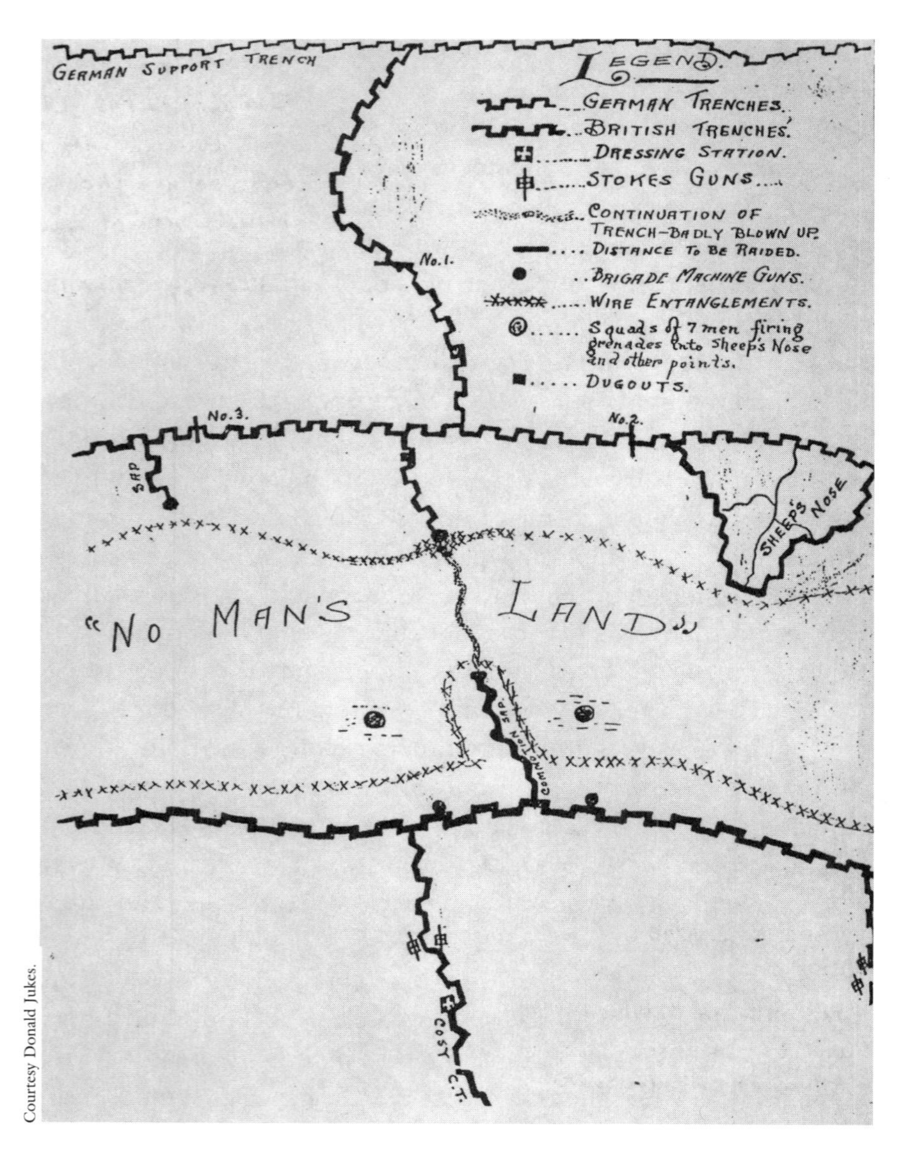

Courtesy Donald Jukes.

The Commotion Sap raid, January 13, 1918, from the autobiography of A.H. Jukes.

forward again and resumed their efforts only when friendly artillery down the line started to fire and covered the noise they were making. By 7:05 P.M., the tube was in position to be fired.

When the first fuse did not set off the tube, a second was made ready. Jucksch and Cormack were lying about seven metres from

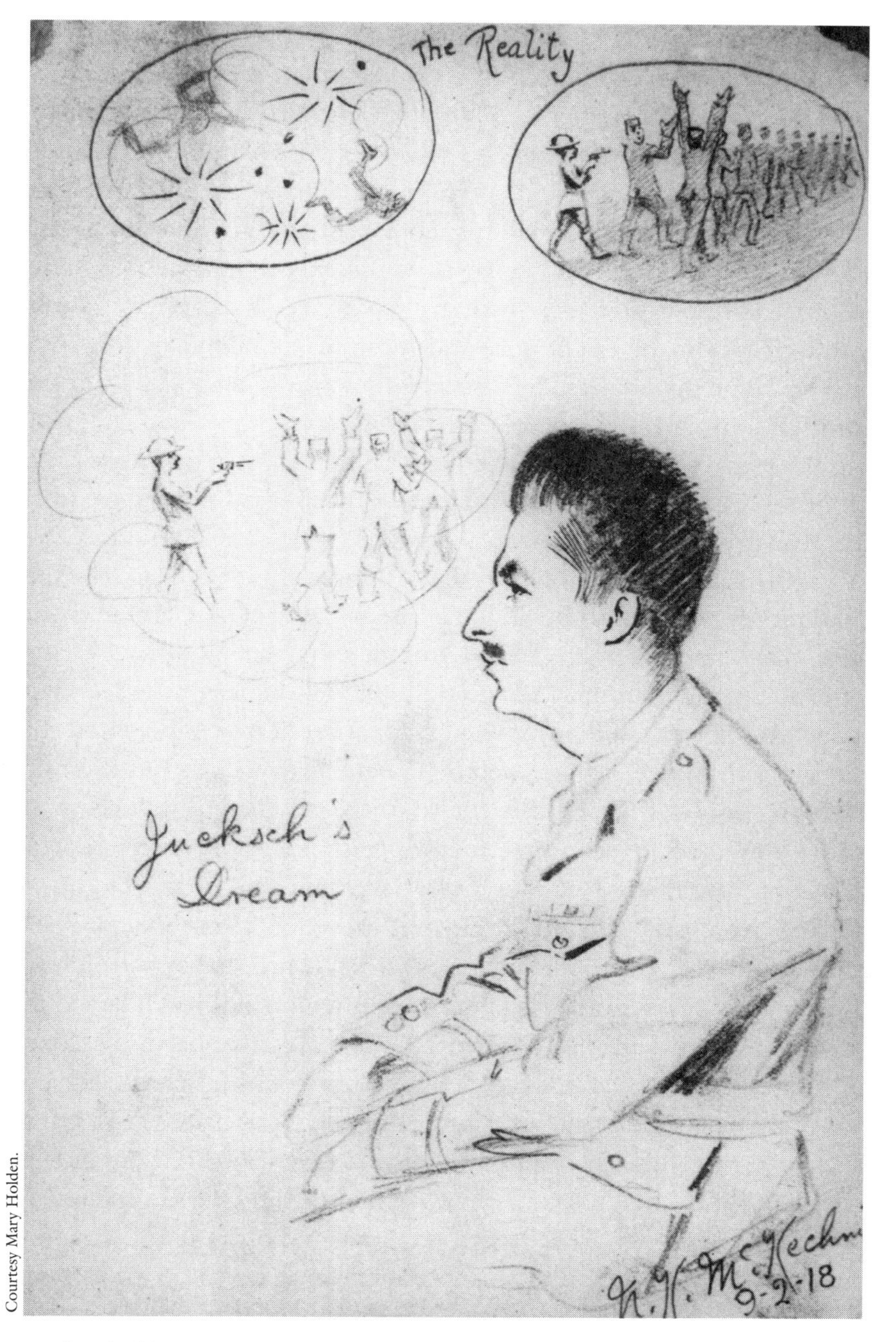

Courtesy Mary Holden.

"Jucksch's Dream," sketched by Lieutenant N.K. McKechnie as Jucksch planned his raid and altered to reflect the number of prisoners captured.

the tube and slightly below it when it went off; otherwise, they would have been wounded. The explosion cut most of the three-metre, heavy wire barrier and lifted Jucksch off the ground, blowing his helmet from his head and his pistol from his hand. The three sections behind him were also stunned, and the enemy was taken by surprise. Jucksch regained his senses first and ran forward to the newly created lane, calling on the three sections to join him. Cormack threw grenades into the sap to keep the enemy away. Jucksch sat on the uncut wire and directed his raiders over it into the sap. The first raiders killed six enemy soldiers in the sap. Jucksch himself went into the sap, followed by the last section and the mopping up party of seven grenadiers led by Lieutenant Walter W. Johnson. The explosion of the ammonal tube had been the signal for the battalion's four Stokes mortars, its Lewis guns, and the Vickers machine guns of the 9th Machine Gun Company in the battalion's trenches to begin a barrage to isolate the German front line from reinforcements. In addition, two parties of seven rifle grenadiers each bombarded the right and left flanks of the German trenches for the same purpose. Canadian artillery was prepared for action with twelve guns trained on the enemy trenches, but the battalion's weapons were sufficient to keep the enemy in check and allow the raiders to continue their operation without interference.

The three raiding sections under Sergeant C.J. Enright, Corporal F. Bearman, and Corporal G. Hooper moved into position to block enemy movement into the section of trench controlled by the raiders. The first section went north along a communication trench linked to Cinnabar, and the other two went right and left respectively along Cinnabar to secure the flanks. The men of Johnson's mopping up party threw grenades and fired into a dugout about halfway along the captured sap. Jucksch stopped them and called into the dugout in German for the defenders to come out. Some did emerge, and seven were taken prisoner. There was a further commotion in the dugout. Jucksch called again, and two more men came up to be made prisoner. Jucksch had been holding a grenade with the safety pin out ready to throw into the dugout when he realized the safety lever had slipped off and he had to throw it away. When the explosion of this bomb caused still more commotion in the dugout, he went down to investigate. About halfway down the steps, he realized he had run into a German who was holding a knife against him. Jucksch pressed his pistol to the soldier's body, and the German surrendered, along with one more companion, bringing the total captured to eleven.

The three raiding squads had gone to work in their respective sections of trench, and when Jucksch went to check on them, he found them "bombing like hell" all around him. He recalled these parties for the withdrawal to their own lines, but they came reluctantly, as they had been enjoying themselves in their frenzy of destruction. The dugout in the sap was now destroyed with more bombs. Several of the prisoners tried to escape, but were recaptured by the riflemen, who used their bayonets to bring the Germans to heel. Jucksch held one by the seat of his pants all the way back to battalion headquarters. The raiders left quickly the way they had come and were back in their own lines shortly after seven o'clock. They had accounted for sixteen enemy killed and eleven captured with no losses of their own.[233] Jucksch immediately began interrogating the prisoners to learn more about the enemy unit in that portion of the line. Congratulatory messages came in from 9th Brigade, 3rd Division, and Lieutenant General Currie. One of the other officers in the 58th had drawn a sketch of Jucksch while he prepared his plans and titled it "Jucksch's Dream." In it, he had drawn three prisoners being herded back to Canadian lines by a pistol-packing Jucksch. On learning of the success of the raid, he changed the sketch and added another section to include the eleven prisoners. The success of the raid, despite the problems with the ammonal tube, was largely attributed to the use of rifle grenades to cover the advance and retreat of the raiders. Staff officers used the raid as an example of how to carry out such actions.[234] Lieutenants Jucksch and Johnson were awarded bars to their Military Crosses. Soon after the raid, Jucksch was promoted to the rank of captain. Scout Cormack was awarded the Distinguished Conduct Medal. Section leaders Sergeant Enright and Acting Corporal Hooper were awarded Military Medals, along with Privates McHardy, Catto, Welch, Game, Clarke, and Mearns.

The front remained quiet the next day, despite the excitement of the previous night. While the unit had covered itself with glory in the raid, one soldier had spent the night in jail contemplating his fate. Private Harry Jennings was facing a court martial for desertion. Jennings had joined the battalion in Niagara on June 30, 1915. Assuming he had come to France in February 1916, Jennings would have been in or near the action for almost two years. During that time, he would have been fortunate to have had one or two leaves of a week or so to get away from the nearly constant threat of death or maiming. One can only speculate whether Jennings had succumbed to the psychological strain of life in the trenches the way some men experienced shell shock and deserted. The battalion daily orders of this period contain many examples of men charged with going Absent Without Leave.[235] Jennings's case was not unique in the Canadian Corps. It is a wonder that more of the men did not desert, given the experience of fighting in the horrible conditions of Passchendaele in October and November and then having to live in the trenches in the cold and wet of the typical European winter. The outcome of the trial is not provided in the Diary, but it is likely he was convicted of his crime and sentenced to death in front of a firing squad. As with the case of Private LeDoux, his sentence was probably commuted to a prison term.

The situation remained quiet until after the battalion was relieved by the 116th Battalion on the fifteenth. A very heavy rain fell that day, and despite an early relief, the communication trenches were in such bad shape that it took until 10:00 A.M. for all companies of the battalion to reach the cellars of Cité St. Pierre. Despite the very tired state of the men, large working parties were detailed. The enemy shelled the area with large-calibre weapons, but caused no casualties. The ground was very muddy when the working parties were sent out the next day. The battalion attended a bath parade that day, and along with the usual issue of clean clothes came rubber boots, in recognition of the wet conditions. On the nineteenth, the enemy shelled the area near battalion headquarters, wounding Lieutenant Horton. Enemy aircraft were observed the next day, and this may have improved the enemy accuracy; five men were wounded and one was killed when a working party was shelled. On January 21, the battalion was relieved by the 1st Battalion of the 1st Division and went into billets at Petit Sains, about six kilometres west of Lens. It rested on the twenty-second and moved further west to Bruay on the twenty-third. On the twenty-fourth, the unit took up billets in the town of Raimbert (Rimbert St. Pierre). The Diary comments that the unit was now on "Army Rest." It appears that the larger formation of which the Canadian Corps was part must have been out of the line to rebuild after the losses of the previous three months.

A pay parade was held on January 25. Training resumed on the twenty-sixth. On the twenty-eighth, half of the companies went to the rifle ranges while the balance carried on with regular training and went for baths. The weather was fine and warm for the training program of the next two days. Major Macfarlane inspected the battalion on the morning of January 30. On the last day of the month, the men trained in the morning and then proceeded a short distance west to Ferfay to watch the Divisional Special Platoon give a demonstration of the new tactics.

NAC PA7377.

Major R.E. Smythe DSO MC and Major A.H. Jucksch DSO and Bar, MC and Bar at Buckingham Palace after receiving decorations for gallantry in March 1919.

 The Human Balance Sheet

	January	Cumulative
Killed	1	355
Wounded	7	1345
Shell Shocked	0	90
Gassed	0	11
Missing	0	234
Sick	0	39
Reinforcements	0	1171

Chapter Twenty-four

February 1918
The Calm Before the Storm

The battalion began the month at Raimbert, about seven kilometres northwest of Bruay. For the seventeen days it was billeted in this small town, there was no mention of rain. Most of the time was taken up with training. Church parades and inspections broke up the training routine. Lieutenant Jucksch returned from the twenty-day leave he was awarded after the raid and was promoted to captain. There were no casualties of any kind during this entire period.

On February 1, Lieutenant Woodyatt took A Company's No. 1 Platoon to the 3rd Canadian Division's school for special training and tests. There is no mention of the syllabus for any of the training in this period, but a reorganization of infantry battalions was taking place about this time, and infantry platoons began to operate with three sections instead of four. The idea was to increase the flexibility of the platoon, and one Lewis gun section was removed from the recommended strength of the platoon.[236] The following afternoon, the men marched the short distance to Ferfay and observed a demonstration by the Divisional Special Platoon. The new three-section tactics could have been the focus of the demonstration.

On February 4, Brigadier General Hill inspected the battalion. On the fifth, the men had an afternoon for recreational training. Only in the army would one find it necessary to train for recreation.

Pay parade was held on the sixth. In the evening, the warrant officers and sergeants held a banquet. Regular training was the routine from then until the fifteenth of February.

On the February 15, Brigadier General Hill was back to lecture the officers and noncommissioned officers about the "Moral of Canadian Troops." The recorded topic could contain a typographical error; the presentation could have dealt with the morale or spirit of the troops. In that case, the intent could have been to make suggestions for the improvement of the men's welfare in order to deal with the problem of men going absent without leave or deserting. It could also have been a Freudian slip by the typist as the Canadians did have a problem when on leave in England. Many men contracted venereal disease from English prostitutes and had to be hospitalized for treatment. The British government ignored Canadian requests to deal with the problem, taking some steps to curb it only after American troops arrived in large numbers in late 1917 and their government also lodged complaints.[237] At any rate, details of the lecture were not included in the attachments to the War Diary. On the sixteenth, the battalion football team showed it still had what it took, defeating the team from the 52nd. It is doubtful that many of the men from the earlier winning teams were still with the battalion. On the same day, Lieutenant Woodyatt returned with the platoon, which had attended the 3rd Division School.

On the eighteenth, the battalion began the move back to the front lines. The first move was a march of roughly twenty kilometres southeast from Raimbert through Houdain to Estrée-Cauchy. Lieutenant G.M. Dallyn was the billets officer for the first night. The next day, the men marched a little more than ten kilometres to Neuville-St. Vaast, near Vimy. The battalion had been here in March 1917. Lieutenant Craig was billet officer for this night, with the responsibility of collecting all training materials used at Raimbert before the unit moved on to Estrée-Cauchy. On the nineteenth, the battalion was back in the front line after relieving the 31st Canadian Battalion at Avion. This was also familiar ground to many of the men, as the battalion had captured sections of trench there in late June 1917. The unit went into the line with 25 officers and 427 other ranks.

The eight days at the front passed without any major incidents. Battalion headquarters at the brewery was shelled by the Germans on the twenty-first, but there were no casualties. The situation was described as quiet the next day. Two men were wounded on the twenty-third. The battalion received six signalers from England as reinforcements. One soldier was wounded on the twenty-fourth. Sixty reinforcements were received to help build up the battalion's depleted numbers. Major Carmichael assumed temporary command of the battalion while Lieutenant Dyke accompanied Major Macfarlane on an inspection tour in Paris. The front was quiet on February 25, and there were no casualties. The enemy directed heavy machine gun fire at B Company's section of the line on the twenty-sixth, and one soldier was wounded. On February 27, the battalion was relieved by the 116th Battalion and took its place in support near La Coulette. Lieutenant R. F. Brazill joined the unit there. No casualties were incurred during the relief or while in support on the last day of the month.

The Human Balance Sheet

	February	**Cumulative**
Killed	0	355
Wounded	5	1350
Shell Shocked	0	90
Gassed	0	11
Missing	0	234
Sick	0	39
Reinforcements	67	1238

Chapter Twenty-five

March 1918
The Storm Breaks

The month began with the battalion at La Coulette fulfilling the role of brigade support battalion. The situation for the five days spent here before the unit moved to Villers-au-Bois was described as either quiet or normal. There was only one casualty in this period: one soldier was wounded on the first. During the next three days, the men were involved in working or salvage parties. On the fourth, the enemy launched a heavy raid on the battalion on the 9th Brigade's left front. There was an artillery barrage lasting about an hour that morning. Later in the day, the unit received a large reinforcement draft of ninety-eight men. The arrival of these reinforcements marked a significant departure from British army policy. The British were reducing the size of their brigades from four battalions to three because they lacked reinforcements. The same policy had been suggested to the Canadians, but General Currie felt it would be a mistake. Instead he proposed that the 5th Division, serving on Home Defence in Britain, be broken up and an extra one hundred men be added to each Canadian battalion in Europe. When the Canadians went into action next, their divisions would have 50 percent more men in them than British divisions. If they had been formed into six divisions, the expansion of the Canadian Corps would have required a new corps headquarters and an army headquarters to manage the two corps, something Currie did not believe the Canadians had the experienced men to staff.[238] He made this decision even though it cost him promotion to the rank of full general and the undying wrath of the Hughes family for denying Major General Garnet Hughes the chance to bring the 5th to France. They would carry on a campaign to undermine Currie's reputation that would culminate in an article in the *Port Hope Guide*, which would accuse Currie of wasting Canadian lives to capture the Belgian city of Mons just before the armistice. In 1928, Currie would take the paper to court and win a libel suit.[239]

There was one casualty on March 6, as the battalion moved into reserve at Villers-au-Bois, taking up billets in Rispdin Camp. The men were transported from La Coulette by light railway. The first day in the camp was spent resting and cleaning bodies and equipment. On the eighth, regular training and the process of integrating the reinforcements began. On the evening of the ninth, the men were treated to a concert at the YMCA. On Sunday the tenth, they attended church parade and then had the remainder of the day to themselves. On March 11, there was regular training and a demonstration by the 3rd Division's Special Platoon in the morning and recreational training in the afternoon. Lieutenant Dalrymple reported for duty with the battalion the same day. The pattern of training continued the following day.

On March 13, the battalion moved north to Neuville-St. Vaast to relieve the 43rd Battalion in brigade support. Eleven platoons were assigned to working parties that day. The same routine was carried out each day until the battalion returned to the front line in the Méricourt Sector south of Lens on March 20. Eight reinforcements arrived on the fifteenth. On the last afternoon in support, the men were given a band concert.

The battalion relieved the 5th Canadian Mounted Rifles in the Méricourt-Left Sub Sector on the evening of March 20. There were several casualties during the relief. One man was killed and two were wounded, probably by shellfire, and Lieutenant Delamere and six men were gassed near Victoria Dump. When the relief was completed at 10:30 that evening, the unit had 27 officers and 683 men in the lines. It was now about 60 percent stronger than when it went into the trenches in February. Normally an infantry platoon had about thirty men, and there were four platoons to a company and four companies to a battalion. The 58th now had two hundred men more than a regular strength battalion.

While the front had been quiet since the cessation of the autumn campaign in early November, spring would arrive the next day, and the Germans were about to launch their last serious drive to end the war on their terms. On March 21, the calm was broken as the German storm troopers unleashed offensive Michael on a sixty-nine-kilometre front south of Arras in the Somme region. Having knocked the Russians out of the war in late 1917, the Germans were able to transfer battle-hardened troops from the Eastern Front to the Western Front, and for a short time, before the troops of the United States came on the scene, they had numerical superiority.[240] This offensive, like the British attack at Cambrai in November 1917, began without the long preparatory barrage that so often warned defenders an attack was coming, allowing them to bring up reserves for a counterattack. The storm troopers were specially trained in infiltration tactics. The leading waves were ordered to bypass strong points and leave them for the second waves of the attack. Speed was the key factor, and the men were to press on to their objectives and not wait for other units to come up on their flanks or consolidate their gains. The stealthy movement forward of these storm troops on the first morning of the attack was aided by early morning mist and by lavish use of gas and smoke shells in the initial artillery bombardment.[241] The Germans had their greatest success at the southern end of their assaulting front and ran into trouble in front of Arras near the Canadian sector. The German High Command was slow to exploit the success near La Fere. Failing to break through around Arras after about a week of fighting, the attack shifted further north near the Canadians around Vimy. The well-prepared defences of General Byng's Third Army stopped this attack cold on March 28, and the Germans shifted their attack south to the sector in front of Amiens. While there were significant territorial gains, and the British lost many men, the Germans had held their men back from Amiens just long enough before launching the attack to allow the British to strengthen the defences and hold the key city. The 58th Battalion was at Méricourt on the twenty-first, about nine and a half kilometres northeast of Arras. The situation was described as quiet all day, and the unit suffered no casualties. In the last hour of the day, the Allied artillery fired gas and high explosive shells into the enemy lines. This attack lasted fifty-five minutes. The next day was also described as quiet, but there was plenty of activity in the enemy lines. Observers in the unit's front line noted that the Germans opposite them had clean helmets, when those observed the day before had had mud-covered helmets. This probably meant fresh troops were in the enemy lines, the prelude to an attack. C Company was relieved by the Royal Canadian Regiment and moved to billets at Chaudiere. The next day, A and B Companies were relieved by the 52nd Battalion, and D Company was relieved by the Princess Patricia's so that the 58th could in turn relieve the 2/7 Duke of Wellington's Regiment.[242] The Canadian Corps' line was being extended to allow the British to create a reserve to stop the German offensive. This manoeuvre was complete by 10:15 that night. The Germans shelled the new positions of A and D Companies with trench mortars, high explosive shells, and some gas shells, causing two casualties: one man was killed and one was gassed. The situation was quieter the next day. Two men were lightly wounded and remained with the battalion. Observers noted increasing enemy movement and the digging of gun pits. These were more signs that the enemy was preparing an attack in the sector. On the twenty-fifth, German troop movement in the support and rear areas increased and there was no attempt to conceal the preparations for the attack. The battalion's front line positions were subject to additional trench mortar bombardment, and the rear areas were placed under harassing fire to interfere with efforts to defend against the coming attack. The situation on the twenty-sixth is described in the Diary as quiet, but enemy movement was still considerable. The unit's Lewis gunners shot down a German aircraft that had flown over their lines. It crashed near the trenches of the battalion to the right. The next night, after being relieved by the 43rd Battalion, the battalion moved to hold a line of trenches running from Farbus north through Vimy to Liéven. At noon on March 27, the 3rd Division was removed from the Canadian Corps and placed under the British XIII Corps in an effort to plug gaps in the British line.[243]

The German attack designed to capture Arras began at 3:00 A.M. the next day with a heavy artillery bombardment on the trenches held by the unit as well as artillery positions behind it at Farbus Wood and on the defensive position known as the Ridge Line. The Canadian artillery responded, and the artillery duel continued through most of the day. The battalion's transport lines were also under fire and had to be moved to Berthonval Wood. The shelling killed one soldier and wounded seven.[244] There were gas shells mixed in with the high explosive shells, and Lieutenant Phin and four men in the front lines were gassed. The German attack went in on the battalion's right and did not come directly at its positions. The attack penetrated the prepared defences known as the Red Line, causing some troops to be withdrawn from the forward trenches, but the attack was defeated on the first day. Enemy activity was still very noticeable the next day, but the battalion went unmolested as the artillery from both sides worked each other over and left the infantry alone. The front went quiet as the Germans shifted their forces for the next phase of their offensive. There were no casualties among the battalion on the last three days of the month. By noon of March 30, the 3rd and 4th Divisions were back under the control of the Canadian Corps.

The Human Balance Sheet

	March	**Cumulative**
Killed	3	358
Wounded	18	1368
Shell Shocked	0	90
Gassed	13	24
Missing	0	234
Sick	0	39
Reinforcements	107	1345

Chapter Twenty-six

April 1918
The Storm Passes

Perhaps in the spirit of April Fools, the month began with a Canadian artillery bombardment on the old front line trench. The barrage was simply a trial by the gunners and lasted about thirty minutes. Because the Diary indicates that the day was a quiet one, the artillery fire may have made the Germans change their minds about attacking when the Canadians could waste enough ammunition for thirty minutes of defensive fire without an attack in progress. The battalion was well back from the front line in Farbus Wood, on the eastern slope of Vimy Ridge. From this location, the men could observe the comings and goings in the German lines. On the second, the enemy was observed to be relocating troops in the reserve area, both by train and by truck. The weather was poorer on the third, and no enemy activity was noted before the 58th moved back to Méricourt to relieve the 43rd that evening. The Germans tried to take advantage of the changeover in the front line and launched a raid on Hudson Trench at 9:30 that evening. They tried to push past the block by covering their raiders with machine gun fire and throwing bombs. The men of the 58th fought back vigorously, repulsing the raiders without casualties.

The next day saw further enemy activity as a patrol approached the Canadian lines through an old communications trench. Captain

Field of B Company decided that this could not be allowed to happen again. At 10:00 the next morning, he set out with Company Sergeant Major Cornelius Enright and fourteen other ranks to re-establish control of No Man's Land. Field took three of the party along Antelope Alley, the same trench used by the enemy to approach the Canadian lines, to a German block, which they found to be unoccupied. Four rifle grenadiers were left there to support the rest of the party as it moved up Antelope to Arleux Loop, the next German trench. They encountered no enemy and continued along the trench to an unoccupied dugout, where three more men were stationed to support the rest of the team. Field and Enright took the last four men with them further along the trench to where four Germans manned a post with a light machine gun. The Germans did not notice the Canadians sneaking up on them and were all killed when Field and Enright sprang up from cover and fired at them with their revolvers. Enright scooped up the machine gun as a trophy of war and passed it to one of the soldiers. The party retraced its steps, Field and Enright covering the four soldiers with their revolvers. The Germans responded to the attack, but the men left behind at various points to cover the raiders did their job and drove off the Germans, inflicting casualties, but suffering none themselves. Field was awarded a bar to his Military Cross, and Enright was awarded the Distinguished Conduct Medal to go with the Military Medal he had won in January. That night, the battalion was relieved by the 5th Canadian Mounted Rifles and moved out to Cellars Camp.

Things were quiet in the camp. There was no training and few parades. Private David Waldron rejoined the battalion on the fifth after taking a reduction in rank to get out of England and rejoin his friends. The men had time to clean up and rest. The German attack then shifted north to the Ypres sector on April 9 and nearly captured the important railway junction at Hazebrouck, southwest of Ypres, before Haig countered the move. The gains made by the British, Anzac, and Canadian soldiers at Passchendaele over a period of four months the previous year were lost in three days in this phase of the campaign. On the tenth, the enemy shelled the rear area, and one man was wounded. It was at about this time that Captain Cusler was wounded for the fourth time: a bullet passed through the left side of his face, causing his subsequent evacuation to hospital in London. He would spend months in hospital undergoing reconstructive surgery. The next day, the unit moved by train to Fosse 11 in the Bully-Grenay area, west of Lens. It completed the relief of the 6th Sherwood Foresters, a British unit in the St. Emile sector at 5:45 A.M. on the morning of the twelfth. The three divisions under the command of Lieutenant General Currie now had responsibility for almost twenty-seven thousand metres of the front line.[245] This was familiar territory to the men of the battalion. Again they wasted no time in establishing their dominance over the front. Under the direction of the sniping officer, Lieutenant J.H.G. Strathy, they scored four observed hits on April 12 and three more on the fourteenth. Strathy issued a memo on hints for snipers at about this time, and it obviously paid off. He commented on the relative merits of the Lee-Enfield and the Ross rifles in the sniping role, mentioning the Ross's superior accuracy at long ranges, but favouring the Lee-Enfield for ease of handling.[246] The battalion's snipers still had to be cautious. Sergeant Rutherford was sniping from a position in a tree when he came under enemy rifle fire. Another sniper was trying to kill him. He pretended to be dead after the shot passed him and hung limply in the tree until dark, when he climbed down to safety.[247] The battalion had one killed and one wounded while in the line. It was relieved by the 116th Battalion on the night of the sixteenth and moved back to Bully-Grenay.

The battalion remained in the reserve sector from the seventeenth to the twenty-third. Time was spent in resting and cleaning up, practicing on the rifle ranges, and carrying out working parties. There was time for a football match with an artillery unit, won by the battalion's team. On April 21, a new sporting challenge was taken up in a baseball game with the Americans, mentioned for the first time in the Diary. There is no indication of the winning team. That same day, the enemy shelled the Bully-Grenay area with high explosives and gas, and there were five gas casualties as a result. The next day, the unit moved back into the St. Emile sector.

The defence of the Canadian Corps' sector was to be bolstered by tanks from the 11th Tank Battalion. The tanks came with crews and weapons, but had no gunners to man the Lewis guns. Men were to be taken from the infantry divisions to man these guns.[248] A second memo arrived on the fifteenth, advising units how to deploy tanks in built-up areas.[249] The War Diary makes no mention of the tanks at this time, but Waldron mentions them in his personal diary on April 14. As the High Command drew off units from other sectors of the British front, the Canadians had to cover a wider area. Having tanks behind the front was expected to give the infantry time to regroup and establish new defensive positions in the event they were driven out of their forward trenches.

Heavy enemy shelling greeted the battalion on its first day back in the lines. One man was killed on this day. A patrol on April 25 found no enemy in the forward posts. The snipers again controlled the area, and four observed hits were reported on the twenty-sixth. The Canadians kept the pressure on the Germans by firing at suspected gas projectors, launching their own gas attacks on the twenty-seventh, and raiding the enemy lines for prisoners. These actions were part of the Canadian effort to deceive the Germans about the strength and location of the Canadian positions.[250] While the front went quiet after that, there were two more casualties on the twenty-ninth, and on the thirtieth, Lieutenant F.J. Hooper and another man were wounded.

The Human Balance Sheet

	April	Cumulative
Killed	3	361
Wounded	6	1374
Shell Shocked	0	90
Gassed	5	29
Missing	0	234
Sick	0	39
Reinforcements	0	1345

Chapter Twenty-seven

May 1918
Preparations for the Counter Stroke

The battalion was at the sharp end of the war for another day or so, and then it moved to a rest area to begin an extended period of training. As the British defences in the north stiffened, the Germans shifted their attack further south to the Rheims area in mid-May and headed for the Marne and Paris. This attack came to a halt with the commitment of American forces at Château Thierry. This series of alternating attacks had produced three bulges in the Allied lines but had nowhere broken through them. The German reserves were depleted from pushing each attack too long after Allied resistance intensified, and a pause occurred as the Germans prepared one last blow to exploit the early successes. The second German offensive in Flanders had petered out, and there was a lull in the fighting for a few weeks. Marshal Foch had been appointed commander in chief of the Allied forces on April 14. One of his first decisions was to create a strategic reserve. The Canadian Corps and the French Tenth Army were selected for this role. Three Canadian divisions, which had been dispersed to act as reserves for hard-pressed British divisions during the early stages of the German offensive in March and April, were brought back under Currie's command, and these battalions were withdrawn to begin training for mobile warfare.[251] Battalion headquarters and the unit's transport section moved to

Valhuon during daylight on the second, while the rifle companies moved that night after their relief by the North Staffords. The men spent the night on buses during the thirty-two-kilometre journey to Valhuon, west of Bully-Grenay. After a day of rest and a chance to clean up, the battalion was on the move again. It marched ten kilometres north to Raimbert (Rimbert St. Pierre), the area it had been in during late January. An appendix to the operation order contained the comment, "The commanding officer wishes that the battalion make a particularly smart appearance on the march."[252] The men were inspected and sent for baths the next day. Training began on the seventh. General Lipsett lectured the officers that evening. The training continued until the thirteenth, when the unit participated in 9th Brigade manoeuvres. The manoeuvres were designed to prepare the senior officers for a war of movement after so many years of static siege operations.[253]

Practice Operation Order No. 5 presented an idea of how the battalion would dispose itself during an attack. It would advance on a two-company front, accompanied by a battery of machine guns from the machine gun company. A lieutenant from a field artillery regiment would be attached as a forward observation officer (FOO); he would travel with the unit to direct the fire of a section of eighteen-pounder field guns. Four Stokes mortars from the 9th Trench Mortar Battery would be with the unit, under the direction of the battalion commander. Mules were available to transport twenty thousand rounds of small arms ammunition and the mortars. Signals had been developed to communicate the need for artillery support. The next operation would be different from the unit's attack on the Somme in October of 1916. The unit would have more firepower at its direct disposal and would be prepared for a more open style of warfare. On the same day as the exercise, the battalion sent seven men to the Canadian Corps Reinforcement Depot as unfit. The Diary does not clarify the situation, but it appears that on the eleventh it had received forty-eight reinforcements from the depot. Thirty-five of these men had the seven-digit ID number that often denoted the conscripted soldier. The politically divisive policy of conscription was now beginning to put men in the reinforcement pipeline. The balance of the men came from other battalions that were being broken up as Currie's plan to strengthen the units in the field was implemented. The War Diary is usually very careful to note the names of newly arriving officers, but seems to have missed the arrival of Lieutenant John H. Way and several other officers from the 119th Battalion out of Sault Ste. Marie. Lieutenant Way came from a military family. His father was about to volunteer for overseas service and his grandfather had served in the British Navy during the Crimean War.[254] He had expected to be sent to France in February, but at the last minute was removed from the draft. One of his fellow officers, Lieutenant Fred Martin, had been sent at that time and ended up with the 58th.[255]

Regular training resumed after the exercise and continued for five days. The weather was fine, with a breeze blowing from the south each day. On the nineteenth, there was a church parade, and there is no mention of training in the Diary. The next day, there was a divisional exercise. Much of the operation order relating to the exercise was similar to that for the brigade order the week before. The difference was in laying out techniques for cooperation with supporting aircraft. The aircraft were to fly over the front and use Klaxon horns, devices capable of making a loud noise, to indicate that they wanted to know the position of the infantry. When the horn sounded three times, the soldiers were to expose their ground panels, large pieces of brightly coloured cloth that could be seen easily from the air, in order to identify the unit to the pilot. Flares and lamps would be used to communicate to the supporting artillery units. Machine gun batteries would be attached to the attacking battalions. At the end of the exercise, there was a conference to discuss the lessons learned.

Training resumed again on the twenty-first and continued until the twenty-fifth. On May 25, the battalion marched north about twenty kilometres to new billets at Wittes. The men rested and were inspected the following day. On the twenty-seventh, the men marched about eighteen kilometres to Bomy. This was the same day as the last German offensive began in the Soissons-Rheims area, well to the south of the battalion's location. While the German

Army made its last, desperate effort to break through the British lines, the Canadians conducted further training exercises at the brigade and divisional levels. On May 31, the battalion marched about thirteen kilometres east to the village of Ham-en-Artois.

The Human Balance Sheet

	May	Cumulative
Killed	0	361
Wounded	2	1376
Shell Shocked	0	90
Gassed	0	29
Missing	0	234
Sick	0	39
Reinforcements	41	1386

Chapter Twenty-eight

June 1918
Honing the Edge

The day after the route march to Ham-en-Artois was spent resting. The battalion moved again the next day, marching to new billets in Blessy, about ten kilometres northwest of Ham. Training resumed the next day with a brigade exercise. The unit was to be ready to move on four hours' notice. There was regular training on the fourth, and on the fifth, the unit participated in training with tanks in the Bomy area. Major Macfarlane returned to the unit after an extended absence and resumed command of the battalion with the rank of lieutenant colonel. Major Carmichael's time as commander would serve him in good stead when the fighting resumed in August.

The training routine was broken the following day by platoon dumbell competitions. The competition, which was likely a talent contest and involved homegrown vaudeville acts and female impersonators, was a real morale booster. Some units had such talented concert parties that they were called to give royal command performances.[256] The contest was won by No. 7 Platoon of B Company.

There were two days of regular training, followed by a church parade on June 9. The next day, the battalion took part in divisional manoeuvres in the Bomy area. Regular training resumed on the eleventh. The next day, the men marched to the airdrome at Serny, about five kilometres southwest of Blessy, for a field day. This was probably a warm-up for what was to follow a few days later. The Diary mentions neither the events nor the winners, but it was just as important to give the men an outlet from training as it was to train them in the new form of attack. On the fourteenth, the signal section, with Captain Field, the adjutant, took part in a divisional exercise. The rest of the men carried on with regular training and that night participated in another manoeuvre.

There was regular training the next morning, and in the afternoon the brigade held football and baseball tournaments, which were won by the battalion. There was a church parade on the Sunday, and the men were given the rest of the day off. On Monday, there was another divisional scheme. During the long hours of that mid-summer evening, the battalion lacrosse team won the brigade championship. There was regular training again the next day, while Captain Field and the signalers were again participants in a divisional exercise. That evening, the football and baseball teams were eliminated in the divisional semi-finals. There was one more day of regular training before the battalion moved into the Nieppe Forest.

In addition to the sporting events, there were "sideshows" for the entertainment of the crowds of soldiers not involved in the events. One of the men posed all day as a "Diving Beauty" in a bathing costume made of shell cones for a brassiere and a towel for a skirt. When the crowd in his tent was large enough, he would dive into a canvas tank full of cold water. Other members of the troupe made up the 58th Battalion Camel Corps. Six camels, each composed of two men under a blanket carrying a stick with a camel head, were led past the judges by six soldiers with blackened faces to represent Arab camel drivers. The camels started in the middle of the parade, but their slow gait caused them to fall behind the other entries in the parade, mostly trucks, and they were dead last by the time they passed the judges. On the command "eyes right," the well-trained camels obeyed and brought the officer judges to tears from laughing so hard. First prize for this part of the event was a barrel of beer, which the "camels" could have used after their stately march, but they had to settle for a box of cigars.[257]

The unit marched about twelve kilometres east to tent bivouacs in the forest on June 20. The area was in range of enemy artillery, and for this reason it was hit by frequent shrapnel strafes and gas attacks. It was not as comfortable as the previous billet in Blessy. Lieutenant Henry Baldwin, great-grandson of the reformer Robert Baldwin, had joined the battalion in late May. A prodigious letter writer, he sent home a detailed description of the scene:

> As we approached our forest I noted little activity in the fields — crops were growing rank — farm houses were occupied solely by the troops. Where Civilians remained they were no longer tolerant hosts, but rather guests (in their own houses) of the soldiery. Casualty clearing stations, dressing stations for walking wounded, transport lines (i.e. the horses and wagons belonging to each Bn.) and Ammunition Dumps soon disposed of any doubts as to the fact that we were on the edge of things. We reached our camp – on the edge of a huge and beautiful forest. Soon everyone was happily settled in tents or under canvas "bivies" (a large canvas sheet made into a tent) and quite concealed from view by the heavy foliage or green boughs placed over exposed bits of canvas – "camouflage" (a word already growing aggravatingly common). Everything peaceful and beautiful, only the "smash" of our own guns to disturb the silence of the woods – but they are very near us.
>
> We crawl tired into our sleeping bags, safe from rain under canvas. Soon our guns grow unpleasantly loud and new and closer batteries begin "battering" the stillness. Then It began – That sickening whine in increasing crescendo ending in a smashing burst or "crump"
>
> They say you don't hear them if they are going to hit you. I don't believe them, and notice that most veterans (honest and unaffected) seem to have the

> same desire as I have – viz, to roll up like a hedgehog and pray for a coat of armour plate. This whining through a forest is particularly disagreeable and lying unprotected in a tent is worse than standing in a more exposed position in the open.
>
> I kept thinking of Faber's Tales of Angels — "Sigh, Sigh, Sigh, said the wind as it swept through the Great Brazilian Forest" — only now it was the Great "Forest De——" and alas! not the end of the world's wind — but man's own Hellish device for ending life.
>
> It was much the same on other nights only most of the shells were gas and made a wobbly sound — at no time did they come nearer than 500 yards short of our billets or as far beyond us. I cannot finish.[258]

The battalion was involved in working parties supporting the XI Corps for the next four days. On June 24, the lacrosse team won the divisional championship. On the twenty-fifth, the men marched back to Blessy and their old billets. The next day, they moved on foot and by train fifty kilometres south to the village of Grand Rullecourt and new billets. This move put them about twenty kilometres west of Arras. After a day of rest following the journey, the unit resumed regular training. They finished the month with a church parade.

The Human Balance Sheet.

	June	Cumulative
Killed	0	361
Wounded	1	1377
Shell Shocked	0	90
Gassed	0	29
Missing	0	234
Sick	0	39
Reinforcements	0	1386

Chapter Twenty-nine

July 1918
Ready!

The battalion was on the move again on Dominion Day. The men marched fifteen kilometres from Grand Rullecourt to Bellacourt, another small village about eight kilometres southwest of Arras. They were to form part of the divisional reserve while in this village. This meant that they were always on four hours' notice to move to specific defensive positions. Between the hours of six and ten o'clock in the morning, they were under one hour's notice to move. They were not called on during this period and so continued regular training from the second to the fifth.

The extended period out of the line, which saw them training and participating in sports days, ended on the night of the sixth, when the battalion moved to the Telegraph Hill Switch Line in relief of the 49th Battalion of the 7th Brigade. The unit was in support at this location, and the men were involved in working parties each day until July 14. There were a number of casualties during this period. Four men were wounded on the seventh. Lieutenant Henry W. Baldwin and another man were wounded on the eleventh. Lieutenant Lockwood and three more men were wounded on the thirteenth. There were two more casualties on the fourteenth.

Baldwin's wound, from stray anti-aircraft shrapnel, was serious enough that he was sent home to Canada before the war ended.

His description of the wounding and its aftermath gives a good idea of how casualties were handled.

> #19 Casualty Clearing Station,
> France, 11/7/18.
> Dear Mother,
>
> I am exceedingly comfortable, between sheets in a hospital tent. I must admit I am rather, aye! very disappointed. It should have been a Blighty (yes I use the above term) instead of a clean little hole in my thigh which will heal up in a week or two. I shall enjoy a rest and then return to the lines and hope for better luck next time. It happened this wise:- I had come up out of the dugout to enjoy the sunshine of a calm and sunny morning. Very little shelling (from either side) was going on. There were several enemy planes scouting above our lines, a rather unusual sight these days. They came directly overhead, (very high up) and we could follow their course by the bursting of shrapnel from our anti-aircraft guns. Some of our men were taking a pot at them with a Lewis gun and I was directing their fire — as I had my field glasses. In order to do this I crouched down in the shelter of the trench and peered up. I heard nothing but felt what I thought was a piece of earth strike my thigh. The Sergeant Major who was sitting on the edge of the trench above me said "Did that hit you Sir?" I was surprised and said, " I don't think so." I stretched out my leg — it seemed alright, then I saw a cut in my breeches and when I investigated with my hand inside my clothes, I found blood — lots of it. No pain. The Sergeant Major at once called to a Stretcher Bearer — who by the way was practically stark naked picking lice out of his clothes — and within two minutes he had cut away my bloody

underclothes, smeared the thigh over with iodine. Having at once decided that no artery had been cut — and then a crowd gathered from every part of the trenches, all envious of my good fortune. It was argued that I must have a good Blighty since there was only one hole in my thigh — and what goes in must come out. Soon a stretcher appeared and as I lay on it surrounded by the envious crowd, I could not resist doing the obvious, and therefore smoked a cigarette – strange to say it really is very comforting and I must have smoked at least ten before I reached this place.... Then the procession started. A guide and six stretcher bearers and my batman. I expected to go <u>through</u> trenches — but they lifted me over the top and started across country which had been heavily shelled only an hour before — it was shorter. So my protests were in vain. Our first stop was at the Regimental Aid Post — a dugout — where the Bn Medical Officer looked at the dressings — decided they were sufficient, and telephoned for an ambulance to take me to an Advanced Dressing Station — so again we proceeded over the open, along a frequently shelled road to a crossroads where the ambulance would call.... At the crossroads there was a bomb-proof cellar in the ruins where they laid me, until the ambulance arrived (after about _ hour). Here I distributed 15 francs to the gratified stretcher party.[259]

Baldwin was then transferred by ambulance to the Divisional Dressing Station and re-examined. He left that facility at 1:30 P.M. and at 4:15 P.M. was at #19 Casualty Clearing Station. Here his leg was X-rayed, and he was admitted to a ward. The next day he was evacuated to England. He was in hospital there for over a month, and the "foolish little wound"[260] refused to heal. After the war he would become Prime Minister King's secretary.

The battalion moved into the front line at Neuville-Vitasse on the fifteenth, in relief of the 116th Battalion. There was some shelling during the relief, and one man was wounded. The battalion's stay in the line was longer than usual, likely reflecting the shortage of manpower available to the High Command as they sought to choke off the last German offensive of the war, which began on this day in the Rheims area. The Canadian divisions were holding a wide frontage and, in order to disguise their weakness, engaged in aggressive patrolling of No Man's Land each night. These patrols usually consisted of two officers and twenty-nine men, roughly a platoon in strength. They would go out at night and travel along the enemy's front line to harass working parties or drive off patrols. The first two nights were uneventful. On the eighteenth, a special patrol was ordered to find a means to identify the German unit opposite their positions. Lieutenant Woodyatt and five men entered the German lines and found an overcoat, which yielded the information they sought. On the way back to their own lines, an enemy patrol was encountered and, in an exchange of hand grenades, two of the enemy were killed while one of the Canadians was slightly wounded. The following night, the brigade on the battalion's right carried out a raid on the German lines. Normal patrolling continued that night and the following two without any other incidents.

The final German effort came near Rheims on July 15. By this time, the British, French, and Americans were expecting the attack and had a good idea where it would fall. The delay had given them time to rebuild their depleted forces by bringing units in from the Italian and Middle Eastern fronts, and they soon halted the German effort and gained the initiative for their own final offensive. The initiative had passed to the Allies on July 18, when Marshal Petain's forces attacked the southern flank of the Marne salient with a force containing large numbers of light tanks. This attack caused General Ludendorff to postpone his second offensive in Flanders, and the Allies began the preparations for their major counter stroke.

On the twenty-first, an operation order required a raiding party to gather additional identification from the enemy in front of the battalion. Again, Lieutenant Woodyatt was to lead, this time with nineteen men in his party and twenty-one men in the support party, led by Lieutenant Craig. A covered way into the enemy trenches had been found, and the plan was to have three groups of men in Woodyatt's party enter the enemy trench, establish blocks, and find equipment or prisoners to identify the unit occupying the trench. They were to be covered by a rifle grenade barrage laid down by Craig's party. Because the enemy's wire obstacles were too well constructed to permit the Canadians to enter the trench, they contented themselves with throwing bombs into it, causing several casualties among the enemy. The battalion had one man killed and another wounded on this day, but it is not clear whether it was as a result of the raid or some other cause.

The battalion was relieved the following night by the 2nd Battalion and marched about seven kilometres west to Dainville. They had a day to rest and clean up after their two weeks in the line. The unit moved to the YMCA Camp the following day, suffering four casualties during the move, one of them fatal. They were far enough from the front that they could resume training. On the morning of July 29, Lieutenant Colonel Macfarlane inspected them. In the afternoon, first Brigadier General Ormond and then Major General Lipsett inspected them.[261] Big things were brewing, but the men were not told of the plans the High Command had for them. The following day, the unit moved to Sus-St. Léger. The next night, they "embussed ... for a point to be notified later."[262]

The Human Balance Sheet

	July	Cumulative
Killed	3	364
Wounded	25	1402
Shell Shocked	0	90
Gassed	2	31
Missing	0	234
Sick	0	39
Reinforcements	0	1386

Chapter Thirty

August 1918
Testing the Edge

The Canadians had not been in action as a corps since Passchendaele. The British army had emptied its manpower cupboard to replace the losses incurred during the German offensive of the spring, and Field Marshal Haig resented the Canadians' desire to fight as a corps and not to allow their divisions to be sent where the action was hottest.[263] Some parts of the British Expeditionary Force referred to the Canadian Corps derisively as the "Salvation Army" and "Foch's Pets."[264] Yet the Canadian policy would pay dividends for the High Command over the next three months. Having learned a lesson from the Germans and from their own experience at Cambrai in November 1917, the High Command was about to launch a surprise offensive of their own, with the best troops it possessed. The Germans knew the Canadians had not been in action. They suspected that wherever the Canadians appeared in the front line would be the main point of any offensive. Because the Canadians were still in the Arras area, they expected the attack to come there. To mislead the Germans, two battalions were moved to the Flanders area, and extra signalers were sent with them to create the impression, through increased radio traffic, that the Canadian Corps was moving north. The rest of the Corps was moved south in total secrecy to take part in the attack planned for August 8. In each man's pay-book was pasted a notice urging him to keep his mouth shut to maintain that secrecy.

The movement of the four divisions of the Canadian Corps and the other units slated for the attack was a major undertaking and had to be done in a way that would not attract the attention of German air observers. The British Fourth Army had 2,034 guns in place for the attack, along with thousands of rounds of ammunition for each gun. There were 560 tanks to hide until the moment came to launch them toward the enemy defences. The combined British and French air forces massed seventeen hundred planes near Amiens to keep the Germans from the learning the secret of the attack preparations.[265]

The 58th boarded buses in Sus-St. Léger at 9:00 P.M. on the evening of July 31. They traveled about fifty-five kilometres as the crow flies to the village of Dromesnil, thirty kilometres due west of Amiens, arriving there at 5:30 in the morning. The day was spent resting and cleaning up before a twenty-five-kilometre night march east to the village of Prouzel. The following night, the men moved east again, crossing the Selle River to Hebecourt and bivouacking in the woods, out of the sight of German air observers. On the night of the fourth, they moved to Bois de Boves. The next night, despite congestion at Boves Bridge, they moved over the river to Gentelles Wood, southeast of Amiens. Here they would make their final preparations before the offensive was launched on the eighth. One soldier described the experience as the "most fantastic thing because in the daytime you were in the woods, you weren't allowed to go outside them, and once dark came it just teemed with transport and men...."[266] The men remained in bivouacs in the woods on the sixth and on the night of their last move into the assembly point for the attack the following morning. They were scheduled to enter the front lines on the night of the sixth, but a German raid at Hourges had captured five Australians, and Fourth Army Headquarters did not want to take a chance that another raid would find the hitherto hidden assault troops in the front line. The order to move was cancelled.[267] Will Bird of the 42nd Battalion described the scene as the various units followed the lines of wire topped stakes to the foot bridges over the Luce River and its marsh:

> It had turned cold and the men were impatient to get moving, but as we were leaving the woods a great rustle of movement stilled them. It was something we had never heard before. All at once no one was speaking or whispering. Thousands of men were moving by us as quietly as possible, and the only thing audible was the soft sound of men jostling in the dark, the swish of feet in grass.[268]

The move began that evening and was completed at two o'clock the next morning, despite the fact that some of the men of C Company were affected by lingering gas fumes. During the move that moonlit night there was artillery fire, and aircraft flew over the lines to mask the sounds of the tanks moving into position to support the attack. The artillery fire was not the preparatory barrage that usually tipped off the Germans to a coming attack. It was mostly the firing of single guns to allow the Canadian artillery to register on the targets they would hit the next day. The wire was to be dealt with by the tanks. If they did not advance, the attack would go badly for the infantry.

By 3:30 A.M., the battalion was in position south of the Luce River near the hamlet of Hourges. Four tanks from A Company of the 5th Battalion of the Royal Tank Regiment, each carrying one of the battalion's scouts, were to lead the way through the marshy ground of the Luce River valley. They were tasked to crush the enemy's wire obstacles and assist in eliminating enemy strong points, as machine gun posts were the main form of the German defences. These posts were usually holes dug half a metre deep by a metre square.[269] B Company, led by Captain C.S. Burrows, was to break through the German outposts about three hundred metres in front of the start line, advance westward to the crossroads on higher ground about one hundred metres south of the Luce River, southwest of Demuin, and then send patrols toward that village. C Company, led by Major Henry Rose, was to move through B Company and take Demuin, which was thought to contain a German brigade headquarters. D Company, led by Captain F.H. Dunham in Captain Jucksch's absence,

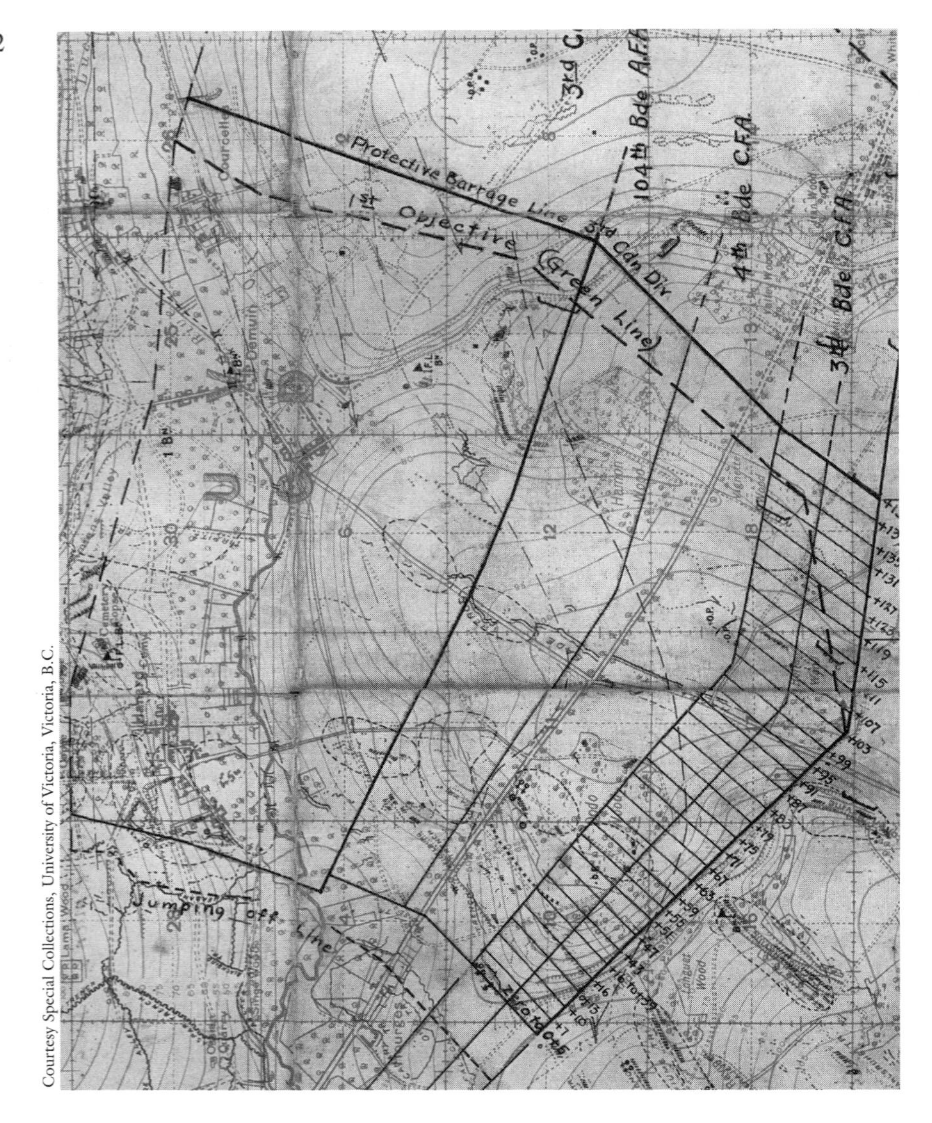

Trench map showing the sector assigned to the 58th between Hourges and Demuin, August 8, 1918.

was to move through the village of Demuin and capture the hamlet of Courcelles. A Company, led by Captain L.J. Carroll, would then move through the village of Demuin, turn to the southwest, and take the high ground overlooking Hamon Wood to assist the 116th Battalion in its attack on this feature north of the Amiens-Roye Road.

The barrage, fired by more than nine hundred guns,[270] began sharply at 4:20 A.M., while a heavy mist covered the ground and obscured the vision of the men both on the ground and in the tanks. The counter-battery work of the Canadians, using the techniques developed before the Vimy attack, was so effective that the German artillery fire did little to hinder the advancing infantry.[271] Because the Canadians had not been able to conduct a reconnaissance of the area in the interests of secrecy, the early going was a bit difficult. By 4:27 A.M., the leading company was under way, and the sun soon dispelled the mist. Lieutenant Andrew Anderson's and Lieutenant Fred Martin's platoons of B Company quickly moved through the enemy's front line about three hundred metres in front of their own lines. Anderson was later described as a fiery Scot who "chewed through the barbed wire and everything else that was in his way."[272] They then had a little difficulty negotiating some marshy ground in front of them while they were under fire from Hangard in the 2nd C.M.R. sector on the left and from machine gun outposts at the crossroads west of Demuin and the main Amiens-Roye Road. The 2nd C.M.R. quickly

Courtesy John Anderson.

Arial photograph of the 58th's start line for the Battle of Amiens. The Amiens-Roye Road runs left of centre, with Dodo Wood on the right and Hamon Wood in the upper left of the photo.

NAC PA2933.

Hourges. Troops of the 9th Canadian Infantry Brigade and Tanks of 3rd Canadian Division.

overcame Hangard's defenders, and the tanks helped eliminate the machine guns on B Company's front. The appendix to the War Diary gives a sketchy account of how things progressed once B Company moved over the marshy ground. The left-hand platoons traveled east on the north side of the road running into Demuin and captured a brick enclosure, which the enemy used as a strong point. The right-hand platoons moved east on the south side of the road and overcame two enemy machine gun posts. The battalion was covering low ground dominated by hills to the southeast, which were the objectives of the 116th Battalion. It was in this stage of the attack that twenty-eight-year-old Corporal Harry Miner, of Cedar Springs, Ontario, carried out the attacks for which he won a posthumous Victoria Cross. As the platoons' lieutenants and sergeants were gunned down, the privates and corporals took over. Corporal Miner rushed one machine gun and, despite being badly wounded in the head and shoulder, managed to kill the entire crew and then turn the gun on retreating Germans. He continued to advance with his platoon, and when the next machine gun tried to hold up the attack, he and two others rushed it and put it out of action. As the company reached the outskirts of Demuin, it encountered an enemy bombing post; again, Miner led the way, bayoneting two of its occupants and driving the rest away. At this point he was wounded again, and, despite being moved to the Casualty Clearing Station, he died of his wounds. One wonders what allows a man to get up and face a firing machine gun. Is it easier to do the second time? Is being wounded something that triggers a battle rage or a desire to close with a tormentor? All of Miner's actions seemed deliberate and showed a disregard for his own personal safety. Could he have been motivated to kill Germans by the briefing about the fate of the men and women aboard the Llandovery

Courtesy Corporal Harry Miner VC Branch 185 Royal Canadian Legion, Blenheim, Ontario.

Corporal Harry Garnet Bedford Miner VC, C. de G. died of wounds on August 8, 1918.

Courtesy Chris McCauley.

Sergeant 453124 James Douglas Rutherford, one of the original members of the 58th, was awarded the Croix de Guerre for actions on August 15, 1918, near Quenoy, France. He was gassed on September 9, 1918, and missed the 58th's last actions.

Castle, a Canadian hospital ship sunk on June 27, whose survivors were machine gunned by the crew of the U-boat that sank them? Miner was one of three men in the Canadian Corps who won the Victoria Cross for similar acts of bravery that morning, and another of them was also wounded early in his action. Private John Croak of the 13th Battalion (Black Watch) died of wounds, and Corporal Herman Good, also of the 13th, survived. They were three of the ninety-five men serving with Canadian units who have won the Commonwealth's highest decoration. B Company suffered additional casualties from machine gun fire as it covered the rising ground in front of the village of Demuin. Major Rose, a British-born banker who had come to France with the battalion in February 1916 as a lieutenant, was close behind with part of C Company. He sent home an account of how things developed from that point:

> When we were nearing Demuin I came upon the O.C. of the Company [Captain Burrows] who was halted with about two of his platoons. I asked him what was the trouble and he stated that he was being held up by a strong Hun machine-gun nest, and had lost a number of men [possibly half his men]. He asked what he had better do, and as time was a very important factor-the barrage was by this time some distance ahead- I decided not to wait for my company to come up, but to outflank the position myself.
>
> I had managed to collect about 30 stragglers on my way up, including a complete Lewis gun crew, so I told the O. C. of the attacking party to get his men under cover, keep his Lewis guns going steadily, and be prepared to support us when we got to close quarters with the Hun.
>
> I led my motley platoon at the double across the Hun zone of fire, with only two casualties, I think, and got fairly close in to the flank of the strong point without being discovered. I was not quite certain where the Hun was, so I went on ahead of my men to reconnoiter. I worked along a sunken road about 150 yards to a bit of bank running at right angles. The patter of the machine guns seemed closer, but I thought I was some distance from them, so I stuck my head over this bank and found the whole thing on the other side. I drew down quickly of course, but not before a Hun bomber had spotted me, and then over came the cylindrical stick bombs. I dropped into a shallow shell-hole and did some hard thinking. I only had my revolver and there were three Hun guns and about 30 of the enemy. While I was wondering

> what to do a Hun bomb dropped on me and lifted me clean out of my cover.
>
> I don't know clearly what happened after this. I found myself amongst the Huns emptying my revolver as fast as I could. Then my men came up and we finished the job. I woke up in hospital a day or two later and found that I had eight wounds including two bad bomb wounds. I could not account for the worst one in the head.
>
> It was not until some time later that I ascertained it was given me by a German who had surrendered.
>
> The net result of the episode was the capture of three enemy machine-guns and the putting out of action of about fifty Germans.[273]

Rose's action was in marked contrast to that of Miner. He had tried to outflank the enemy and then approach them unobserved. When he was observed, he tried to think of what to do. It was only after he was wounded that he charged into what seemed like certain death, at odds of thirty to one, with only his revolver. No doubt his action inspired his men, who charged the position and rescued him. Rose was subsequently awarded the Military Cross.[274]

After Major Rose's action, three of his platoons entered Demuin from three sides and moved through the built-up area to form a line to the east of the village. They had cleared it by 6:30 A.M. D Company then moved through Demuin, one platoon moving toward Courcelles along the south bank of the Luce River, one assaulting it frontally, and two moving up on the eastern flank, capturing the hamlet by 7:05 A.M.[275] Lieutenant Ineson fearlessly led his platoon against a series of enemy positions and captured thirty-one prisoners.

Lieutenant Way sent home a stirring account of the action that morning:

> France Saturday Aug 10/18
> My dear Laura, Ernie & Billie
>
> Was so glad to receive your letter dated July 14

this am as it is the first Canadian mail I have received for over ten days.

Well Laura no doubt you have heard of our great advance and what a wonderful part the Canadians played. Our brigade & battalion were in the front and we "jumped off" behind our barrage at 4:20 am Aug. 8 and really started the whole affair. It was wonderfully terrible. The noise of our guns was deafening and added to that we had Fritz's shells bursting all around. One could only wonder how anyone could live thru it all. On the start it was misty and all I remember was rushing ahead behind our shells then I struck the river and waded through. After a time german prisoners started to come through. Some were big strapping fellows, others small, some old, some very young and of course a lot were wounded. We made the prisoners carry out our wounded. We surely took them by surprise and Canadians took thousands of prisoners. They were surely glad to be taken and handed over everything they had including watches, money, iron crosses, revolvers, belts &c and our boys took them all. [The Germans had been facing the Australians in this sector and knew that they liked to collect "souvenirs" from their prisoners, so they had their loot ready for their captors.[276]]

We reached one of the Headquarters and found coffee boiling. We also got wine, cauliflower, carrots, potatoes &c also lots of glasses & dishes evidently taken from French houses. Suffer it to say we reached our objective almost an hour before schedule.

Our tanks were fine & talk about scared fritzies, why they ran when they saw our tanks coming a mile away.

You know now the extent of our advance and have read all about it in the papers. I was glad to be in so big a show, but it was some experience to see

> so many dead & dying men. Of course we lost some men killed & wounded, but not nearly as many as Fritz. ... I think this drive will go a long way towards ending the war but it will go on for a while longer I think.[277]

A Company now began the final phase of the battalion's attack by moving south to face Hamon Wood and support the advance of the neighbouring 116th Battalion. They rapidly overcame enemy resistance in an old trench and established a post that allowed them to bring small arms fire to bear on an enemy field artillery battery, compelling the Germans to abandon their guns. At this stage of the attack, Major Carmichael led a small party forward to capture a German regimental headquarters and sixty prisoners. On this occasion, he dispensed with his slogan of "Take no prisoners."[278] The 116th Battalion, which occupied the wood, reported the capture of an 8-inch howitzer and a battery of 5.9- and 4.1-inch guns.[279]

At just after 7:10 A.M., the battalion had captured all of its objectives in a three-kilometre advance, along with four hundred prisoners, forty machine guns, and some trench mortars. The Diary states that the men gave credit to the tanks "for their excellent work in clearing up enemy machine gun nests and strong points."[280] This may explain how the Diary could consider casualties of 15 men killed, 10 officers and 137 men wounded, and 1 man missing "light." Two of the dead were men who had distinguished themselves in earlier actions. Company Sergeant Major Connie Enright had been awarded the Military Medal and the Distinguished Conduct Medal for his actions in previous raids. Private John S. Danbrook, a stretcher-bearer, had won the Military Medal at Passchendaele in October 1917. Captain Burrows, slightly wounded in the assault, was mentioned for heroism, as was Corporal Miner and his action in silencing a machine gun post. Scout Sergeant Lue Bishop was awarded the Distinguished Conduct Medal for carrying out reconnaissance during the attack and killing the four-man crew of a German machine gun position. When he saw the post holding up the advance of the platoons, he crawled up behind it and shot the crew with his revolver.[281]

This was only the opening stage of the attack. The success of the operations assigned to the 58th and 116th opened the way for the 7th Brigade to move into the attack.[282] The 58th Battalion now went into reserve. The attack continued through the remainder of the day, with other brigades of the 3rd Division moving further into German territory until they were on their objectives, and the 4th Division finishing off the day's actions, almost thirteen kilometres behind the initial front lines of the Germans. This was the farthest advance of any of the forces attacking that day. The Australians, on the Canadians' left flank, had advanced eleven kilometres. The French, on the Canadians' right, had advanced eight kilometres. The British, on the Australians' left, advanced three kilometres. General Ludendorff was very distressed with the way his troops failed to repel the attackers. August 8 became known as "the Black Day" of the German Army. The success of this attack brought home to the German General Staff that the war could not be won by Germany. Within three days Kaiser Wilhelm II was declaring that the war must be brought to an end.[283]

The 58th was only a bit player as efforts continued over the next four days to turn the initial success into a breakthrough. The Germans hurriedly brought up reserves, and the gains came at a higher cost to the infantry. By August 10, the major Canadian attacks had come to an end, replaced by smaller efforts designed to break into the trench lines of the 1916 Somme Front. The total Canadian casualties for the Amiens offensive were 11,822.[284]

On the evening of the eighth, the battalion bivouacked in Hamon Wood and remained there until the afternoon of the tenth, when they moved to Le Quesnel. On the eleventh, they moved up to support the 116th Battalion. In this role, they suffered three killed and thirteen wounded on the thirteenth. Major Carmichael and six men were wounded on the fourteenth. Two more men were killed and three wounded on the fifteenth. On that day, Scout Sergeant Rutherford led a small patrol toward Le Quesnoy. He attacked and killed the defenders of a German post that was holding up the advance of a French unit on their right flank. He was awarded the Croix de Guerre. That night, the battalion relieved the 116th in the line at the village of Damery.

B, C, and D Companies were in the line, with A Company in reserve. By 9:30 that morning, an outpost had been established in front of the main line, and a patrol had moved within forty-five metres of Blavet Wood. That afternoon, as the 16th Battalion moved patrols along Regulus Alley, the 58th sent a ten-man patrol, led by Lieutenant Andrew Anderson, along Thorn Alley for almost two hundred metres. When they encountered opposition, they drove the Germans away and captured four light machine guns. The 16th Battalion attempted to capture Schwartz Wood but had trouble moving their right flank forward. Lieutenant Anderson led his platoon of B Company forward to support the patrol in Thorn Alley. When enemy opposition increased, the advance in Thorn Alley had to be halted, and the men were withdrawn to a point 180 metres from their furthest advance, where a line was formed along the main Parvillers-Goyencourt Road. They captured three enemy machine guns. Enemy mortar and machine gun fire from the town of Fresnoy forced the men to stay in their trenches. That night, the 10th Battalion relieved them, and they bivouacked in Beaucourt Wood. The day's efforts had cost the unit one killed and nine wounded.

In the Diary, Captain Smythe's entry for August 17 sums up the performance of the battalion from the eighth to the sixteenth: "The conduct of the operations during this period reflected the greatest credit on all ranks concerned, the men showing initiative, eagerness and coolness under fire." In addition to the Victoria Cross won by Miner and the Military Cross won by Rose, a Distinguished Service Order was awarded to Major Carmichael, and a Military Cross to Captains P.R. Dunham and C.S. Burrows and Lieutenant D. Ineson. Lieutenant A.A. Anderson was awarded the Military Cross for his actions in the capture of Demuin and a bar to the decoration for the patrol in Thorn Alley at the end of this eventful week. He had been a corporal in Lieutenant Jucksch's platoon and an acting company sergeant major at Passchendaele, where he won the Distinguished Conduct Medal. Jucksch considered him the bravest man he knew.[285] Ineson too had been promoted from the ranks and won the Military Medal while a sergeant. Six enlisted men won Distinguished Conduct Medals, twenty-one were awarded Military Medals, three received bars to the M.M., and a total of five French Croix de Guerre were awarded.[286]

Another lesson had been learned after four long years of war. For perhaps the first time, the High Command on the Allied side stopped pushing an attack after it ran out of momentum instead of waiting for the weather to halt it. The Germans had been caught by surprise on the first day of the attack, and all conditions favoured the attackers. The German soldiers had not prepared continuous trenches for their defence and were tired after their own advances. As the Canadians continued their drive to the east, they encountered the churned-up battlefield of the Somme from 1916 and more German divisions. The British generals decided not to push the men into futile attacks on enemy barbed wire at the cost of heavy casualties and shifted the effort to a new sector. There would be no repeat of Passchendaele, but the fighting to come would still be costly in human lives.

The men spent three days in Beaucourt Wood. They rested and cleaned up from the action of the previous week. On the eighteenth, a church parade was followed by a pay parade. On the nineteenth, there was a muster parade, and then the men had the balance of the day to themselves. That night, they formed up in full marching order and moved to Maison Blanche, a hamlet on the Amiens-Roye road, where they boarded buses for the secret fifty-five-kilometre trip to Bourquemaison, due north of Amiens. They arrived there at 5:30 A.M. on August 20. The transport section of horse-drawn General Service Wagons arrived on the twenty-first. The men spent the twentieth and twenty-first resting. There may have been reinforcements waiting for them here. The personnel records of Private Hubert Elver indicate that he was taken on strength at this time, but the Diary does not mention reinforcements.[287] On the twenty-second, they participated in exercises in the morning and had an afternoon for recreation. At 10:30 that night, they formed up in full marching order and departed for Gouy-en-Ternois, about fifteen kilometres away, arriving there at 4:30 A.M. Thirty or forty stragglers drew the attention of Brigadier General Dan Ormond. He sent a memo to Lieutenant Colonel Macfarlane praising the 58th for its fighting record, stating that no unit in the army had a better one, but adding that he expected it to do as well on the march. He recommended that the officers use their horses to better observe and control the men on the march. Private Gibson of C Company was singled out for the poor excuse he gave for dropping out of the column.[288] Ormond stated that the reason Gibson gave for falling out was that he had not had sufficient to eat, and Ormond wanted an inquiry with the company commander to determine if Gibson was lying. He also attached a list of names of men who dropped out on the march who he thought were just trying to put one over on their officers. They moved again on the night of August 23, this time to Hermaville, about twelve kilometres away from Gouy and about ten kilometres northwest of Arras. They were warned to move the next day, but the order was cancelled. They marched the short distance east to Etrun the following day. They were given baths and paid again in the afternoon.

After the success of the attack at Amiens, Field Marshal Haig believed (correctly, as it turned out) that the Germans' ability to resist further attacks was beginning to crumble. He wanted to keep the pressure on them, rather than allowing them time to recuperate as the Allies prepared another offensive in the old style. The French Third

Courtesy Geoff Stead.

"Wire in the Hun Line near Queant."

Army struck further south on August 20, and the French Tenth Army struck to its north the following day. The British Third Army, under General Byng, launched a successful attack near Albert on the twenty-third. The British Fourth Army with the Australian 1st Division advanced on Haig's right flank. It was the turn of the British First Army and the Canadian Corps to deliver the next blow on August 26.

The task of the Canadians was to break a key German defensive position known as the Drocourt-Quéant Line, which was situated east of Arras and blocked the approaches to Cambrai. This line connected with the Hindenburg Line at Quéant and was designed to contain any Allied attempt to advance across the Douai plain. In the operation that followed the Canadian capture of Vimy Ridge in April 1917, the British lost 158,000 men trying to force a way through this hilly, wooded country because the Germans had been given ample time to prepare for defence, unlike at Amiens.[289] The strategy of General Ludendorff was to stage a fighting withdrawal to the Hindenburg Line, giving the German Army time to fully prepare this last line of defence while recovering from the recent defeat at Amiens. "With the enemy expecting attack, except for the actual hour of the assault, surprise was clearly impossible. It would be a case of launching successive frontal, grinding assaults against well-established lines manned by tenacious, alert troops."[290]

The 3rd Division's attack began early on the morning of the twenty-sixth with an assault on Orange Hill and Monchy-le-Preux by the 8th Brigade.[291] These objectives were taken by 7:40 A.M. The Germans counterattacked in an attempt to retake Monchy. Their attack was beaten back, but this resulted in the end of the Canadian advance for the day.

At 3:00 A.M. that day, the 58th had been ordered to be ready to go forward to the battle. After forming up in battle order at 9:00 A.M., it moved to the area around Orange Hill to await instructions. Two hours earlier, one officer and eight men from each company had been sent forward to conduct a visual reconnaissance of the Bois du Vert area. The battalion began the move to its start line at 2:30 A.M. on the twenty-seventh. The 58th was to attack Bois du Sart, just north of Bois du Vert, at 4:55 A.M., supported by four tanks of the 3rd Tank Brigade and divisional artillery. A Company was to lead the assault and capture the enemy defences west of the wood. D and C Companies would then advance side by side and clear the wood, with B Company in support.

Rain that night obscured the moon's light and meant the men had to advance to their start line in the dark over six and a half kilometres of unfamiliar terrain. Major Jucksch, now second in command of the battalion, had located the start line only minutes before the attack was to begin. He had received word of the impending attack at 2:00 A.M. and had to hustle up to the front through an enemy artillery barrage falling in the village.[292] The companies arrived on time, and A Company jumped off from Cartridge Trench on schedule at 4:55 A.M. following about one hundred metres behind the supporting barrage. The men of the 1st Platoon bombed their way forward through Keel and Pear Trenches to Tree Trench. The 2nd Platoon cleared Bois des Aubepines and connected up with 1st platoon in Tree Trench. The 3rd Platoon outflanked Twin Copse to the right and occupied Poodle and Foal Trenches. D Company on the left, under the command of Lieutenant Ineson, and C Company on the right advanced into the main body of the wood and, by 6:50 A.M., after heavy fighting, drove out the enemy. D Company sent a patrol into Hatchet Wood, a long narrow wood connecting Bois du Sart to Jigsaw Wood. The enemy still controlled Tusk Trench and the portion of Cartridge Trench between the 58th and the Princess Patricia's on their left. D Company's patrol was driven out of Hatchet Wood at 7:00 A.M., and the enemy counterattacked Bois du Sart and gained a foothold in it before being driven out by the combined efforts of A and D Companies. Another counterattack came in from the southeast and pushed C Company back on D Company, threatening to surround them. B Company was ordered to counterattack in conjunction with D and C Companies; together, they pushed the Germans out again by 7:30 A.M. One company of the 49th Battalion came up on A Company's left flank to offer support and help extend the line north toward the ground held by the Princess Patricia's. The battalion remained in the Bois du Sart overnight. The cost was higher than in the first day at

Amiens. D Company had suffered heavy casualties in the see-saw struggle and was still under fire from machine guns in the village of Pelves to the north of their position. It may have been at this stage of the battle that Lieutenant Ineson was killed. He had received a facial wound early in the attack on the wood, but continued to lead his men until it was cleared. Soon after, he was wounded in the face again, this time fatally. Lieutenant John H. Way, also of D Company, and thirty men were killed. Way had been advancing with his platoon through an area of barbed wire obstacles hidden by long grass when he stopped to help a man entangled in the wire and was hit by shrapnel and mortally wounded.[293] Lieutenants Stevenson, Ashwell, Springford, Avery, Martin, and Anderson and 104 men were wounded. Seven men were missing.

Lieutenant Fred Martin, a forty-three-year-old former Crown Attorney from the Algoma District, had been leading his men through a series of shallow communication trenches in advance of B Company when a machine gun bullet struck him. Sergeant William Russell (later killed while acting as a tripod for a Lewis gun) and two other men dragged him out of the trench on a board; otherwise, Martin would have been taken prisoner. His batman, Private Harrison, and several other men took him back to Casualty Clearing Station No. 7, where he was operated on immediately, but he died on August 30, just one week after his birthday.[294] He had been selected for a three-month tour at headquarters just before the attack and had sent a note to Lieutenant Colonel Macfarlane begging to be allowed to stay with his men.

Lieutenant Anderson was wounded after he entered a German dugout with a party of his men. In preparation for the attack that morning he had noticed the dugout's entrance. Inside was a group of German officers gathered around a map, possibly preparing a counterattack plan. Anderson demanded their surrender, but one of the seated officers fired a shot from under the table, striking Anderson in the right groin and shattering his pelvis. Anderson fired as he fell and killed the German.

Major Jucksch left a detailed account of his part in the action that day:

Courtesy John Anderson.

Newly commissioned Lieutenant Andrew A. Anderson with three wound stripes on his left sleeve and the ribbon for the Distinguished Conduct Medal on his left breast. He would win the Military Cross and Bar at Amiens and be seriously wounded on August 27, 1918.

As the attack started, I sat down for a breathing spell my work finished (as I thought) when suddenly I noticed the men bunching up & bewildered under the enemy's heavy retaliation [artillery fire] in rear, & also two or three officers being killed. So I once more jumped into the fray & got them spread out & into smaller groups & pointed out their objective to them, in the distance & away we all went stumbling over wire, trees, dead, through muddy holes, what a glorious sight at the beginning but not so later on for me. I was enamoured with it and with taking so much new territory & prisoners, when I was suddenly brought to my senses by the absence of voices & lo and behold I was alone in big open fields with no

> one on my right or left & the Huns in front. I rushed like a madman to the right & to the left to find men to fill the gap, but could find none, so I continued on my way thinking sooner or later I would find some. I was in an open spot, some hundreds of yards from the big wood when a quick succession of whistling & spitting bullets passed by my bewildered head, one or two passing through my clothes. I recognized the pit-pit of a German machine gun. At this moment I was becoming weak from thirst & hunger, so I fell flat on my stomach.

Jucksch then began a one-sided duel with a German machine gun nest, drawing his revolver and emptying it at them twice as they fired two belts of machine gun ammunition at him. He again found himself failing from hunger and thirst and tried to revive himself by plunging his head into the water at the bottom of the trench he occupied. At this juncture one of his men joined him:

> I noticed a little pale faced chap who was shouting, "Wait, I'll help you" and came running up just as I became quite sick as my tongue was getting thick. I will remember his name always, Collins. He poured water into my mouth from his water bottle. This really helped & gave me the strength I needed. By this time I was well up on the Huns, so I called to him to follow me & up we were & running at the Huns both firing as carefully as we could on the run. We hit some of them and scared the rest & I had no trouble in taking three machine guns from under their noses. They were caught by surprise & could hardly speak. It was done so quick & they thought they had gotten us when we fell. Collins and I herded them back after I ordered them in German to stack up their rifles etc. I sat down and had a good drink from Collins' water bottle.

> Before I had been there a few minutes I noticed one of the companies [possibly D Company] having trouble on the left flank, held up for some reason. I soon saw the reason-a strong point of Huns, I imagine about 60 of them were holding them up. So I took the German machine guns & loaded them quickly & enfiladed the Huns & chased them out. So the company got on its objective. The tanks should have assisted us but were nowhere in sight. [295]

Jucksch and his men captured about fifty prisoners, and he was awarded the Distinguished Service Order for his actions that morning.[296]

General Currie hoped to use a fresh brigade from each division each day as his plan to break the Drocourt-Quéant Line unfolded. The strength of the German resistance and the ferocity of their counterattacks quickly forced changes to his plan. In the first two days of fighting, all three brigades of the 3rd Division saw action. The 42nd Battalion of the 7th Brigade moved up to the Bois du Sart to relieve the 58th early in the morning so that it could support an attack by the 52nd Battalion of the 9th Brigade in conjunction with the 4th C.M.R. of the 8th Brigade. The objective of the assault was to clear the village of Boiry-Nôtre Dame of enemy and to capture Artillery Hill. This feature of higher ground lay just at the northern edge of the village, in the centre of the Fresnes-Rouvroy Switch Line. This line was in front of the main Drocourt-Quéant Line.

The attack was launched at 11:00 A.M. on August 28, supported by all the artillery of the 3rd Division. The 52nd Battalion cleared the trenches southeast of Boiry and then moved past the village to the north. The 58th remained under the command of Acting Major Smythe. He selected D and B Companies to advance through the village, and they cleared it by 1:00 P.M. The two companies moved to the north side of the village to take Artillery Hill. When they experienced some trouble at this point and requested support, A Company was moved forward. Initially, this restored the situation, but then two pillboxes began to pose a threat to the advance, and battalion headquarters requested that one company of the 42nd be added to the assault to outflank the pillboxes. The response was immediate, and the pillboxes and their garrisons were quickly captured. The battalion advanced its line in the direction of Branch Farm (Bench Farm) and held a position from Artillery Hill on the left in an arc around to the northeast corner of Boiry on its right. The Germans were seen massing for another counterattack in Victoria Copse, a small wooded area northwest of Boiry. They advanced toward the battalion's position at 5:30 P.M., and the situation looked serious until the requested artillery fire landed almost directly on the enemy's assembly area. Fire from the battalion's Lewis and Vickers guns, combined with the artillery support, quickly reduced the threat. By 6:15 P.M., the situation had stabilized. The battalion gave up some ground under enemy artillery fire, but returned to the forward area after the shelling ceased and was back in the captured positions at 9:00 P.M. "This attack by the 58th was tremendously successful and by cracking the northern flank, endangered the whole German line."[297] They had captured three hundred prisoners, fifty machine guns, and an anti-tank gun. The cost to the 58th for this achievement was sixteen killed, Captain Field and Lieutenants Andrews, McAdam, McGrath, and George and fifty-two other ranks wounded, four men missing, and twenty-four men gassed. Among the dead was Private Walker G. Gibson, likely the man that Brigadier General Ormond had singled out for slackness on the march during the night of the twenty-second. Major Smythe was awarded the Distinguished Service Order for his skillful handling of the battalion throughout this operation.

The high number of gas casualties could have been the result of the men making a conscious decision to leave their respirators off as they moved to the attack. The standard small box respirator would have had eye pieces that fogged up in action, and the filters would not have allowed for the amount of air need by men straining to move forward and drive the enemy from prepared defences. The Germans had tried to saturate the area under attack with gas, but the Canadians were actually aided by the rain, which fell overnight and reduced the effectiveness of the gas. The men wore their respirators only in the highest concentrations of gas.[298]

Early the next morning, the 4th British Division and elements of the Canadian Machine Gun Corps relieved the battalion. The relief was accomplished by four o'clock, and the unit moved about seven kilometres west to Feuchy. As they arrived in the village, an aerial bomb struck A Company, leaving eight men dead and sixteen wounded. The same night, they moved to the "Y" hutments near Arras. On the thirtieth, they received a visit from Brigadier General Ormond, who praised them for the way they captured and held their objectives against enemy counterattacks. They remained in the hutments for the last day of the month.

The fighting to capture the rest of the Fresnes-Rouvroy Line and the Drocourt-Quéant Line behind it continued until September 2. The task now fell to the fresher units of the 1st and 4th Divisions. The 58th suffered a total of 480 casualties in leading the 9th Brigade's assault at Amiens and in the two days of hard fighting to capture Bois du Sart and Boiry-Nôtre Dame. Some of the wounded remained with the unit, but the fighting strength was significantly reduced, despite the extra reinforcements received in March 1918. While veterans had the battle skills to improve their chances of survival in this new style of combat, they were not immortal. They would continue to fall right up to the battalion's last major attack in October.

The Human Balance Sheet

	August	**Cumulative**
Killed	82	446
Wounded	356	1758
Shell Shocked	0	90
Gassed	24	55
Missing	12	246
Sick	0	39
Reinforcements	0	1386

Chapter Thirty-one

September 1918
The Edge is Blunted

The 58th was now at rest near Etrun, west of Arras. Other units in the Canadian Corps continued to attack the remaining German defensive line in front of Cambrai. The 1st Canadian and 4th British Divisions relieved the 2nd and 3rd Divisions on the night of August 28 and prepared to launch the next phase of the attack on September 2. On August 31, the 4th Canadian Division arrived from Amiens and moved into the line. After three and a half years of war, General Currie's staff was capable of handling the rapid movement of the troops available and creating a sound plan in a short period of time. It concentrated a powerful artillery barrage on the German front and planned to use tanks to crush the wire not destroyed by the heavy artillery shells armed with the 106 fuse. The hammer that set off the explosive in the shell was mounted to protrude through the nose of the shell when it was armed. It would be triggered on contact with the ground before the shell proper penetrated below the surface, thus allowing the force of the explosion to strike the barbed wire obstacles and not merely throw up a fountain of earth.[299] The attack on the Drocourt-Quéant Line went in at dawn on September 2. The tanks helped to break paths for the infantry. German resistance was not as fierce as it had been in late 1917, and enemy soldiers surrendered in large numbers. Despite not achieving its first day objectives in terms of territory gained, the battle had taken its toll on the Germans. On resuming the advance the next morning, the Canadians found they had the battlefield to themselves. The Germans had withdrawn to the east bank of the Canal du Nord and the positions of the Hindenburg Line. The success of the Canadian attack meant the Germans had had to withdraw their troops from a wide area, allowing other British formations to advance unmolested by enemy fire. By September 3, the Germans had retreated from all of the territory they had captured in their spring and summer offensives. The total Canadian casualties for the three days of fighting were 5,500.

The High Command began preparations for a series of attacks from Cambrai in front of the Canadians on the north to St. Quentin, about thirty kilometres due south. The Canadian Corps would attack on a frontage of sixty-four hundred metres from north to south, along the west bank of the Canal du Nord. A flooded bog covered thirty-eight hundred metres of the front, and another twenty-three hundred metres were obstructed by an incomplete, but dry, section of the canal. General Currie decided to funnel all four divisions over the incomplete section of the canal and have them fan out on the other side of the obstacle, driving the enemy away from the breach by attacking north and south. To succeed, the plan required perfect coordination between artillery, engineers, and infantry. Once the defences along the east bank of the Canal were subdued, the next phase of the attack would be to break through the Marquion trench system and capture Bourlon Wood. Then the Canadians would tackle the Marcoing Line in front of Cambrai itself.

The attack was to begin on September 27 with the 1st and 4th Canadian Divisions leading the way, each with two battalions forward. In a carefully scheduled sequence, fresh battalions from each of the lead divisions were to move forward until the Marcoing Line was in sight. Then, the 3rd Division would come forward to breach that line and advance on Cambrai. The 2nd Division expected to be the reserve.

The 58th Battalion moved to Tilloy-les-Mofflaines on the Arras-Cambrai Road on September 2. The next afternoon, the men marched to Vis-en-Artois in order to be in reserve if the Germans staged a counterattack. On the fourth, the battalion moved to Saudemont and relieved the 47th Battalion of the 10th Brigade in support on the line formed after the capture of the Drocourt-Quéant Line on the previous day. The 58th were supporting the 116th Battalion, a sister battalion of 9th Brigade. Major Dougall Carmichael had been promoted to take the place of Lieutenant Colonel George Pearkes, who had been wounded for the fifth time in the battle for Amiens. The historian of the 116th described Major Carmichael as "one of the outstanding officers of the 9th Brigade."[300] Two men were wounded during the relief, and there were four more casualties over the next two days. There were no casualties on the seventh, but three more on the eighth. Sergeant Rutherford was seriously wounded by gas on the ninth while sleeping in a trench. He started to walk to the Casualty Clearing Station, but managed to get a ride to medical attention, probably saving his life. The battalion moved to Wancourt on the eleventh and suffered two killed and six wounded — its heaviest losses while in reserve. The Diary comments that it had been a quiet stay in the lines.

Wancourt was about six kilometres southeast of Arras and had been the scene of heavy fighting in the early stages of the Battle of Arras. Now it was quiet enough for the men to rest, clean up, and engage in some training. Two of the companies were able to go to rifle ranges, while the remainder of the companies carried out regular training. On September 18, the battalion moved back to the "Y" Hutments, west of Arras.

While in the "Y" Hutments, the men had time for recreational training and equipment inspections to bring their equipment up to standard. Regular training and time on the rifle ranges continued until the battalion moved to Hauteville, eleven kilometres west of Arras. It had two days there to rest and prepare to return to the fray. There were no casualties during this period out of the line. George Bell later related a story about the "death" of one Ferguson from A Company that happened about this time. A man in 58th uniform died at a casualty clearing station, and a photo of his corpse was sent to the battalion in the hope that he might be identified. Ferguson's section from A Company positively identified the corpse as their mate. Intelligence soon learned that Ferguson was alive and a prisoner of the Germans. The photo was sent back and again Ferguson's comrades identified him, this time in sworn affidavits. Again Intelligence reported that Ferguson was a prisoner. There the matter stood until Bell met Ferguson in London after the Armistice. He had, indeed, been a prisoner. The corpse was never positively identified.[301] A major change in command took place during this rest period. Major-General Louis Lipsett was returned to the British army to command the 4th British Division. Major General F.O.W. Loomis, formerly commander of the 2nd Canadian Infantry Brigade, assumed command of the 3rd Canadian Division.

On September 26, the battalion marched twenty-five kilometres to Wancourt to entrain for the trip to the Hendicourt-Cagnicourt area. The thirty-three-kilometre train journey took nine hours. The men de-trained at two o'clock in the morning in the village of Quéant and marched to trench billets at Riencourt-les-Cagnicourt. At 11:00 A.M. that same day, they moved to the Canal du Nord in battle order. The opening assault on the Canal had started earlier at 5:20 A.M., and the Canadians quickly broke through the first line of defences. At 1:40 P.M., the 58th crossed to the east side of the Canal and took up forward positions, where the men rested overnight. Lieutenant W.E. Brown and two other men were killed, and twelve men were wounded that day. The battalion was now ready to take its turn in its last major attack with the Canadian Corps.

At five o'clock in the morning on September 28, it moved off in support of the 52nd Battalion and was to pass through the 52nd when it had captured its objectives. Both the 52nd and the 43rd Battalions ran into difficulties before they could carry out their assigned tasks. The decision was made by the brigadier to have the 58th launch a second attack at 7:00 that evening, supported by a heavy artillery barrage, to break through the Marcoing Line itself. This defensive position had two belts of barbed wire twenty-seven metres thick, machine gun posts every nine metres, and a pillbox every eighteen metres.[302] The plan was a measure of how far things had improved since 1916. The men were not ordered to attack entrenched enemy with only their rifles and bayonets. Artillery would be used to soften up the defenders, and the Canadians would follow close behind it to catch the defenders before they could return to their positions. Lieutenant Colonel Macfarlane and Major Carmichael conducted a reconnaissance together, as the 116th would carry the attack beyond the Marcoing Line. It was decided to make it a two-company attack, with A Company taking the left flank adjacent to the 7th Brigade and C Company taking the right flank along the railway adjacent to the Cambrai-Bapaume Road.

The softening-up barrage commenced on schedule at 7:00 P.M., and the two companies moved to the attack at 7:05 P.M. As Major Jucksch described it, "... the air was filled with the devil himself, the bursting of thousands & thousands of shells. It was a seething mass of hellfire."[303] A Company on the left made good progress and cleared the section of the Line in front of it. C Company on the right ran into trouble from heavy machine gun fire originating along the railway line. Lieutenant Archie Venn led a platoon over the railway and the Cambrai-Bapaume Road twice before they could establish good positions to defend the right flank of the battalion. By the time they secured this last objective, the company was virtually wiped out. Once the 58th had secured its objectives, the 116th moved through it to tackle the hamlet of St. Olle on the outskirts of Cambrai. The 116th had to withdraw in the face of heavy machine gun fire

Courtesy Kelly Campbell.

Lieutenant Frederick Stockhausen, killed in action near Cambrai, France on October 1, 1918.

Lieutenant Lorne Bean Craig MM, March 7, 1917, wearing sergeant stripes. Killed in action on September 30, 1918.

from the hamlet, and it was decided to resume the attack in the morning. The fighting that evening had left the battalion with heavy losses. Captain Robert Pollock, who had reverted from the rank of major to join the battalion, and Lieutenant Fred Stockhausen[304] were killed along with sixteen men. Stockhausen had been wounded in the leg by shrapnel at the start of the attack, but refused to leave his men and seek medical attention out of the line. He continued to lead the platoon until he was struck again by shrapnel, this time in the head.[305] Lieutenants Legard, Finney, Church, and Kress and 170 men were wounded. In the back and forth of attack and withdrawal, another seven men were missing. Honourary Captain S.E. McKegney, one of the unit's chaplains, was tireless in his efforts to rescue the wounded in the two days of the attack. He would continue to look after the injured the next day and was awarded the Military Cross for his gallantry and devotion to duty under very heavy fire.

The attack to take St. Olle resumed the next morning at six o'clock. The 116th led off from the left flank and was again badly mauled by machine gun fire. Two companies of the 116th were nearly destroyed by the well-prepared enemy.[306] The 116th did not give up the attack. It appealed to a nearby field artillery battery for support, which was duly provided. The combination of fire from its own Lewis guns and the artillery enabled it to capture the village. The 58th moved up on the right flank and again crossed the railway and Bapaume-Cambrai Road. Twice driven back from the road to the railway, D Company, reinforced by the remnants of C Company, managed to complete the clearing of that section of the Marcoing Line by one o'clock in the afternoon. Contact was established with the King's Liverpool Regiment of the 57th British Division. A Company helped the 116th clear enemy-held houses east of St. Olle. By three o'clock, the situation was under control. The casualties were lighter than on the first day of the operation, but the battalion had less to lose. Lieutenant Venn of C Company, Lieutenant Lorne Craig, Lieutenant J.B. Swarts, and another sixteen men were killed. Craig had been an acting sergeant during the Battle of Mount Sorrel in the Ypres Salient and won the Military Medal for his work as a runner during that attack. Private Chester Baker was also killed that day. Like his friend, David Waldron, he had lied about his age to enlist in 1916, and was only eighteen when he was killed. He may have survived the battalion's many costly actions to this point by being kept out of harm's way until he turned eighteen. Now he paid the price for being in the adventure he had sought three years earlier. Other casualties included Lieutenants Dallyn and Woodyatt, who were wounded along with seventy-three other ranks, and eight more men were missing.

The heavy losses of the previous two days necessitated a reorganization of the battalion, and B Company was amalgamated with C Company. The total fighting strength of the unit was down to about 320 men. Three officers and 29 men from the band came up as reinforcements to bring the total up to 352. The 58th moved into reserve behind units of the 8th Brigade, which moved up to take over positions in the Marcoing Line. That night, orders arrived for the 58th and 116th Battalions to resume the attack the next morning.

The Human Balance Sheet

	September	Cumulative
Killed	42	488
Wounded	276	2034
Shell Shocked	0	90
Gassed	0	55
Missing	15	261
Sick	0	39
Reinforcements	0	1386

The entry in the War Diary for October 1, 1918, lists 46 killed in action, 89 missing in action, and 245 wounded during these operations.

Chapter Thirty-two

October 1918
One Last Effort

The 58th had to participate in one last effort to drive the enemy from the Cambrai area. General Currie called on all four divisions of the Corps to attack in line and capture a bridgehead over the Canal de l'Escaut northeast of Cambrai on October 1. The attack began at 6:00 A.M., and despite some initial success, the Canadians found the Germans unwilling to give up their defence of Cambrai. Currie's old division, the 1st, was unable to achieve all of its objectives on the left flank. This jeopardized the operations of the 4th and 3rd Divisions. General Loomis assigned the 9th Brigade the task of taking the high ground east of Tilloy and establishing a bridgehead over the canal at the town of Ramillies. Colonel Sutherland, temporarily in command of the 9th Brigade,[307] gave the first part of the operation to the 52nd and 43rd Battalions. They quickly took the high ground and captured 350 prisoners.[308]

The 116th and the 58th moved through them in broad daylight and attacked down a slope devoid of cover against enemy troops entrenched along the canal bank. The 116th advanced along the left flank toward the town of Ramillies. The 58th headed for the Pont d'Aire between Ramillies and Morenchies. Struck by very heavy machine gun and artillery fire coming from the woods on the far side of the canal near Morenchies, the attack faltered, and the two exhausted battalions dug in about halfway to their objectives.[309] The diarist noted, "Trained Bosche snipers and machine gunners accounted for a great number of our men and the use of forward sections of artillery by the Bosche was turned to great account."[310] He also recorded that many of the new men had not learned to take advantage of what cover there was, resulting in needless casualties. The Diary indicates that four men were killed and thirty-one wounded in this last effort, but an examination of the C.E.F. Roll of Honour shows at least forty-two killed in action on this date, over half of them conscripts newly arrived on the Western Front. Captains C.S. Burrows and W.W. Johnson and Lieutenant S. Kemp were reported missing. Johnson and Kemp had been with the battalion from the beginning and had risen from the ranks. Johnson won the Military Cross and two bars after being promoted. Burrows was reported killed soon after, and Kemp died in captivity after the Armistice. Johnson survived thanks to medical treatment received from his captors and returned to Canada. He was awarded the Distinguished Service Order for his bravery in the fighting in these final days of the war. Major Carmichael was awarded a bar to his Distinguished Service Order for his leadership of the 116th Battalion in the St. Olle and Tilloy attacks. He was wounded in the face during the second attack, but remained with his men for another two hours until he could no longer carry on.[311] Private Elver was wounded in both legs. The 58th was finally withdrawn from the line at 11:55 P.M. when the 24th and 27th Battalions moved into the line.[312]

The attack of October 1 did not accomplish all the objectives General Currie set for it. It did bring the high ground around Tilloy under Canadian control, and from this position the Canadians were able to dominate Cambrai and the valley of the L'Escaut River. The German hold on the city was made precarious by this development. The strength of the German resistance to the Canadian assault caused Currie to stop the attack. It would later be learned that the Germans had deployed a quarter of their forces on the Western Front against the Canadians to protect the Drocourt-Quéant Line, the Canal du Nord, and Cambrai, and yet they had been unable to stop the four Canadian divisions from advancing thirty-seven kilometres in a little over a month.[313] Developments elsewhere on the front hastened the conclusion of the war even though the Canadian commanders thought the Germans still had plenty of fight left in them.

During the next two days, the men rested and cleaned up after their ordeal. They moved from Fontaine-Nôtre Dame to Bourlon Wood on the third. On the fifth, the officers carried out company inspections, and shortages of equipment were made good. They were back at regular company training on the sixth and continued with that until the twentieth. On the seventh, Lieutenant Colonel Macfarlane was transferred to England to assume a training command while Acting Major A.H. Jucksch was appointed to temporary command of the battalion. On the tenth, it marched about eight kilometres west to Pronville, where the men were quartered in billets in the village and in dugouts. On the seventeenth, Lieutenant General Currie inspected them and the rest of the 9th Canadian Infantry Brigade. On the nineteenth, Major R.E. Smythe assumed command of the battalion and was promoted to acting lieutenant colonel.

The period of recuperation came to an end on October 21. The battalion was bused to the village of Hornaing, about eight kilometres west of Valenciennes. Travelling near the front in busses was a new experience for the men. They were pleased to be greeted by grateful French people who hung flags from the buildings and covered the vehicles in flowers in their excitement at being freed from the German occupation.[314] Here the battalion was in support of the 1st Division. It moved into Raismes on the twenty-second. The enemy was in retreat, so there was very little action. The next day the men resumed company training and inspections, which continued until the twenty-seventh. There had been no new casualties in the prior three weeks.

They moved up to L'Escaut Canal on the twenty-seventh. One man was killed and another wounded during the move to the front line in relief of the 43rd Battalion. They moved back to Raismes the next day when relieved in their turn by the 1st Canadian Mounted Rifles and moved into support. They were inspected again on October 29, and on the thirtieth they moved to the hamlet of

Cataine, located ten kilometres northwest of Valenciennes. The 58th was not directly involved in the Corps' last major action, the capture of Valenciennes. It closed out the month doing regular training.

The Human Balance Sheet

	October	Cumulative
Killed	5	493
Wounded	32	2066
Shell Shocked	0	90
Gassed	9	55
Missing	3	264
Sick	0	39
Reinforcements	0	1386

Chapter Thirty-three

November 1918
The End

The battalion enjoyed the comfort of their billets in Cataine for the next five days. These were located near a factory, which the Germans had used as a prisoner of war camp. The local population reported that the Germans had been cruel captors. While in reserve, the battalion marched to Aremberg for baths and carried out regular training. On the third, there was time for an afternoon of sports. The next day, there were company inspections and, in the evening, a battalion concert. The men's morale was reported as very good. When rain fell all day on the fifth, the men were kept indoors and given a lecture on the general situation on the Western Front. The situation was changing rapidly, and victory was in the air. The German High Seas Fleet had mutinied on October 29 when ordered to put to sea for a final confrontation with the British Grand Fleet. Revolution threatened to destroy Germany from within before her enemies could penetrate her borders. The French, Americans, and British continued to move forward all along the front.

On November 6, the battalion moved about ten kilometres east in full marching order to the town of Bruay-sur-l'Escaut on the northern outskirts of Valenciennes. Battalion headquarters was established in a local chateau. The old German billets in town had been left in a poor state, perhaps a symptom of the decline in morale of a once proud army. The next day, the men marched five kilometres east to the suburb of Onnaing to take over billets that were previously used by the 49th Battalion. The civilian population was very "war worn," but friendly toward their liberators. The Germans had destroyed all aspects of the railways in the area and damaged the major crossroads in order to hamper pursuit — and, seemingly, as a last malicious gesture before they gave up territory they had controlled since the summer of 1914. On the eighth, Edward, Prince of Wales, paid a visit to the Headquarters Mess. The following day, the battalion crossed the Belgian border and moved to Boussu. It marched into the town's Grand Place with its surviving bandsmen playing and received a rousing reception from the civilians. The officers were the guests of the Burgomaster. The same day, Germany's ruler, Kaiser Wilhelm II, abdicated his throne. A German delegation had previously been sent to accept any terms the Allies cared to offer to end the hostilities. The whole corps was on the move along the road to Mons. Even the artillery observation balloons were moving while in the air over their transport as wires and other obstacles were cleared from their route.[315] The next day, the men marched three kilometres east to the suburb of Quaregnon and, again, they received the joyous welcome bestowed on liberators. The billets were good, and the health and morale of the men were excellent. The men may have sensed that the end of more than four long years of slaughter was at hand, but there was still plenty of artillery fire. They were on the outskirts of Mons, where the British army had first fought the Germans in the summer of 1914. The Canadian advance to Mons was the furthest penetration of the German lines by any British troops.

In an operation that would prove to be very controversial after the war, General Currie received orders from the Allied High Command that Mons be captured on the morning of November 11, even though the Armistice had been signed and was to go into effect at eleven o'clock that morning.[316] The men of the battalion later remembered the arrival of orders from Currie:

> . . . the despatch rider pulled up on his motorcycle and handed over the regular envelope containing

> the morning despatch from Brigade. Among all the routine mail dealing with horses, rations, men's leave and the dozen and one things we receive daily was a single signal message form.... A typical cold army message, no expression of joy, triumph, or relief. As a matter of fact a very business like note casually mentioning that the war was over but for us to carry on with reliefs, marches, etc."[317]

Thus the battalion received official word that the fighting would end, at least temporarily, at 11:00 A.M.[318] After the 42nd Battalion captured Mons, the 58th moved through it to the new front line east of Obourg. A and B Companies relieved the cavalry unit in the front line and set up strong points to ensure that no one other than advancing British troops or returning prisoners of war should get through the lines. D Company went into the support position while C Company formed the reserve in Obourg. That afternoon, Captain Thomas F. Lamb, one of the battalion's originals, led a group of fifty all ranks, including the bandsmen, to the central square of the city for a ceremony celebrating the relief of Mons. There, the men marched past Albert I, King of the Belgians, and the Prince of Wales with similar parties from other battalions. The rest of the battalion could hear the cheers six and a half kilometres away in Obourg. The sound of German munitions being destroyed provided a somber accompaniment to the celebrations in the city.

The 116th Battalion relieved A Company on the twelfth, and it moved up to the suburb of St. Denis. There were no sightings of the enemy, but his demolition of ammunition could be heard at a greater distance. The support and reserve companies were engaged in training. There may have been a sense that the Armistice was only temporary, as the Diary records that the men didn't trust the enemy. Fifteen reinforcements arrived. Training continued the next day. Louder explosions could be heard coming from a great distance. The Diary makes several comments about the situation of the local population. They are reported as grateful for their liberation and relieved to see the last of the undisciplined

German troops. The Diary also notes that they were desperate for food. Sixteen reinforcements arrived on November 16. On the eighteenth, the 1st Division passed through the line on its way to the Rhine and the zone of occupation in Germany. Brigadier General Ormond inspected the battalion. The next day, the battalion moved to Mons for baths. The battalion commander inspected them the following day. The Diary comments that their appearance had improved, no doubt due to the relief from the strain of war and the fresh clothes issued after the baths. Their appearance contrasted favourably with that of men who had escaped from German prison camps and now found their way back to Canadian lines. These men complained of harsh treatment and looked the worse for wear. Training and sports occupied the men for the next few days. On the twenty-fourth, there was a special church service attended by the people of Obourg. They presented Major Smythe with a bouquet of flowers as a token of their thankfulness. On the twenty-sixth, the brigade arranged to send a party of eighteen officers and NCOs to Brussels and Waterloo. The Battle of Waterloo

Courtesy R. Horne.

Medal awarded to Private 452965 Arthur James Horne by the people of Mons in gratitude for their liberation by the Canadian 3rd Division.

had taken place over a hundred years before and was something all men of the British Empire would have known in some detail. The battlefield had passed unchanged, except for the elimination of the sunken road that sheltered Wellington's reserves from the French artillery bombardment. Its banks had been lowered to provide earth for the Lion Mound at the centre of the British line. It would be interesting to know how these veterans compared it to the places over which they fought. The next day, two hundred officers and men were assigned to police the streets of Mons during the visit of the King of the Belgians to the city. On November 29, Lieutenant Neil K. McKechnie was appointed Battalion Education Officer, and the process of readying the men of the battalion for civilian life began in earnest. On the last day of the month, Major General Loomis inspected the battalion. This would not be the last inspection before the men finally returned to their civilian pursuits.

The Human Balance Sheet

	November	Cumulative
Killed	0	493
Wounded	0	2066
Shell Shocked	0	90
Gassed	0	55
Missing	0	264
Sick	0	39
Reinforcements	39	1425

Chapter Thirty-four

December 1918 – March 1919
Going Home

By the beginning of November, it was evident that the fighting would soon cease, and plans to return the men to Canada were formulated. While the Canadians hoped to return home directly from France, the British would not provide the shipping for this to happen. Consequently, the Canadian Corps first returned to England before departing for Canada.

Even this move did not take place immediately, for it took time to organize. The 3rd and 4th Divisions originally expected to move to Germany to join the 1st and 2nd Divisions in the Zone of Occupation. However, the damage done to the railways by the retreating Germans made it very difficult to transport supplies to the first two divisions and the Belgian and French populations in the territory previously under German control. As a result, the 58th remained in Belgium.

Once hostilities ceased, the next question was what to do to keep the men occupied. By December, the battalion had a regular schedule of educational training or parades in the morning and sports in the afternoon. The University of Vimy, which was a 3rd Division initiative in the winter of 1917 and 1918, was re-established as the Khaki University and copied by some of the other Allied armies. Leaves were granted to large groups of the men.

There were social events such as a 3rd Division ball at the Palace D'Aremburg in Brussels, and a battalion dance was given by the Mayor of Ecaussinnes-d'Enghien. The battalion changed location several times, until finally it was located near Corps Headquarters in Brussels. Lieutenant Colonel Macfarlane and Major Carmichael returned to the battalion in December.

The Christmas of 1918 was a memorable one. The men of the battalion joined their celebration with that of the local population, and everyone had plenty to eat and drink. The officers held a ball at Maison Haute. At midnight, the regimental sergeant major decided that the men should serenade the officers from the ballroom balcony. This action was well received, with many toasts from the officers. The next morning, the officers and men were so hung over they could not change locations as ordered by Corps Headquarters.[319]

The battalion spent New Year's Day at Renaix and moved the following day to Templeuve, on the French-Belgian border, where it remained for the rest of the month and for the first six days of February.[320] The same pattern of lectures or training in the morn-

January 1919, officers of the 58th Battalion.

ing and sports in the afternoon continued here at Templeuve. The pattern was broken occasionally by special events: a lecture by Major General Loomis to the officers of the 9th Brigade or an inspection of the battalion by Lieutenant General Currie. The evening could bring a concert put on by the Belgians or a show by the 3rd Division's concert troop, the famous Dumbells.

The process of returning to Canada began in earnest in February. On the first day of the month, the horses were delivered to the Horse Demobilization Camp at Renaix. The next day, surplus equipment, Lewis guns, and small arms ammunition was turned into the 3rd Division Supply Depot. Leave was granted to five hundred men before the battalion moved to Le Havre on February 7. The men and their records were prepared for embarkation to England, which occurred on February 10. They sailed on the S.S. *Lorina* from Le Havre to Weymouth that night and arrived the next morning. The battalion spent the day in a rest camp before moving to Bramshott Camp on the twelfth. It was almost three years to the day since the battalion had left England for France in 1916 from this same camp.

The next thirty days would see the men of the battalion firmly embraced by military bureaucracy. Their days would be replete with form filling, clothing, bath, pay, medical, and battalion parades as the army tried to ensure that each man's documents were in order. From February 13 to 28, there were five medical parades or inspections. The Canadians were again in close proximity to English women of loose morals, and General Currie had decreed that no one suffering from venereal disease would be sent home while exhibiting any symptoms of the disease. This was a tactic to keep the men under control until shipping could be found to send them home. The units of the 3rd Division were extremely fortunate in that regard. By a quirk of fate, they were closest to the embarkation point for the journey to Canada. It made more sense to send them home first rather than the more senior 1st and 2nd Divisions.

The weather at the beginning of March was rainy, and much of the outdoor activity had to be cancelled. The educational program was discontinued on the first. By the fourth, the books of the school were distributed to anyone interested in them. Every effort was made to ensure that each man had proper documentation for the return to Canada. On the fifth, the battalion received a favourable report on this score, and on the tenth, after the battalion had been warned to prepare for embarkation to Canada on the twelfth, Dominion representatives made one last check of the men's documents. The next day saw the culmination of three years of war service for the battalion. Lieutenant General Sir Arthur Currie presented the 58th Battalion with its regimental colours. The battalion had begun life as a composite unit made up of twenty-one regiments from the Central Militia District and, as such, had brought no colours to England in the winter of 1915. Many other units had made the pilgrimage to Westminster Abbey on arrival in England and left their colours on General Wolfe's tomb. Brigadier General William Taylor, Chaplain General of the British Forces, conducted the ceremony. Lieutenant Colonel Robert A. Macfarlane, twenty-two officers, and about five hundred other ranks attended the ceremony. Lieutenant Andrew A. Anderson, Lieutenant H.L. Thorpe, Sergeant Perritt, Sergeant Larivee, and Sergeant J. Young formed the colour party. Major

NAC PA6086.

March 13, 1919, Bramshott Camp, England. Presentation of the battalion's King and Regimental Colours by Lieutenant General Sir Arthur Currie. Major Jucksch on the left, with Major Carmichael on Currie's left and Lieutenant Colonel Macfarlane with his back to the camera.

Dougall Carmichael and Major Arnold H. Jucksch handed the colours to General Sir Arthur Currie. "The corps commander made a short speech thanking the battalion for the splendid work done by them and wishing them good speed and a happy time in Canada. The battalion then marched past and the ceremony was complete." The next morning, the battalion moved to Liverpool by train. By four o'clock that same afternoon, the 33 officers, 55 sergeants, and 619 men of the battalion were on their way home, having been seen off by Major General Loomis, commander of the 3rd Division.

The battalion was to demobilize in Toronto. On March 22, its trains were held up outside the city in order to provide for a daylight welcome on the following morning. The previous day, one of the Toronto papers had carried a story describing the unit's achievements. The headline ran, "OLD 'FIFTY-EIGHTH' HONOURED BY FRANCE — Fighting Toronto Battalion, Returning To-morrow, is Only Unit in Canadian Corps Entitled to Display Croix de Guerre on Colours."[321] The word spread quickly that the men would be returning the next morning, and a large crowd gathered early at the North Toronto railway station, an unusual occurrence in those days. The crowd, estimated at one hundred thou-

NAC PA83767.

Soldiers of the 58th coming home, Toronto, Ontario, March 23, 1919.

Courtesy Mary Holden.

Tiny, one of the 58th's regimental mascots, in dress uniform.

sand, was made up of mothers, fathers, wives, children, and comrades who had returned earlier. At the Armoury downtown, more celebrants awaited the actual dismissal parade. The railway platform was lined by one thousand previously returned veterans. As the trains came into view at quarter to nine, a great cheer resounded and echoed along Yonge Street. Then men came off the trains and were organized into companies for the march down Yonge Street. Of the 1,100 men who had gone to England in November 1915, only 147 returned with the battalion.[322] One of the wounded veterans, Private James H. Rawlinson, blinded at Vimy, declined the offer of a ride with other disabled veterans and joined his comrades on their last march. Led by two bands and joined by "Tiny," one of the 58th's canine mascots, the men of the 58th and the 2nd Canadian Mounted Rifles swung down Yonge Street in column of fours, and then west along Queen Street to the saluting stand in front of the City Hall. The men marched with the precision of well-drilled troops. With their steel helmets on their packs, their rifles sloped on their shoulders, and their bayonets sheathed, they still had the look of fighters.

The press of people was so great that General Gunn, who took the salute, found himself unable to enter the Armoury. People were held back from the centre of the Armoury floor by a thin line of soldiers and some ropes on stands. Others were in the balconies surrounding the upper walls, waving flags and cheering as the soldiers arrived at the entrance to the building.

As A, B, and C Companies entered the building to the strains of "Tipperary," the crowd could contain its enthusiasm no more and broke through the slender restraints to offer their returned loved ones a personal welcome. The formal program, including Mayor Tommy Church's speech, had to be abandoned. Lieutenant Colonel Macfarlane made a brief speech and then, after dismissing the men, jumped from the dais into the crowd, shaking hands and wishing his men well. His announcement that they would proceed immediately to the Exhibition Grounds for demobilization was greeted with wild cheers.

The reporter from the *Daily News* moved among the happy mass of humanity, gathering quotations and vignettes from the throng of officers, men, and their families. Major Reg Geary, ex-mayor of Toronto, firmly embraced his mother as he expressed his joy at returning home. Other members of the battalion described the bold leadership of Macfarlane and Lieutenant Andy Anderson and the incidents where Major Carmichael had blown up the Letter Box and the band had gone into action at Cambrai. Someone expressed the opinion to the reporter that "while there had been a wonderful esprit de corps in all the Canadian battalions, it is doubtful if ever the sentiment was developed to the high degree that prevailed in the 58th."

Epilogue

The 58th Battalion went to England as a group of enthusiastic amateur soldiers. A large number of the men had previous military experience, but few of them, even those who had seen action in the Boer War of 1899 to 1901, were prepared for what they found in the trenches of the Western Front. Those who survived the first months of mud and rain, the almost constant shelling, and the experience of Mount Sorrel and the Somme developed a professional approach to the war. The first officers of the battalion were often prominent men who came from the Canadian upper class. As they were eliminated through death, injury, or assignment, they were replaced by men who had survived the first clashes with the enemy and who would lead their men with a better understanding of what was possible. Dougall Carmichael rose from the rank of captain to command the 116th Battalion. Robert Macfarlane rose from the rank of lieutenant to command the 58th. Walter Johnson, Lorne Craig, Dick Ineson, Andrew A. Anderson, and Thomas Lamb were just some of the men who rose from noncommissioned rank to officer rank and who led their men from the front, several of them being killed in action in the latter stages of the war. A number of privates rose to noncommissioned rank through the demonstration of skill and courage; Doug Rutherford is but one example.

The result of this winnowing process was the creation of a very effective fighting unit. The attack at Mount Sorrel was successful because of artillery preparation, while the actions on the Somme were unsuccessful because artillery preparation had not been effective. The first raids conducted by the battalion were inconclusive affairs. However, by the time of the battle for Vimy Ridge, the whole Canadian Corps, including the 58th Battalion, was a seasoned fighting force. The 58th led the furthest advance at Avion in June 1917. They conducted the successful daylight raid at Nun's Alley in August of that year. While they did not capture all of their objectives at Bellevue Spur in front of Passchendaele on October 26, 1917, they had started from the toughest ground, their backs to the flooded Marsh Bottom. The showed their resilience by returning to the front in early November and holding Vindictive Crossroads against the German counterattack on November 13. Their record in 1918 was one of almost unbroken success. The raid by Lieutenant Jucksch was a model action, but it was not the only one as the battalion strove to carry on the Canadian Corps tradition that their territory started at the German wire. The only failure came in the last attack at Tilloy on October 1, 1918, when the planning of the acting brigadier seemed to revert to the 1916 style of attack. Two under-strength battalions were to assault prepared enemy positions, in the middle of the day, over open ground, and without proper artillery support. The results were similar to those experienced on the Somme in 1916, and many of the newly arrived conscripts lost their lives in this futile attack.

When the war was over and most of the survivors were back in Canada, the cost of the war continued to be paid. The battalion War Diary lists a cumulative total of 493 killed in action and 254 missing. Men who served with the unit continued to die of war injuries. Sergeant George Gray, who had gone to England as a private in 1915, is the last recorded death. He passed away in Canada on October 6, 1921, from endocarditis. He would be fatal casualty 938 of the battalion. This figure is eighty-seven more than the battalion commemorated on its plaque in the Church of the Transfiguration in 1927. The fact that the record keepers at the battalion would not know the fate of those who left the battlefield wounded or those who died of wounds or disease after the cessation of hostilities may explain the discrepancy. Including Sergeant Gray, seventeen men died after the battalion returned to Toronto.

But what legacy did the men who formed the battalion leave behind them? Did the end of the war mean the end of the associations formed in its crucible of fire and mud? How was it remembered by those who survived its various actions, and how did they transmit that memory to others?

The 58th Battalion was officially disbanded on September 15, 1920. It was a wartime creation, and, despite its accomplishments, Canada did not need it after the fighting ceased. Because many of the men who served in the battalion had come from Toronto, it was perpetuated as the 1st Reserve Battalion of the Royal Grenadiers of that city. By that time, Lieutenant Colonel Robert A. Macfarlane was commanding officer of the Royals and he had Major Reg Geary and Major Arnold Jucksch with him as company commanders. Macfarlane was transferred out of Toronto in 1921, and command of the Royals returned to Lieutenant Colonel E.A. Gooderham until Major Geary was promoted on March 31, 1924. For a short time, at least, there were men from the 58th to impart some of their spirit to a surviving military unit.

It was not until 1935 that the veterans formed an association, with an executive and various committees to maintain the connections among these comrades-in-arms. Prior to that date, the members of the battalion had kept in touch informally with Christmas parties for the children, family picnics, and "smokers" for the men. A newsletter of high quality was published to report on issues of interest to the members. The new association would try to lobby on behalf of its members and all veterans during the tough economic times of the so-called "Dirty Thirties." It was also involved in organizing the pilgrimage of some its members to the unveiling of the Vimy Memorial and the Corps Reunion Dinner in 1938. For these occasions, it obtained berets and armbands in French grey, the colour of the 3rd Division-patch. After the Second World War, the quality of the newsletter diminished, the content becoming more about what was happening to the members than about the history of the fighting unit. Over time, the old soldiers died off, and the memory of their achievements began to fade away

For most of the men, the return home meant a return to civilian pursuits. Major Dougall Carmichael began a short career in politics. He joined the United Farmers of Ontario and served the government of Ernest Drury as Minister Without Portfolio from 1919 to 1923. He was re-elected in 1923 despite the defeat of the Drury government. He resigned his seat in 1925 to run unsuccessfully in the federal election of that year. In 1930, he left the family farm in Collingwood to go to Ottawa as one of three appointees on the War Veterans Allowance Board. From that post, he could look after the needs of all his comrades in the Canadian Expeditionary Force. He returned briefly to the army to command a training centre at Brockville early in the Second World War. His final rank was colonel. He passed away in September 1940.

Carmichael's daughter, Mary Holden, remembers her father meeting once a year with several other men from the 58th and pulling out the old maps to relive the battles. Generally, the men did not talk about their war experiences with their families. Even when members of the next generation went to their war, the older men kept silent about the horrors of life in the trenches.

One of Carmichael's visitors in Ottawa was Walter Johnson. Johnson had been wounded in the battalion's last attack at Tilloy on October 1, 1918, and taken prisoner by the Germans. While he survived his captivity, he did lose the sight of one eye. Being captured by the Germans may have deprived Johnson of the Victoria Cross. The High Command may have feared for his safety had he been awarded that decoration and instead he received the D.S.O. Johnson would also have another stint in the Canadian Army, rising to the rank of colonel and commanding Military District No. 2, the area from which the 58th was raised in the First World War. In 1945, the Conservative government of George Drew appointed him Assistant Manager, Navigation, for the T.&N.O. Navigation Company, part of the Ontario Northern Railway. In that position, he worked at developing tourism in the north.

Lieutenant Colonel R.A. "Alex" Macfarlane rejoined the Canadian Army during the Second World War, finishing with the rank of brigadier. He was decorated with a United States Presidential Citation for his service during that war. He seems to have had a successful career in business, serving on the Board of Directors of Barclay Distillery.

Major R. Eric Smythe returned to Canada with the 58th and then went home to the Niagara area. In 1920, he was appointed brigade major of the 5th Infantry Brigade. He graduated from the University of Toronto in 1926 with a Bachelor of Applied Science (Civil) degree and then went to work in Detroit. He returned to Canada in 1928 as Director of the Technical Service Council of Toronto, finding work for graduating engineers in Canada to stop them from leaving the country (an early manifestation of the "brain drain"). In 1934, he was promoted to colonel and given command of the 5th Infantry Brigade. He rejoined the Canadian Army during the Second World War and ended it with the position of vice-quartermaster general stationed in Ottawa. After the Second World War, he returned to the Technical Service Council. In 1947, he began work on three reports for the Ontario Government dealing with the availability of electric power, rural telephone companies, and the formation of a water commission. In 1948, he formed a construction company and was responsible for the erection of schools, factories, and institutional buildings in southern Ontario. He used his pistol from the war years to guard the company payroll. He died on January 30, 1969.

Captain Hedley, one of the unit's chaplains, returned to the Anglican Church in Toronto and, soon after the war, was involved in the establishment of a new church in north Toronto. The Church of the Transfiguration would become the focal point of the 58th's annual memorial services. Hedley had established the 58th Scout Troop and Wolf Cub pack at the church in honour of the battalion. On September 25, 1927, in an extremely moving ceremony attended by the two commanding officers of the battalion and 600 of the surviving men and their families and the families of the fallen, the King's and Regimental Colours of the 58th Battalion were deposited in the church, and a memorial plaque to 851 men of the battalion who had died during the war was unveiled. Major Warner Elmo Cusler approached the door of the church and addressed the rector and the wardens:

> Sir, I have been commanded by Lieutenant Colonel Macfarlane, commanding the 58th Canadian Infantry Battalion to inform the authorities of this church that he has repaired here today with the colours of the battalion and desires permission to prefer a request that they be deposited herein.

Hedley died while trying to put out a bush fire at a family cottage in the Kawarthas in May 1938.

Major Arnold Homer Jucksch was appointed to the staff of Sunnybrook Hospital, but he found the peacetime army pay less than adequate to cover his bills and soon resigned from the position. He changed his last name to Jukes and began a singing career under the stage name The Great Arnoldi. This career took him to concert halls and stages across North America. A man of many talents, he eventually became a wood carver for William Randolph Hearst, the newspaper tycoon, and decorated the interior of the Hearst Mansion in California. Later in life, he worked as a builder of models for an American aircraft manufacturer. He wrote his unpublished autobiography in 1954 and died on August 7, 1958.

Major Warner Elmo Cusler returned to Canada much later than the rest of his companions in the 58th. He had to spend many months in England undergoing reconstructive surgery necessitated by the wound that destroyed the left side of his face. Soon after his return home, he married Dorothy Frier, a Canadian nurse whom he had met during his stay at Ramsgate Military Hospital after he was wounded in June 1916. When he was able to return to Canada, Cusler rejoined the Imperial Bank of Commerce and had a twenty-year career there, finishing as manager of one of the Toronto branches. He served for a time as president of the 58th Battalion Association and tried to create interest in a written history of the unit. Having spent the last twenty-eight years of his life in pain from his numerous wounds, he died suddenly on July 28, 1946, at the family farm he had left thirty-one years earlier to join the 58th. Jane Cusler has clear memories of her parents, both of them veterans of the war, talking at length to each other about their military experiences

Richard Joyce left the 58th on June 20, 1916. He admitted to his diary that he was suffering nervous strain after four months in the trenches, but his prime reason for leaving the battalion was his dislike of Captain David McKeand. On arriving in England, he was sent to the Machine Gun School at Grantham and joined the British Expeditionary Force. In March 1917, he was in France and soon found himself with the 62nd Division in the Somme sector, where so many of his comrades had been killed or wounded the previous year. In September, he was promoted to captain and given the command of the 201st Machine Gun Company. He was with this unit through the first major tank attack of the First World War at Cambrai in November 1917. His diary reflects the excitement felt after the early gains and the disappointment when the Germans counterattacked and took back those gains. Having been in action for about for about nine months., he again found his nerves failing him. At the urging of friends he put in for a transfer to the Canadian Expeditionary Force Machine Gun School in England, and it was granted just before the major German offensive of March 1918. He remained in England until August 1919, when he returned home to Toronto, having spent several months touring the British Isles seeing family and friends. He had a successful career in business, operating a paper mill in Toronto. A lifelong bachelor, he led an active social life and belonged to many of the city's most prestigious clubs. He also kept in touch with his comrades in arms, particularly Gerry Cosbie, the original medical officer of the 58th. Dr. Cosbie came to the Joyce home the night before Dick died and put a stop to his transfer to a local hospital. He told his friend, in the straightforward fashion of men who have seen death many times, "Dick, you will be dead in the morning," to which Dick replied, "I know." Richard Joyce passed away on March 21, 1967.

Captain Waring Gerald Cosbie survived his wounding and went on leave to Canada. On board ship he met Billy Bishop before he became a famous ace. He returned to the front with No. 8 Casualty

 Clearing Station because his old commanding officer had not requested he return to the 58th. He won the Military Cross rescuing wounded during the attack at Vimy Ridge in April 1917. At the end of the war he was with the 3rd Division as it liberated Mons. After the war, he returned to graduate school at the University of Toronto and specialized in gynecology. He pioneered certain medical treatments and became a recognized expert in his field. One of his most high profile patients was Eva Peron, whom he attended in secrecy at the Mayo Clinic in Rochester, Minnesota. He died on April 22, 1987, at his home in West Vancouver. His body was returned to Toronto for burial in the Cosbie family plot in St. James Cemetery. The Book of Common Prayer he used to bury his dead comrades in the absence of the chaplain was used in his burial service.

Sergeant James Douglas Rutherford survived the gas he had inhaled in the fall of 1918. He returned to the farm in northern Ontario after the war. His family moved to Toronto, but he remained on the farm and married in 1935. He and his wife, Minnie, were very active in their local community. Rutherford worked as Clerk-Treasurer in Hudson Township and was a member of the Legion, and Minnie operated a general store. The gas had affected his health quite badly, and this necessitated regular trips to the Christie Street Veterans' Hospital to drain his sinuses. In later years, the treatments and drugs that became available were better able to deal with his illness, and his daughter remembers him as active almost until his death of heart failure in 1976.

Sergeant George Thomas Bell returned to work for the City of Toronto and, over time, rose to become parks commissioner. In 1963, he was given the task of overseeing the completion of the new Toronto City Hall. That task was accomplished just before he retired from the city in 1965. Because he was in a prominent position in the city and easy to locate in his downtown offices, he became an essential part of the network for the men of the 58th. The son of one of them remembers receiving his first job as a summer counselor at a city park and finding himself surrounded by co-workers who were the children and grandchildren of the men of the 58th. The ranks of the survivors thinned over the years, and he was the only member of the bat-

Courtesy of the Bell family.

Sergeant George T. Bell

talion to attend the fiftieth anniversary Remembrance Day service in Ottawa in 1968. Bell was a battalion clerk during the war and, as such, managed to accumulate a large collection of documents relating to the battalion. Several of the people who have assisted in the writing of this book have mentioned chance encounters with Bell that resulted in his sending them information about their relatives from those files. Bell's daughters donated the papers to the Royal Canadian Military Institute after his death in 1979. Unfortunately, it seems that the records were destroyed after a reorganization of the Institute's library in 1985.

Three Campbell brothers served with the 58th. Jack died of wounds while in hospital on October 28, 1918. Fred and Lewis both survived the war. Lewis had enlisted underage like David Waldron. The manpower shortage was so critical that his mother's written request that he be returned home was denied. Mrs. Campbell received a letter informing her that Lewis was being kept "well back of the line and in a position of safety...,"[323] which was not quite true. He was acting as a stretcher-bearer, a role that could be extremely dangerous. After the war, Lewis took the possessions of his friend, Lieutenant Fred Stockhausen, back to Toronto where he arranged to deliver them to Stockhausen's family. There he met the youngest sister of his comrade, and they subsequently married. He remained active with the 58th Battalion Association, serving on the executive during and after World War II.

Courtesy Lewis G. Campbell, Jr.

The three Campbell brothers who served in the 58th: Jack C. Campbell (back row, extreme left); Frederick C. Campbell (front row, extreme right); and Lewis G. Campbell (front row, second from right), who would marry Fred Stockhausen's youngest sister.

Archie MacKinnon arrived home in Toronto in March 1917. His father came down from the farm to greet him and wrote a letter to Archie's brother, Ronald, still serving overseas, describing Archie as "...looking fine & not very lame but he is not the boy he was when he went away."[324] Archie went for therapy at the Christie Street Military Hospital once a week for three months for a problem called "foot drop." He always had problems from his leg wound, especially in cold weather. He married and had four daughters, but he told his family little of his wartime experiences and did not participate in the 58th Battalion Association. He worked for Canada Customs in Toronto until his death in 1947.

Private Hubert Elver survived his leg wounds and was back in Canada in January 1919, attached to the Canadian Army Dental Corps. On his discharge from the army in October 1919, he went to work at Sunnybrook Veterans' Hospital until his retirement in March 1953. While there, he may have seen Arnold Jukes and David Waldron. He died of a heart attack at the hospital on September 13, 1954. His granddaughter Donna George remembers a man who loved gardening and never talked about his wartime experiences.

Private Robert Henry McKee survived the wound he had received during the attack on Regina Trench. He was sent to the 3rd South General Hospital in Oxford, England, and soon met Margaret, the sister of his platoon mate, Fred Rosser. Bob was in the hospital for a number of months and underwent fourteen operations to clean the wound to his hip before the final operation to remove the shrapnel ball that had caused the damage. All of these procedures were necessary to drain the wound and remove infected tissue in the days before antibiotics. He returned to Canada for rehabilitation and was discharged just before the end of the war. He and Maggie were married in Toronto in April 1920. His wound eventually led to a condition known as Thrombo angiitis obliterans, and this diagnosis resulted in the granting of a full disability pension. He died at Sunnybrook Veterans' Hospital on March 15, 1961.

Lieutenant Albert T. Skill left a widow and three young daughters when he was killed at Passchendaele. His grandson, Benjamin Keevil, says that the family never spoke about him. Benjamin was a member of the 58th Cub Pack at the Church of the Transfiguration, but made the connection to the 58th Battalion only as he assisted the author with this history. In memory of the men of the battalion, Benjamin has created a website under the title "The Canadians at Passchendaele."

Private John Carter's body was never found, and he is commemorated on the Vimy Memorial. He also left a wife and three young children. His widow found it difficult to raise the children and deeply regretted her loss. She hated the war and the governments that had allowed it to happen. She hid all her husband's papers relating to his military service. His grandson, Don, wrote that the death of John Carter hung like a pall in his household until after the death of his mother in 1996. The effect of the war was felt for a long time in many families.

David Waldron was pulled out of the battalion in March 1917 and returned to it in April 1918. He was an instructor in various courses in England while he was away. On April 27, he submitted his name for a posting to the Artillery Observation Section. From his acceptance on the thirtieth until the end of the war, he would

Courtesy Benjamin Keevil.

The Skill family in 1916. Lieutenant Albert Skill was killed in action at Bellevue Spur on October 26, 1917.

serve in one of six observation posts looking for signs of enemy artillery and directing the fire of Canadian artillery on them. He would be gassed once in this role and nearly killed on another occasion when the observation post was shelled. After the fighting stopped, he went to Germany with the 1st Division. He returned to England on March 2, 1919, and embarked for Canada a week later. On his return to Canada, he enrolled in evening classes at the Technical Schools of Toronto. At one time, there had been talk of his entering the ministry, but he felt his war experiences rendered him unsuitable to be a "messenger of God's love." On completion of his Senior Matriculation in 1926, he went to work for Masco Electric as a purchasing agent, a position he held until his death in 1965. In 1923, Waldron married Agnes Murdoch, a girl who had been his neighbour on Jones Street during their childhood. He named their first-born son David Craig Waldron after his good friend, Lorne Bean Craig, who had died at Cambrai in 1918. Waldron's children agree that their father's mind was consumed by his memories of battle, but that he seldom spoke with them about the tragic losses he had experienced. Agnes Waldron told her children privately about a number of frightening nights in the early years of their marriage when he would leap to his feet on their bed and act out a bayonet attack. She attributed these lingering hallucinations to the effects of gas poisoning, but perhaps his nightmares were simply a response to remembered horrors. Waldron's four sons also recall quite clearly their mother's refusal to allow toy guns and weapons in the house and assume this to indicate a respectful deference to their father's discomfort. They also remember a Prussian helmet and bayonet, souvenirs for which their father traded his own weapons after the Armistice. During the war, Waldron was in the habit of sending coins and stamps to his younger brother, and these formed the beginnings of extensive collections, which continue to be extended by two of his sons. His daughter has fond memories of the battalion Christmas parties held during the Depression. The children received a Christmas stocking, which always contained a very special treat: a Florida orange. All of the children recall their father's loyalty to the battalion, for he attended all of the church parades, memorial services, and reunions as well as taking his turn on the battalion Association Executive. Sunday afternoons were faithfully observed as the opportunity to visit ailing comrades from the 58th at Christie Street Veterans' Hospital and later Sunnybrook Veterans' Hospital. In the last years of his life, Waldron carried with him a list of surviving battalion members published in 1950, and, as the men of the 58th passed away, he inscribed the dates of their deaths in this personal Roll of Honour. If David Waldron were in any way disillusioned about the futile sacrifices of the "war to end all wars," he never ceased to wear the pin of the battalion's double blue colours with dignity and pride.[325]

There are physical memorials to the men of the battalion dispersed across France, Belgium, Great Britain, and Canada. The Menin Gate on the edge of Ypres has the name of 153 men of the battalion inscribed on the wall of one of its staircases. Other names are commemorated on the base of Canada's monument at Vimy Ridge. These represent the men who have no known grave. There are headstones for those whose bodies were recovered, and they are all clearly marked with the battalion number in the beautifully maintained cemeteries of the Commonwealth War Graves Commission. For those with access to the Internet, there is a website that enables a researcher to locate the memorial to any soldier commemorated in its cemeteries. Here in

Canada, municipal cenotaphs often carry the names and battalions of men from their communities who lost their lives in the Great War. Brantford has a school in memory of Major Ballachey because he was the only school trustee to lose his life overseas. Anna Durie later raised a very impressive monument to her son, William, in St. James Cemetery on Parliament Street, near Bloor Street in Toronto. It is very similar in shape to the Cross of Sacrifice erected in the Commonwealth War Graves Cemeteries, but it lacks the bronze sword embedded in the originals. Schools such as the University of Toronto, Upper Canada College, and Earl Grey Public School frequently have a Roll of Honour that lists the students who gave their lives in the war. Fort York Armoury in Toronto, home of the Royal Regiment, which now perpetuates the 58th, has a plaque in memory of those who died. The Church of the Transfiguration on Manor Road still displays the colours of the 58th above the plaque dedicated to the battalion's 851 killed and missing. A plaque on the grounds of the Cedar Springs United Church in Cedar Springs, Kent County, Ontario commemorates Corporal Miner's actions on August 8, 1918.[326] His medals, including the

Kevin Shackleton.

Grave of Corporal Miner VC, Crouy British Cemetery.

Victoria Cross, are the property of the Blenheim Branch of the Royal Canadian Legion and are lent out to museums in southwestern Ontario on a regular basis.

Unfortunately, most Great War service medals, engraved with the names and numbers of the men, are stashed in metal boxes or jewelry cases gathering tarnish. For the families of those who died overseas, there is a plaque from the government to help remember the lost one. Sometimes, there are collections of buttons and badges, bullets and shell fragments. Many families retain more ephemeral mementos. Discharge papers, faded photographs, letters, Field Service postcards, and trench maps are tucked away half forgotten. Often found among them are small obituary notices announcing the passing of a man from the 58th with those numbers appearing directly after his name.

Written references to the deeds of the 58th Battalion are very rare. The lack of an official history soon after the war meant that it was difficult for authors of other histories to include its exploits in their works. Arnold Jukes's colourful autobiography might well have raised the profile of the battalion, but it was written in the 1950s while Jukes was living in the United States, far from its natural market. James Rawlinson's slim volume about his experiences as a blind veteran still circulates among collectors of Great War material, but it has little about the actions of the battalion. A rare volume of poetry by Anna Durie eulogizes her only son, but provides little concrete detail about his career.

This slim volume is offered in the hope that it may validate in some small way the inscription on the altar of sacrifice in the Commonwealth War Grave Cemeteries: "Their Name Liveth for Evermore."

Endnotes

1 The ranks of the men referred to in the book are the ranks they held at the time of the events described. The references to rank after the war indicate the highest rank achieved by the individual, frequently an acting rank.

2 Goodspeed, D.J., *Battle Royal.* Brampton, 1979, p.277.

3 Col. Geo. H. Cassels, "Formation of the 58th Battalion Twenty-five Years Ago". *58th Battalion News.* Volume 6, March 1940, p. 1.

4 NAC, RG 9, Vol.4696, folder 62, file 3.

5 NAC, RG 150, Vol. G90, file Harry Augustus Genet.

6 Tunnell, A.L., *Canadian Who's Who.* Vol. II, 1936-7, Toronto, p. 182.

7 NAC, RG 150, Acc. 1992-93/166, Box 2246-1.

8 Roll of Honour, *Royal Bank Magazine.* March 1922, p.32.

9 Canadian Bank of Commerce, *Letters from the Front.* Vol.2, Toronto, Canadian Bank of Commerce, 1921, p. 386, p. 391. Ryerson was a descendant of William Egerton Ryerson

10 Desmond Morton, *When Your Number's Up, The Canadian Soldier in the First World War.* Toronto, Random House of Canada, 1993, p. 278.

11 Arthur Guy Empey, *Over the Top.* New York, Popular Library, 1963, p. 10.

12 58th Battalion Nominal Roll.

13 Cassels, "Formation of 58th Battalion Twenty-five Years Ago," *58th Battalion News.* Volume 6, 1940 p.5.

14 86 men listed some military service. 29 had service with Imperial Forces, Territorial units or the Royal Navy. Canadian Expeditionary Force Nominal Rolls, 58th Battalion and Reinforcing Draft.
15 Richard H. Joyce, "Pinky Campbell, a Portrait." Undated notes from a speech given about 1960.
16 R. H. Joyce, Unpublished Diary. Courtesy Geoff Stead.
17 Ibid.
18 Cassels, "Formation of the 58th…" *58th Battalion News.* Vol. 6 p. 5.
19 NAC, RG 9, Vol.4197, folder 1, file 7.
20 Morton, *When Your Number's Up.* p.18.
21 NAC, RG 9 Vol. 4696, Folder 62, file 3.
22 Ayton Richey Leggo Fonds Diary November 15, 1915. NAC, MG30, E559.
23 Ibid.
24 Cassels. "Formation of the 58th…" *58th Battalion News.* Vol. 6 p.5.
25 NAC, RG 9 Vol.4696, Folder 62, file 3.
26 Letter of Capt. W. G. Cosbie to his mother November 23 to November 29, 1915.
27 RG 9 DIII-I Vol. 4696 Folder 62, file 3.
28 Leggo Diary Nov 27, 1915.
29 Letter from Private James D. E. Rutherford to his sister December, 1915.
30 Letter of Capt. W. G. Cosbie to his mother December 4, 1915.
31 Letter of Archie MacKinnon Dec. 2, 1915 NAC MG30, E547
32 Letter from Lieutenant W. E. Cusler to his family December 5, 1915.
33 R. H. Joyce, Unpublished Diary.
34 Letter from Private James D.E. Rutherford to his sister December 1915.
35 Leggo Diary Jan. 3, 1916.
36 Morton, *When Your Number's Up.* p.182. Total fatal casualties in the C.E.F. from disease would be 6,767.
37 R. H. Joyce, op.cit. Saturday, January 15, 1916.
38 Ibid. Thursday, January 27, 1916.
39 Leggo Diary Febebruary 16, 1916.
40 Letter from Lieutenant W. E. Cusler to his family February 6, 1916.
41 Leggo Diary February 16, 1916 p. 46, NAC, MG 30E559.
42 Letter of Archie MacKinnon, February 19, 1916.
43 David H. Waldron, Unpublished Diary.
44 Ibid.
45 Ibid.
46 Letter from Capt. W. G. Cosbie to his mother March19, 1916.

47 David H. Waldron, Unpublished Diary.
48 Joyce, Unpublished Diary.
49 Ibid.
50 Archie MacKinnon, Mar. 26, 1916. NAC MG 30 E 547
51 Cosbie letter, April 1, 1916.
52 "First World War Disease Has Come Back To Threaten Homeless AIDS Patients." P/S/L Consulting Group Inc, 2000.
53 Letter From Lieutenant W. A. P. Durie to Miss H. Durie April 4, 1916. Durie collection, City of Toronto Archives.
54 R. H. Joyce, Unpublished Diary. Joyce had earlier been assigned to the Machine Gun Section.
55 Major C.B. Pridham, *Lewis gun Mechanism Made Easy.* Aldershot, Gale & Poldern, 6th Ed. November, 1940, p.1.
56 The Adjutant kept up the War Diary. The person holding the office changed throughout the course of the war. Not being sure who was writing at any particular time, I have chosen to refer to the person keeping the diary as the diarist. The use of a capital letter D always indicates a reference to the War Diary.
57 R. H. Joyce, Unpublished Diary.
58 David H. Waldron, Unpublished Diary.
59 R. H. Joyce, Unpublished Diary. Had the ammunition been used in action it would likely have caused problems with the Ross rifle.
60 Canadian Bank of Commerce, *Letters from the Front.* Vol. 1, Toronto, Canadian Bank of Commerce, 1920, p. 108
61 Cosbie letter to his mother April 17, 1916.
62 R. H. Joyce. Unpublished Diary.
63 *Hamilton Spectator,* April 26, 1916, p.1
64 Cosbie letter to his father April 24, 1916.
65 Archie MacKinnon, April 19, 1916. NAC MG 30E547.
66 Gwynne Dyer, *War.* New York, Crown Publishers, Inc. 1985. P. 144.
67 Desmond Morton, *When Your Number's Up. The Canadian Soldier in the First World War.* Toronto, Random House of Canada, 1993. p 198.
68 R. H. Joyce, Unpublished Diary. Joyce put in for a transfer to the Machine Gun Corps the next day.
69 *Hamilton Spectator.* May 1, 1916.
70 Author's emphasis. For the metric generation one yard is slightly shorter than one metre.
71 *Trinity War Book, A Recital of Service and Sacrifice in the Great War.,* Toronto, Trinity Methodist Church, 1921, p. 136
72 Shrapnel shells were fired from light artillery pieces, and while still

in the air, the shell discharged a hail of small pellets. In the Second World War, shell fragments were called shrapnel. In the First World War the men distinguished between shrapnel and shell splinters.

73 Archie MacKinnon, May 13 to 16, 1916. NAC MG 30 E 547.

74 David H. Waldron, Unpublished Diary. May 1, 1916.

75 Counter battery fire took place when the artillery units of one side fired at the other side's artillery units in an effort to disrupt or destroy them.

76 R. H. Joyce, Unpublished Diary. May 19, 1916.

77 Ibid. April 30, 1916.

78 Ibid.

79 Ibid. May 27 to May 31, 1916.

80 Col. W. W. Murray, *The History of the 2nd Canadian Battalion.* Ottawa, the Historical Committee 2nd Battalion C.E.F., 1947, p.90.

81 Richard H. Joyce, "Pinky Campbell, a Portrait." Undated notes from a speech given about 1960.

82 Letter from Lieutenant Warner E. Cusler to his family May 27, 1916.

83 Ypres was a walled medieval town which grew rich on the wool trade. The B.E.F. knew it as "Wipers" and it is now known as Ieper

84 Jeffrey Williams, *Byng of Vimy. General and Governor General.* London, Leo Cooper, 1983, p. 121.

85 Three officers out of 22 and 73 men out of 680 answered the Roll Call on June 4. S. G. Bennett, *The 4th Canadian Mounted Rifles 1914-1919.* Toronto, Murray Printing Company Limited, 1926, pp. 19-20.

86 Lieutenant Cusler was wounded in the right foot and left thigh, likely by shrapnel, on this day and evacuated to hospital. Personnel Records, Box 2246.

87 David Waldron's Diary June 6, 1916. The diary contains references to Matthews's burial and to the placing of a cross on the grave on June 8. Waldron's papers contain a hand-drawn map that appears to locate the Matthews grave near Railway Dugouts.

88 Ibid. June 7, 1916.

89 The author's great uncle, Private Frederick G. Rosser was wounded by shrapnel while on sentry duty that morning. Also among the wounded, although not mentioned in the War Diary, was Capt. Cosbie the medical officer.

90 Letter from Lieutenant Cusler to his family, June 8, 1916.

91 Williams, *Byng of Vimy.* p. 124.

92 Archie MacKinnon, September 3, 1916, NAC MG 30E547.

93 R. H. Joyce, Unpublished Diary. June 12, 1916.

94 Archie MacKinnon, November 10, 1916 NAC MG 30E547.

95 Richard H. Joyce, "Pinky Campbell, a Portrait." Undated notes from a speech given about 1960

96 Richard H. Joyce letter to Geoffrey Stead, his brother-in-law dated April 25, 1917. He did not confide this story to his diary, perhaps in recognition of the danger it could pose to him if he were captured.

97 Waldron's diary contains two references to Sergeant Le Seur or Lesuer, but there does not seem to have been a man by this name in the C.E.F. The correct spelling could be Le Sueur as there was a Sergeant Le Sueur in the 52nd Battalion. There was a Sergeant Harry Joseph LaTour with the 58th, but he is not recorded in the June 1916 section of the War Diary as having been awarded a Military Medal.

98 Ibid.

99 MacKinnon op.cit..

100 Letter from Major MacKay to friends of Mrs. Ewan Nicol, *Stratford Daily Beacon*. Nov. 22, 1916.

101 Henderson's father learned of his death on June 16th just after giving a speech in Hamilton advocating conscription to increase Canada's manpower commitment to the Empire. *The Globe,* June 17, 1916.

102 The Canadian attack on the 13th made *The Daily Mail and Empire* on June 14, 1916. The story mentioned the recapture of portions of the old British front, including Sanctuary Wood, but it didn't mention the 58th Battalion's role in the operation.

103 *Trinity War Book*. p. 137

104 R. H Joyce, Unpublished Diary. Joyce would not return to the 58th, but he did survive the war.

105 Tim Cook, *No Place To Run. The Canadian Corps and Gas Warfare in the First World War.* Vancouver, UBC Press, 1999, p. 42.

106 F. W. Noyes, *Stretcher Bearers...at the Double!* Pp. 111-112.

107 Will R. Bird, *Ghost Have Warm Hands.* Nepean, Ontario, CEF Books, 1997, p. 144.

108 Bill Rawling, *Surviving Trench Warfare. Technology and the Canadian Corps, 1914-1918.* Toronto, University of Toronto Press, 1992. p.68.

109 The author noted a small collection outside the wall of the Courcelette Cemetery in May 2000.

110 Reginald H. Roy, Ed. *The Journal of Private Fraser.* 1985, Victoria, Sono Nis Press. p. 55.

111 NAC, RG 9, Volume 4201, folder 12, file 2.

112 The loss of Singapore in early 1942 cost the British a garrison of 85,000 men in a week of fighting.

113 Malcolm Brown, *The Imperial War Museum Book of the Somme.* London, Pan Books, 1997. p.72.

114 A. H. Farrar-Hockley, *The Somme.* London, Pan Books, 1966, p.253.

115 Archie MacKinnon, October 19, 1916 NAC MG 30E547.

116 *Letters from the Front.* Vol. 2, p. 392.

117 David H. Waldron, Diary. September 21, 1916.

118 Col. G.W. L. Nicholson, *Canadian Expeditionary Force 1914-1919.* Ottawa, Queens' Printer and Controller of Stationery, 1962, p.172.

119 Correspondence with Don Carter.

120 Col. G.W. L. Nicholson, *The Gunners of Canada.* Vol. I Toronto, McClelland and Stewart Limited, 1967, p. 267.

121 Col. G.W. L. Nicholson, *Canadian Expeditionary Force 1914-1919.* Ottawa, Queen's Printer and Controller of Stationery, 1964, p. 186.

122 Lieutenant General E. L. M. Burns, *General Mud.* Toronto, Clarke, Irwin & Company Limited, 1970, p.28.

123 N. M. Christie, *For King and Empire. The Canadians on the Somme September-November 1916.* Winnipeg, Bunker to Bunker books, 1996, p. 72.

124 Col. G.W. L. Nicholson, *Canadian Expeditionary Force 1914-1919.* Ottawa, Queen's Printer and Controller of Stationery, 1964, p.184.

125 Bill Rawling, *Surviving Trench Warfare.* p.38.

126 "Canadian Dash On Foe Lines," *The Globe.* Friday October 13, 1916, p. 1.

127 The author's grandfather, Private Robert Henry McKee of B Company, was wounded by a shrapnel ball in the left hip on October 8. The diary mentions a carrying party led by Private Proctor of B Company just before the attack started. Enemy shelling killed three men, sent two missing and wounded two more who Proctor brought to safety. It is just speculation that one of them was Private McKee. He survived his wound and was discharged from the army just before the Armistice.

128 Nicholson, *Canadian Expeditionary Force.* p. 185.

129 "Canadian Dash On Foe Line," *The Globe.* October 13, 1916, p.4.

130 A. M. J. Hyatt, *General Sir Arthur Currie, a Military Biography.* Toronto, University of Toronto Press, 1987, pp. 59-60.

131 Williams, *Byng of Vimy.* p.141.

132 Battalion Daily Orders September 1, 1917, page 2.

133 Desmond Morton, *When Your Number's Up. The Canadian Soldier in the First World War.* Toronto, Random House of Canada, 1993, p. 249.
134 Ibid.
135 Ibid.
136 Archie MacKinnon, November 8, 1916, NAC MG 30 E 547
137 Tim Cook, *No Place To Run*. p.88.
138 Address by John Kendall Cornish at Trivitt Memorial Church Exeter, June 28, 1970.
139 Letter from Lewis G.Campbell to the author, September 12, 2000. Frost placed ads in the inter-war battalion newsletter.
140 Lieutenant W. A. P. Durie rejoined the battalion in December, but his return is not mentioned in the War Diary.
141 Cpl. Archie MacKinnon's brother Ronald was serving with the Princess Patricia's, another 3rd Division battalion. In a letter to their sister dated December 30, 1916 he mentions a Christmas truce and that the "...Germans were quite friendly. They came over to see us and we traded bully beef for cigars." The line about no fraternizing in the 58th War Diary may have been for the benefit of the High Command. NAC MG30 E547 file 3.
142 From an oral account received by John Anderson after the death of his father.
143 War Diary of the 58th Battalion, January 1, 1917.
144 David H. Waldron, Diary January 11 to 18, 1917.
145 The permeable nature of the chalk subsoil meant there was very little ground water for sources of drinking water. Water had to be piped considerable distances from wells to proved water for the men and the horses, which were their main source of transportation power. Peter Doyle, "The Mud of Flanders" *Military Illustrated Past and Present.* Issue 139, pp.44-49.
146 War Diary 58th Battalion, April 10, 1916.
147 Rawling, *Surviving Trench Warfare.* p.127.
148 David H. Waldron, Unpublished Diary, February 2, 1917
149 Capt. J. Roy Cockburn, from the University of Toronto had worked out the range for the Stokes mortars of the battalion. Military Service of R. E. Smythe Cockburn later transferred to the new scientific sound ranging unit and eventually ended the war in the Middle East. Military service of J. Roy Cockburn University of Toronto Archives A73-0026/062(73) .
150 NAC, RG 9, Vol. 4696, folder 62, file 8.
151 "Canadians Gazetted For Gallant Service", *The Hamilton Spectator.*

April 18, 1917, p. 5.

152 Will R. Bird, *Ghosts have warm hands.* Ottawa, CEF Books, 1997, p.15.

153 David H. Waldron, Unpublished Diary, March 2, 1917.

154 Pte David H. Waldron was sent to Le Havre on March 5th. An underage soldier when he enlisted, he ended up in England on April 16th despite having his 18th birthday on November 4, 1916.

155 R. E. Smythe Military Service Synopsis.

156 Nicholson, *The Gunners of Canada.* Vol. 1, pp311-317.

157 Pierre Berton, *Vimy.* Toronto, McClelland and Stewart Limited, 1986. p.183

158 John Keegan, *The First World War.* Toronto, Key Porter Books Limited, 1998. p. 324.

159 Leslie W. C.S. Barnes, *Canada's Guns. An Illustrated History of Artillery.* Ottawa, National Museums of Canada, 1978. P.73.

160 The Pimple, a small rise on the northern end of Vimy Ridge, remained in German hands for two more days

161 The massive shock and heavy bleeding of a compound fracture of the thigh very often proved fatal.

162 Unpublished letter from Douglas Martin to the author dated November 23, 1999.

163 Letter to the author from Lewis G. Campbell August 2, 2000.

164 A.H. Jukes, Unpublished Autobiography, 1954, p. 18. Jucksch changed his name to Jukes after the war.

165 The Adjutant, *The 116th Battalion in France.* Toronto, E. P. S. Allen, 1921, p.15.

166 Letter from Sergeant George T. Bell to Isabel Bell dated May 2, 1917.

167 Letter from Lieutenant Cusler to his family dated May 9, 1917.

168 Cook, *No Place To Hide.* P.111.

169 James H. Rawlinson, *Through St. Dunstan's to Light.* Toronto, Thomas Allen, 1919, p. 2.

170 A. H. Jukes, Unpublished Autobiography, 1954 p. 29.

171 "Canadians in Outskirts of Last Defence of Lens", *The Globe.* June 29, 1917, p,1 and 2.

172 Letter from Lieutenant W. A. P. Durie to Anna Durie, July 25, 1917. Durie Collection, City of Toronto Archives

173 Letter from Lieutenant Cusler to Dorothy Frier written July 1, 1917.

174 "Hun holds to Village of Avion", *The Globe.* June 28, 1917, p.2.

175 John Keegan, *The First World War.* Toronto, Key Porter Books Limited, 1998 p.338.

176 Toronto Star, September 20, 1917.
177 Harry Garnet Bedford Miner 823028, Casualty Form- Active Service, NAC, RG 150, Vol. 6235 Acc. 1992-93/166
178 Lewis G. Campbell, unpublished letter to the author, August 2, 2000.
179 Larry Worthington, *Amid the Guns Below.* Toronto, McClelland and Stewart Limited, 1965. Pp100-101.
180 James H. Pedley, *Only This.* Ottawa, CEF Books, 1999, p.14.
181 A copy of the medal was provided to the author by his grandson John Settle.
182 A. H. Jukes, Unpublished Autobiography, 1954.
183 The St. Mary's Journal, *Remembering '96.* p. 28.
184 Worthington, *Amid the Guns Below.* p.102.
185 Letter from Lieutenant Cusler to his family 13 September 1917.
186 Ibid.
187 D. J. Goodspeed, *Battle Royal. 2nd Ed.,* p. 289.
188 NAC, RG 9 Vol. III, C3-4198 Folder 3 File 1.
189 Cook, *No Place To Run.* p.120
190 Ibid. p.122.
191 N. M. Christie, *Futility and Sacrifice. The Canadians on the Somme, 1916.* Nepean, Ontario, CEF Books, 1999, p. 34.
192 James H. Pedley, *Only This.* Ottawa, CEF Books, 1999, pp73-74.
193 B. H. Liddell Hart, *The History of the First World War.* London, Pan Books, 1970, p. 353.
194 The author's great uncle, Private F. G. Rosser 452025, was wounded on June 8, 1916 while in the Ypres Salient. He was soon transferred to hospital in England. On September 29, 1916 he was considered recovered from his wound and assigned four weeks physical training. He rejoined the battalion almost a year later.
195 Keegan, *The First World War.* p. 354
196 Unpublished letter in the possession of Douglas Martin.
197 Toni and Valmai Holt, *Major and Mrs. Holt's Battlefield Guide to the Ypres Salient.* London, Leo Cooper, 1997, p.72.
198 H. Jukes, Unpublished Autobiography, 1954, pp.38-39.
199 G.W.L. Nicholson, *Canadian Expeditionary Force 1914-1919.* Ottawa, Queen's Printer and Controller of Stationery, 1964, p.318.
200 Robin Prior and Trevor Wilson, *Passchendaele the Untold Story.* New Haven, Yale University Press, 1996, p. 174.
201 Nicholson, *Canadian Expeditionary Force.* p. 319.
202 Daniel G. Dancocks, *Legacy of Valour. The Canadians at Passchendaele.* Hurtig Publishers, Edmonton, 1986, p. 130.

203 D.J. Goodspeed, *Battle Royal.* 2nd Ed. The Royal Regiment of Canada Association, Brampton, 1979, p. 290.

204 NAC, RG 9, Volume 4942, Reel T-10, 749,"Report on Operation carried out by the 58th Canadian Battalion October 25/26th 1917 till 9:25 P.M. October 27/28th 1917."

205 "Passchendaele Ridge A New Canadian Epic," *The Brantford Daily Expositor.* October 29, 1917, p. 1.

206 D. J. Goodspeed, *The Road Past Vimy.* Toronto, Macmillan of Canada, 1969. p. 117.

207 Letter from Lieutenant D. Cameron to Miss Gissing, University of Toronto Archives, A73-0026/358 (12)

208 Jukes, p.39.

209 Nicholson, p. 320.

210 *The Globe.* October 27, 1917, p. 1.

211 Elliot G. Strathy, Unpublished Diary.

212 Ibid.

213 Ibid.

214 Ibid.

215 Capt. Jack Affleck, personal diary entry for November 13, 1917.

216 "Huns cannot oust Canadians," *The Globe.* November 15, 1917, p. 1 and 5. This article described the events of November 13 without mentioning the 58th Battalion.

217 The War Diary gives the total killed as two, but an examination of other records shows that 8 men were killed in action that day and one died of wounds.

218 Elliot G. Strathy, Unpublished Diary, November 14, 1917. When offered a drink of rum as a stimulant he refused it as he was a temperance man and took water instead.

219 Jeffrey Williams, *Byng of Vimy. General and Governor General.* London, A Leo Cooper book 1983, p.177.

220 Nicholson, *Canadian Expeditionary Force 1914-1919.* pp. 230-231.

221 In a number of provinces women had the municipal franchise. The three prairie provinces gave them the vote in 1916 and B.C. and Ontario gave them the vote in April 1917. On May 24, 1918 all female citizens over age 21 received the right to vote in federal elections. While the vote had been given to the women with relatives overseas in the C.E.F. it was taken away from citizens who had immigrated to Canada from enemy countries before the war.

222 NAC, RG 9, Volume 4201, folder 13, file 3.

223 Op. Cit.

224 Affleck diary entry for December 6, 1917.

225 NAC, RG 9, Volume 4201, folder 13, file 1.
226 Christie, N. M. *Slaughter in the Mud. The Canadians at Passchendaele 1917.* pp. 28-29.
227 NAC RG 9, Volume 9 III C-3 4198 folder 3, file 1.
228 NAC, RG 9, Vol. III C 3-4198 folder 3, file 1.
229 Harry Garnet Bedford Miner NAC, RG 150, Vol. 6235 Acc. 1992-93/166.
230 D. J. Goodspeed, *Battle Royal.* Brampton, 1979. p. 279.
231 James H. Pedley, *Only this.* Ottawa, CEF Books, 1999, p. 169.
232 Arnold H. Jukes, Unpublished autobiography. pp.42-47.
233 NAC, RG 9, Volume 4696, folder 62, file 9.
234 Bill Rawling, *Surviving Trench Warfare. Technology and the Canadian Corps, 1914-1918.* Toronto, University of Toronto Press, 1992, p. 172.
235 NAC, RG9, Volume 4200, folder 9, file 1.
236 NAC RG 9, Volume 4696, folder 6, file 1.
237 Desmond Morton, *When Your Number's Up.* Toronto, Random House of Canada, 1993, p. 201.
238 John Swettenham, *To Seize The Victory. The Canadian Corps in World War I.* Toronto, Ryerson Press 1965, p.194
239 Ibid. pp.1-20.
240 Liddell Hart, *History of the First World War.* p.363.
241 Ibid. p.368.
242 The numbering for this unit indicates that it was a second line Territorial battalion, not usually placed in the front line. This suggests how desperate the British manpower situation was at this time.
243 *Report of the Ministry Overseas Military Forces of Canada, 1918.* London, The Ministry, Overseas Military Forces of Canada, undated, p. 112.
244 Lance Corporal George William Fretwell 453786, died of wounds on August 28. His father had died of wounds just over two years earlier.
245 *Report of the Ministry Overseas Military Forces of Canada 1918.* London, the Ministry, Overseas Military Forces of Canada, undated, p.116.
246 NAC RG 9 III C3 4201 Folder 12, file 3.
247 Interview with the family of Sergeant J. D. Rutherford.
248 NAC RG9 III C3 4201 Folder 11, file 15.
249 Ibid.
250 *Report of the Ministry of Overseas Military Forces of Canada 1918.* p.116.

251 Larry Worthington, *Amid the guns below. The story of the Canadian Corps (1914-1918).* Toronto, McClelland and Stewart, 1965, p.131.
252 58th Canadian Battalion, Operation Order No.127 May 5, 1918.
253 *Report of the Ministry Overseas Military Forces of Canada 1918.* London, The Minister, Overseas Military Forces of Canada, p. 124.
254 *The Roll of Honour of the Empire's Heroes.* London, The Queenhithe Publishing Co. no date or pagination.
255 Letter of Lieutenant J. H. Way to his family Feb. 25, 1918.
256 Jeffrey Williams, *Princess Patricia's Canadian Light Infantry.* London, Leo Cooper, 1972, p.26.
257 Lieut. N. K. McKechnie, "The Fifty-Eighth Camel Corps" *58th Battalion News.* Volume 4, March 1940, p2.
258 H. W. Baldwin Letter 52, June 26, 1918 NAC MG 30 E65
259 Letters of Harry Baldwin NAC MG 30 E 65
260 Ibid. Letter of July 21, 1918.
261 Arnold H. Jukes, Unpublished Autobiography. 1954, p. 61. Captain Jucksch's D Company was regarded as the best turned out company in the Brigade.
262 58th Battalion War Diary, entry for July 31, 1918.
263 Nicholson, *Canadian Expeditionary Force 1914-1919.* p.380.
264 Daniel G. Dancocks, *Spearhead to Victory.* Edmonton, Hurtig Publishers, 1987, p. 18.
265 James McWilliams and R. James Steel, *Amiens Dawn of Victory.* Toronto, Dundurn Press, 2001, p.24.
266 Dancocks, *Spearhead to Victory.* p. 32.
267 McWilliams and Steel, *Amiens Dawn of Victory.* Pp. 54-55.
268 Will R. Bird, *Ghosts Have Warm Hands.* Ottawa, CEF Books, 1997, p.101.
269 James H. Pedley, *Only This.* Ottawa, CEF Books, 1999, p.222.
270 Colonel G. W. L. Nicholson, *Canadian Expeditionary Force 1914-1919.* Ottawa, Queen's Printer, 1964, p. 398.
271 Ibid.
272 The *Toronto Daily Star* March 24, 1919.
273 Canadian Bank of Commerce, *Letters from the Front.* Vol. 1, Toronto, Canadian Bank of Commerce 1920, pp310-311.
274 Goodspeed, *Battle Royal.* p.292.
275 Arnold H. Jukes, Unpublished Autobiography, 1954, p. 61. Capt. Jucksch returned to the company despite suffering from the flu. He joined the attack and wrote in his autobiography that he captured a German general.
276 McWilliams and Steel, *Amiens Dawn of Victory.* p.130.

277 Letter of Lieutenant J. H. Way to his family August 10, 1918.

278 "Proud Record of War Recalled by Reunion"

279 The Adjutant, *The 116th Battalion in France.* Toronto, E.P.S. Allen, 1921, p. 70.

280 58th Battalion War Diary, entry for Aug. 8, 1918.

281 London Gazette 31128, Jan. 16, 1919.

282 Dancocks, *Spearhead.* p.51.

283 McWilliams and Steel, *Amiens Dawn of Victory.* p.256.

284 Norm Christie, *For King and Empire. The Canadians at Amiens August 1918.* Ottawa, CEF Books, 1999, p.30.

285 A.H. Jukes, Unpublished Autobiography. p.33.

286 Goodspeed, *Battle Royal.* 1962, p. 292.

287 Elver spent about six months in England before being sent to France and had little time to be seasoned before being thrust into battle. NAC RG 150 Acc. 1992-93/166 Box 2897-49.

288 NAC RG 9 III C3 Vol. 4198, folder 2, file 9.

289 Desmond Morton and J. L. Granatstein, *Marching to Armageddon. Canadians and the Great War 1914-1919.* Toronto, Lester & Orpen Dennys, 1989, p.218.

290 Nicholson, *CEF.* p. 427.

291 The speed with which the Canadian Corps changed fronts for its next action caught Lieutenant Col. Macfarlane by surprise. He went on 10 days leave to England, expecting to be back before the next offensive and left the battalion under the command of the adjutant, Capt. R. E. Smythe as Major Carmichael was in hospital after being wounded.

292 A.H. Jukes, Unpublished Autobiography, p.62.

293 *The Roll of Honour of the Empire's Heroes.* London, The Queenhithe Publishing Co. no date or pagination.

294 Letter from Lieutenant F. G. Dyke to D'Arcy Martin, University of Toronto Archives A73-00261308-93

295 A.H. Jukes, Unpublished Autobiography, pp. 63-65

296 London Gazette 31158 1.2.1919.

297 Norm Christie, *For King and Empire. The Canadians at Arras August-September 1918.* p.57. Jukes stated that the whole battalion was mentioned in despatches for this action. A.H. Jukes, Unpublished Autobiography, p. 71.

298 Cook, *No Place To Run.* p. 196.

299 Col. G. W. L. Nicholson, *The Gunners of Canada. Vol. 1 1534-1919.* Toronto, McClelland and Stewart, 1967, p. 279.

300 The Adjutant, *The 116th Battalion in France.* Toronto, E. P. S. Allen, 1921, p. 80.

301 George Bell, "Why Orderly-Room Sergeants Go Grey", *58th Battalion News.* Volume 5, March 23rd, 1939, p.4.

302 "D.S.O. Tells of Fight," *The Toronto Daily Star.* March 24, 1919, p.8.

303 A.H. Jukes, Unpublished Autobiography, p. 83.

304 The War Diary clearly states that Lieutenant Stockhausen was killed in action on September 28th, but the Commonwealth War Graves Commission records his death as occurring on October 1, 1918.

305 *The Roll of Honour of the Empire's Heroes.* London, The Queenhithe Publishing Co. no date or pagination.

306 Ibid. p. 82.

307 Dancocks, *Spearhead to Victory.* p. 166.

308 Nicholson, *Canadian Expeditionary Force.* p. 453.

309 Ibid.

310 Appendix, Narrative of Operation in Cambrai Sector, 58th Battalion War, Diary September, 1918.

311 J. F. B. Livesay, *Canada's Hundred Days.* Toronto, Thomas Allen, 1919. P.261.

312 Sergeant William J. Groves, recipient of the Military Medal and two bars was captured in one of these last attacks and died of wounds a prisoner of the Germans on October 1, 1918.

313 *Spearhead to Victory.* p. 168.

314 "With the 58th on Armistice Day 1918", *58th Battalion News.* Volume 2, December 1935, p.4.

315 "With the 58th on Armistice Day 1918", *58th Battalion News.* Volume 2, December 1935, p.4.

316 See Swettenham's account of the libel action Lieutenant General Currie won against the *Port Hope Guide* in *To Seize the Victory.* Chapter one.

317 "With the 58th on Armistice Day 1918", *58th Battalion News.* Volume 2, December 1935, p.4.

318 Ibid.

319 "Down Through the Years With the 58th Battalion", *58th Battalion News.* Volume 2, December 1935, p.1.

320 Some men were away from the battalion in England. The author's great uncle went absent without leave on New Year's Day. Perhaps he wanted a longer stay with his family in Oxford. Being a married man he had priority to return to Canada and was home and discharged on March 20, several days before the rest of his comrades.

321 Efforts were made to learn the circumstances of the grant, but the French Military Archives have no records relating to the 58th

Battalion. The men of the battalion were entitled to wear a lanyard signifying the unit's receipt of the award. Private David Waldron added a note to his diary to the effect that the 58th Battalion was the only battalion mentioned in the German press for bravery in the field. He also referred to the attack at Avion in June 1917.

322 "Stirring Scene When Veterans Met Troops," *The Toronto Daily Star.* March 24, 1919, p.8.

323 Letter from Alistair Fraser to Mrs. John Campbell April 21, 1918.

324 Letter from Archibald MacKinnon to Ronald MacKinnon April 5, 1917. NAC MG 30 E 547

325 From a letter written by Ian Waldron, David's youngest son, September 11, 2000.

326 Arthur Bishop, *Our Bravest and Our Best. The Stories of Canada's Victoria Cross Winners.* Toronto, McGraw-Hill Ryerson Limited, 1995, p. 106

Honour Roll

Service No.	Rank	Surname	Decorations/Alias	Given Names	Date of death	Cause of Death	Previous Unit
451061	Pte.	Abbott		Robert Stanley	1919 02 28	DOD	
451772	Pte.	Abram		Arthur William	1916 08 19	KIA	
3106012	Pte.	Adams		Robert Walpole	1918 08 27	KIA	
211045	Pte	Adams		William Alogins	1916 10 08	Missing	98th
654294	Pte.	Aitchison		Cleveland	1917 02 17	Pneumonia	161st
141367	Pte.	Akam		John	1916 10 08	KIA	
226876	Pte.	Allen		Frederick James	1918 10 01	KIA	
451338	Pte.	Allen		Sydney Percy	1916 10 07	Missing	
	Lieut.	Allen		William Alexander	1917 04 18	KIA	
654359	Pte.	Allin		Lorne William John	1917 10 26	KIA	161st
210047	Pte.	Alward		Clarence Cecil	1916 10 08	Missing	98th
3030039	Pte.	Anciello	aka Devis, Charles	Carlo	1918 08 27	KIA	
451391	Pte.	Anderson		Albert	1916 05 01	KIA	
3106970	Pte.	Anderson		John	1918 09 29	KIA	
755009	Pte.	Anderson		Karl John	1918 09 09	DOW	57th, 119th
453709	Pte.	Apps		William	1918 08 30	DOW POW	
427493	Pte.	Armstrong		Edward	1916 11 04	KIA	46th
189819	Pte.	Armstrong		John William	1918 10 13	DOW	
452973	Pte.	Arnold		Robert Ashmore	1916 10 08	Missing	
404988	Pte.	Ash		John	1916 06 07	KIA	35th
427661	Pte.	Atkinson		Robert Halls	1917 04 12	KIA	46th
210051	Pte.	Atkinson		William	1916 10 08	KIA	98th
648039	Pte.	Ayre		Arthur	1917 08 28	DOW	159th
681497	Pte.	Bachelor		Arthur Walter	1917 10 26	KIA	170th
451339	L/Cpl.	Bailey		Edward	1916 10 08	KIA	
451153	Cpl.	Bailey		James	1916 09 20	KIA	
451780	Pte.	Baker		Chester Danes	1918 09 30	KIA	
451340	Pte.	Baker		William George	1916 06 13	KIA	
727673	L/Cpl.	Baker		William John	1917 10 26	KIA	110th
784378	Pte.	Ball		Ellery Harold	1918 08 27	KIA	129th
401680	Pte.	Ball		Frank Milton	1917 03 21	DOD Phthisis (TB)	33rd

Service No.	Rank	Surname	Decorations/Alias	Given Names	Date of death	Cause of Death	Previous Unit
401126	Pte.	Ball		William	1916 10 08	Missing	33rd
	Maj.	Ballachey		Panayoty Percy	1916 06 14	KIA	
925214	L/Sgt.	Ballantyne	MM	James	1918 09 28	KIA	1
42067	Pte.	Balliston		Alfred Meeton	1916 10 05	KIA	
210162	Pte.	Banwell		William Rowland	1916 10 08	KIA	
1066273	Pte.	Barber		Wilfred	1918 08 12	KIA	248th
727591	Pte.	Barclay		Alexander	1917 10 26	KIA	110th
		Lieut.	Barclay	Lindsay Traill	1916 10 08	KIA	
727605	Pte.	Barclay		William	1916 10 26	KIA	110th
654005	Pte.	Barker		Joseph Henry	1917 10 26	KIA	161st
3030745	Pte.	Barlow		Harry Witton	1916 10 01	KIA	
451393	Pte.	Barnes		Charles	1916 05 01	KIA	
210148	Pte.	Barr		John	1916 10 08	KIA	
754115	Pte.	Barr		Roy W.	1918 08 08	KIA	
925250	Pte.	Barrett		William George	1917 04 17	DOW	152nd
211173	Pte.	Barton		Edward James	1916 10 05	KIA	98th
427688	Pte.	Barton		Frank Boyle	1916 09 18	KIA	46th
451054	Pte.	Batchelor		Frank David	1918 10 01	KIA	
228344	Pte.	Bates		David Clements	1917 09 18	KIA	
654347	Pte.	Bates		John Henry	1917 07 17	DOW	161st
727063	Pte.	Bayley		Ralph Thomas Percy	1918 10 01	KIA	110th
210155	Pte.	Bean		William	1917 06 29	KIA	98th
678756	Pte.	Beardwood		Wilfred	1918 08 27	Missing	169th
754103	Pte.	Beaton	MM	Angus	1919 03 01	DOD pneumonia	119th
451181	Pte.	Beaton		Hector Blake	1916 06 14	Missing	
3314127	Pte.	Beatty		Nelson	1918 09 28	KIA	
681265	Pte.	Beer		Harold Russel	1917 10 26	KIA	170th
	Lieut.	Bell		Charles Arthur	1916 10 08	KIA	Eaton MGB
838834	Pte.	Bell		Frederick Russell	1918 09 28	KIA	248th
838834	Pte.	Bell		Frederick Russell	1918 09 29	KIA	38th, 147th
1066094	Pte.	Bell		John Alexander	1918 03 24	KIA	248th

Service No.	Rank	Surname	Decorations/Alias	Given Names	Date of death	Cause of Death	Previous Unit
1066206	Pte.	Bell		Neil Cameron	1918 08 27	KIA	
452984	Pte.	Bender	MM	James Charles	1918 08 26	KIA	
3106990	Pte.	Bennett		Edwin Henry	1918 10 01	Missing	
453253	Sgt.	Bennett		John Samuel	1917 04 12	KIA	
427023	Pte.	Bennett		Thomas Cameron	1916 10 08	Missing	46th
679024	Pte.	Benson		John	1917 05 22	DOW	169th
445215	Pte.	Bernard		James	1916 09 16	DOW	55th
	Lieut.	Bertram		Aimers Stirling	1917 07 10	KIA	
142383	Sgt.	Best		Robert Harry	1917 05 22	KIA	
453244	Sgt.	Birchenough		Benjamin	1916 06 13	KIA	
3107096	Pte.	Birtley		Thomas	1918 09 29	KIA	
249050	Pte.	Black		Samuel	1918 08 08	KIA	208th
678770	Pte.	Blackburn		James	1917 10 26	Missing 1	69th
405604	Pte.	Blackman		Albert	1916 06 13	KIA	35th
453724	Pte.	Blackman		Thomas	1916 10 08	Missing	
453725	Pte.	Blair		Alexander	1918 03 28	KIA	
427304	Pte.	Blair		Thomas Herbert	1916 10 08	KIA	46th
444923	Pte.	Blais		Alphonse	1916 09 20	Missing	55th
427682	Pte.	Blake		Patrick John Lacelles	1916 09 16	KIA	46th
138128	Pte.	Blanche		John	1916 07 09	KIA	75th
451787	Pte.	Blaney		Norman	1916 09 22	DOW	
210158	Pte.	Blunden		Charles Albert	1916 10 08	KIA	98th
210082	Pte.	Boddington		Percy	1916 11 01	DOW	98th
451185	L/Sgt.	Borrett		William George	1916 09 17	KIA	
3106184	Pte.	Borrows		Charles Edwards	1918 10 06	DOW	
453180	Pte.	Boucher		Henry	1916 10 08	KIA	
681106	Pte.	Boulton		Percy	1918 09 30	KIA	170th
445123	Pte.	Bourgoin		Joseph Alcide	1916 08 19	KIA	55th
838241	Pte.	Bowen		William Ralph	1918 08 18	KIA	147th
451048	Pte.	Bower		Albert Edward	1916 06 13	KIA	
727019	Pte.	Bowling		Sidney	1917 07 27	DOD	110th

Service No.	Rank	Surname	Decorations/Alias	Given Names	Date of death	Cause of Death	Previous Unit
406676	Pte.	Boyce		George Frederick	1916 07 16	KIA	36th
453254	Pte.	Boyd		Robert Malcolm	1916 06 13	KIA	
451124	Pte.	Boys		Reginald	1916 05 01	KIA	
451187	Pte.	Bracey		Alfred Ernest	1916 06 13	KIA	
451976	Pte.	Breadon		Joseph	1920 10 10	Phthisis (TB)	
211286	Pte.	Brewis		Stanley	1917 04 13	DOW	98th
249215	Pte.	Brick		Daniel	1919 02 09	Influenza	208th
453705	Pte.	Briggs		Arthur William	1916 08 19	KIA	
252979	Pte.	Brinsmead		David Horace Alexander	1918 08 08	KIA	
681333	Pte.	Briscoe		Alfred	1917 04 12	KIA	170th
654260	Pte.	Brombley		Charles Edward	1917 10 26	KIA	161st
452541	Sgt.	Brooks		George	1916 10 19	DOW	
727021	Pte.	Brown		Albert Gordon	1917 11 01	DOW	110th
654142	Pte.	Brown		Bernard	1918 09 12	KIA	161st
228119	L/Cpl.	Brown		John Howard	1917 04 14	DOW	13th CMR
189450	Pte.	Brown		Robert Alfred	1917 10 26	KIA	
678279	Pte.	Brown		William	1917 04 15	DOW	
141631	Pte.	Brown		William	1916 10 08	KIA	
	Lieut.	Brown		William Eberts	1918 09 28	KIA	227th
453604	Pte.	Browne		Wilfred Ewart	1916 10 08	DOW	
754051	Pte.	Browne		William	1918 10 01	KIA	119th
406686	Pte.	Buckthorpe		William	1916 06 05	KIA	36th
124055	Pte.	Bugg		George David	1916 08 16	KIA	
451799	Pte.	Bunn		Morris Roy	1918 07 25	KIA	
400803	Pte.	Burdett		Thomas	1916 08 19	KIA	33rd
3030815	Pte.	Burns		Robert	1918 09 29	KIA	
451801	Pte.	Burrell		Ernest	1918 08 27	KIA	
	Capt.	Burrows	MC	Charles Stuart	1918 10 01	KIA	180th
453732	Pte.	Burrows		William Henry	1916 09 16	DOW	
453255	Pte.	Burt		Samuel	1917 10 26	KIA	
211302	Pte.	Butler		John Hickman	1916 10 08	KIA	98th

Service No.	Rank	Surname	Decorations/Alias	Given Names	Date of death	Cause of Death	Previous Unit
452658	Pte.	Cade	aka Sully, George	George	1916 09 25	DOW	
452552	Pte.	Cairns		William Hugh	1916 09 17	Missing	
249391	Pte.	Calladine		Charles Henry	1918 08 29	KIA	208th
452992	Pte.	Calver		Alexander Dick	1918 10 31	Influenza	
654275	Pte.	Cameron		Robert Franklin Gordon	1918 08 27	KIA	161st
452590	Cpl.	Campbell		Daniel	1916 10 14	DOW POW	
190027	Pte.	Campbell		Emerson	1917 08 23	KIA	
451095	Pte.	Campbell		John	1916 06 13	KIA	
249503	Pte.	Campbell		John	1918 10 28	DOW	208th, 50th
754221	Pte.	Campbell		Russell Clark	1918 08 27	KIA	119th
249913	Pte.	Cannon		Ernest Harold	1918 08 27	KIA	208th
649347	Pte.	Carboy		John	1917 10 26	KIA	159th
754162	Pte.	Carr		William Thomas	1918 08 27	KIA	119th
249963	Pte.	Carroll		James	1918 09 25	Drowned	
850727	Pte.	Carroll		Michael Joseph	1917 04 12	KIA	176th
3107062	Pte.	Carroll		Thomas Owen	1918 09 30	KIA	
451195	Pte.	Carson		Samuel Lewis George	1917 02 15	Acc Killed	
452396	Pte.	Carson		Thomas	1916 10 05	KIA	
211119	Pte.	Carter		John	1916 10 06	KIA	98th
654662	Pte.	Carter		John Edward	1917 10 26	KIA	161st
3105320	Pte.	Cartwright		William Baden	1918 09 29	KIA	
3105911	Pte.	Cavanaugh		Harry	1918 10 01	KIA	
839005	Pte.	Cavelle		Charles Alexander	1917 10 26	KIA	147th
210180	Pte.	Chadwick		Herbert	1916 10 05	KIA	98th
3106616	Pte.	Chamberlain		Frank David	1918 10 22	DOW	
427188	Pte.	Chamberlain		William James	1917 06 17	DOW	46th
452956	Sgt.	Chambers		Charles Gibbon	1916 06 13	KIA	
451068	Pte.	Chambers		William Henry	1916 07 06	DOW	
727744	Pte.	Chamney		Harold Glendening	1917 10 26	KIA	110th
678552	Pte.	Chapman		James Hartwell	1917 04 12	KIA	169th
452398	Pte.	Chapple		Frederick James	1916 09 16	KIA	

Service No.	Rank	Surname	Decorations/Alias	Given Names	Date of death	Cause of Death	Previous Unit
839160	Pte.	Cherry		Lorne (Harold)	1917 10 26	KIA	147th
3314283	Pte.	Church		Kenneth Roy	1918 10 01	KIA	
123183	Pte.	Clanachan		Alexander	1916 09 17	KIA	
	Lieut.	Clapperton		George	1916 06 13	KIA	
451350	L/Cpl.	Clare		William	1916 03 17	KIA	
452400	Pte.	Clark		Edward Wells	1916 09 16	KIA	
453257	Sgt.	Clark		Peter	1918 09 28	KIA	
427761	Pte.	Clark		Wilfred	1916 10 08	KIA	46th
654800	Pte.	Clarke		Arthur Edward	1917 06 15	KIA	161st
444727	L/Cpl.	Clarkson		Robert Stanley	1917 10 27	KIA	55th
406495	Pte.	Cole		Thomas	1916 09 28	DOW	36th
123504	Pte.	Coleman		Edgar	1916 09 17	DOW	
427056	Pte.	Coleman		John	1918 08 09	DOW	46th
427518	Pte.	Coleman		Victor Albert	1919 01 20	Pneumonia	46th
406265	Pte.	Coles		Albert John	1916 10 08	KIA	36th
678292	Pte.	Collins		Francis William	1917 06 18	Missing	169th
3030177	Pte.	Commons		John	1918 10 01	KIA	
445060	Pte.	Condo		Barney	1917 08 30	KIA	
405610	Pte.	Conlon		Benjamin	1916 09 22	KIA	35th
123207	Pte.	Connell		Frederick Samuel Austin	1916 09 17	Missing	
250138	L/Cpl.	Conroy	MM	Michael	1918 09 29	KIA	
679046	Pte.	Cook		Ernest	1917 04 17	DOW	169th
453790	Pte.	Cook	MM	George William	1918 09 29	KIA	
654279	Pte.	Cook		Rollo Elmer	1918 09 29	KIA	161st
648198	Pte.	Cooke		Frank	1917 11 15	DOW	159th
678790	Pte.	Cooke		Frederick William	1917 04 12	DOW	169th
427770	Pte.	Cookson		James Russell	1916 11 20	DOD	46th
452041	Cpl.	Coombe		Alfred John	1916 06 13	KIA	
451203	Pte.	Coombes		Thomas	1917 01 22	KIA	
123820	Pte.	Cooper		Edward	1916 09 17	Missing	
249270	Pte.	Cooper		Ernest William	1918 10 01	KIA	208th

Service No.	Rank	Surname	Decorations/Alias	Given Names	Date of death	Cause of Death	Previous Unit
678792	Pte.	Cooper		James Calderwood	1921 05 23	Pneumonia	169th
451353	Pte.	Cordner	MM	Thomas henry	1917 11 17	DOW	
452548	Pte.	Cornish		Angus	1916 05 26	KIA	
249301	Pte.	Corrigan		Robert	1918 08 10	DOW	208th
444863	Pte.	Cosseboom		Clinton William	1916 06 06	KIA	55th
141174	Pte.	Cowan		George	1916 09 17	KIA	
453682	Pte.	Cowan		James McCaul	1916 04 10	KIA	
602450	Pte.	Cowell		John J	1916 10 08	KIA	34th
123155	Pte.	Cowie		David	1916 07 07	KIA	
727723	Pte.	Crabb		Hugh John	1917 10 26	KIA	110th
453609	Lieut.	Craig	MM	Lorne Bean	1918 09 30	DOW	
250020	Cpl.	Craigie		Lewis	1918 08 28	DOW	
681454	L/Cpl.	Cranfield		Harry	1917 10 26	KIA	170th
451811	Pte.	Crawford		Gilbert	1917 11 13	KIA	
727494	Pte.	Cross		Peter	1920 07 20	Endocarditis	
342082	Pye	Croydon		Frederick Harold	1918 08 29	KIA	
838255	L/Cpl.	Cumberland		Charles	1918 08 27	KIA	147th
126750	Pte.	Cummins		Thomas	1916 10 08	KIA	
681538	Pte.	Currell		William George	1917 10 26	Missing	170th
681700	Pte.	Curry		Francis Samuel	1917 10 26	Missing	170th
452407	Pte.	Curtis		Wiiliam	1916 10 08	DOW	
452561	Pte.	Dakes		Robert Duncan	1916 12 29	KIA	
453845	Pte.	Dale		Edward	1918 10 01	KIA	
1066253	L/Cpl.	Danard		Harold Parsons	1918 10 20	KIA	248th
727668	Pte.	Danbrook	MM	John Stanley	1918 08 08	KIA	110th
453186	Pte.	Darmody		Michael Joseph	1916 06 13	KIA	
453258	Pte.	Dart		George	1916 10 07	KIA	
	Lieut.	Dashwood	MC	John Lovell	1917 04 13	KIA	
1004052	Pte.	Davall		Claude	1918 08 28	KIA	227th
678562	Pte.	Davis		Arthur Henry	1917 11 13	KIA	169th
681858	Pte.	Davis		Frederick Lorne	1917 04 23	DOW	170th

Service No.	Rank	Surname	Decorations/Alias	Given Names	Date of death	Cause of Death	Previous Unit
249720	Pte.	Davis		Joseph Steel	1918 08 27	KIA	
	Lieut.	Daw		Herbert Bethune	1916 04 26	KIA	
	Lieut.	Dempsey		James Daniel	1917 04 14	DOW POW	
210250	Pte.	Denison		John Richard	1916 10 08	KIA	98th
452560	Pte.	Dennes		Reginald	1916 05 05	KIA	
3106248	Pte.	Dennison		John	1918 10 15	DOW POW	
124566	Pte.	Dent		Fred John	1918 10 01	KIA	
427086	Pte.	Denton		William	1916 09 22	KIA	46th
452557	Pte.	Derbyshire		Frank	1916 05 06	DOW	
649458	Pte.	Devine		Lauchlin	1917 10 26	KIA	159th
1066135	Pte.	Devlin		Earl Louis	1918 08 29	KIA	248th
727730	Pte.	Dewar		Waldren	1917 06 28	KIA	110th
445696	Pte.	Dewitt		Ralph Edward	1917 11 12	KIA	55th
452559	Pte.	Diamond		Reginald	1916 10 08	KIA	
211049	Pte.	Dibble		Frank	1916 10 08	Missing	98th
453661	Pte.	Dicker		James Norman	1916 06 03	KIA	
452556	L/Cpl.	Dickson	MM	Alexander	1918 09 28	KIA	
124261	Pte.	Dinning		John	1916 08 28	KIA	
451757	Sgt.	Diver		John Walter	1916 04 23	KIA	
681522	Pte.	Dodds		William Allan	1917 10 26	KIA	170th
678808	Pte.	Dodson		Thomas	1918 08 27	KIA	169th
452416	Sgt.	Doig		John George	1916 05 26	KIA	
210256	Cpl.	Dolby		William Thomas	1917 06 28	KIA	98th
727389	Capt.	Doupe		William Ivan	1918 10 02	KIA	110th
491279	Pte.	Down		Arthur George	1916 10 23	DOW	33rd
648257	Pte.	Doxsee		Arthur Edward	1918 08 09	DOW	159th
444681	Pte.	Doyle		Harry	1916 10 08	KIA	55th
444913	Pte.	Doyle		John Thomas	1916 09 18	KIA	55th
210273	Pte.	Drinnan		George Andrew	1916 10 08	KIA	98th
648265	Pte.	Dubroy		Edward	1917 08 30	KIA	159th
451086	L/Cpl.	Dunbar		Robert S.	1916 04 26	DOW	

Service No.	Rank	Surname	Decorations/Alias	Given Names	Date of death	Cause of Death	Previous Unit
727074	Pte.	Dunham		George	1917 04 09	DOW	
249328	Pte.	Dunlop		James Charles	1918 06 24	DOD	208th
678304	Pte.	Dunlop		Joseph	1917 04 13	DOW	169th
678501	Pte.	Dunn		Herbert William	1917 10 26	KIA	169th
678305	Pte.	Dunn		James Sidney Herbert	1917 04 14	DOW	
	Capt.	Durie		William Arthur Peel	1917 12 27	KIA	
452044	Pte.	Durst		John William Tinewell	1916 04 25	KIA	
644443	Pte.	Dusome		Patrick	1918 08 18	KIA	157th
451405	Pte.	Dwyer		Ray Michael	1916 09 20	KIA	
1055185	Pte.	Earhart		Thomas Britton	1918 08 28	KIA	248th
451106	Pte.	Earl		Thomas George	1916 05 31	KIA	
189311	Pte.	Eberlee		George Hastings	1918 04 23	KIA	
678307	Pte.	Ede		Arthur James	1919 02 19	Peretonitis	
427621	Pte.	Edgecombe		Frederick Allison	1919 05 17	Pulmonary TB	
451155	Sgt.	Edmison		Harry Gardner	1916 10 08	KIA	
2042552	Pte.	Edwards		Edward Philip	1918 10 01	KIA	
678815	Pte.	Elkington		Frederick	1917 10 27	Missing	169th
657847	Pte.	Elliott		Howard Hollingshead	1917 07 03	DOW	162nd
451829	Pte.	Ellis		Harry	1916 06 13	KIA	
414104	C.S.M.	Embree		David Thornton	1917 12 29	KIA	40th
	Lieut.	Empson		Lancelot William	1917 01 01	KIA	
210311	Pte.	England		Frank Charles	1916 11 02	DOW	98th
754285	Pte.	England		Nicholas	1918 08 10	DOW	119th
678309	C.S.M.	Enright	DCM MM	Cornelius Joseph	1918 08 08	KIA	169th
754278	Pte.	Ensworth		Clyde Nugent	1918 10 02	KIA	119th
1066097	Pte.	Ervin		Henry D.	1918 08 27	KIA	248th
427090	L/Cpl.	Esson		Edward	1917 10 26	KIA	46th
	Lieut.	Ewens		George Arthur	1917 10 22	KIA	
427375	L/Sgt.	Eyre		Joseph	1918 10 01	KIA	
2528359	Pte.	Fadil		Haseeb Abou	1918 10 02	KIA	
445288	Pte.	Fairweather		Charles White	1916 06 13	KIA	55th

Service No.	Rank	Surname	Decorations/Alias	Given Names	Date of death	Cause of Death	Previous Unit
654492	Pte.	Fallis		Robert John	1917 07 19	KIA	161st
401786	Pte.	Fenton		Francis George	1917 08 27	KIA	
	Lieut.	Finley		Charles Arthur	1917 10 26	KIA	
	Lieut.	Finney		Sylvester Webster	1919 12 25	DOD	
123308	L/Cpl.	Finnie		William	1918 09 30	KIA	38th, 70th
451408	Sgt.	Fitton	MM	George	1917 04 13	DOW	
453026	Sgt.	Flatt		Alfred	1916 10 08	KIA	
142088	Pte.	Fleming		Albert Henry	1916 10 08	KIA	
226834	Pte.	Fletcher		Frederick	1918 09 30	DOW	
427065	L/Cpl.	Flint		Alfred William	1917 04 12	KIA	46th
249041	Pte.	Foley		William	1918 08 28	KIA	208th
727244	Pte.	Forbes		William Thomas	1917 10 26	Missing	110th
453031	Pte.	Ford		Frederick George	1917 10 26	KIA	
654770	L/Cpl.	Forrest		Charles B.	1917 10 26	KIA	161st
654177	Pte.	Forsyth		Ross Frederick	1917 06 06	DOW	161st
240669	Pte.	Fortune	MM	Frank Harold	1919 07 17	DOS	
451218	L/Cpl.	Foster		John	1917 10 26	KIA	
838943	Pte.	Foster		William Earl	1918 08 18	KIA	147th
453034	Pte.	Fountain		George	1916 09 21	KIA	
451410	Pte	Fowler		Percy	1916 05 03	DOW	
3030926	Pte.	Fox		Harold	1918 10 01	KIA	
3105359	Pte.	France		William Edward	1918 10 10	DOW	
451412	Pte.	Fraser		George Alexander	1916 06 19	DOW	
654868	Pte.	French		Alexander Charles	1917 10 30	DOW	161st
452428	Pte.	French		Herman Roy	1916 06 06	KIA	
445543	Pte.	Frenette	MM	Adelard	1918 10 28	DOW	55th
453035	Pte.	Fretwell		George	1916 03 20	DOW	
453783	L/Cpl.	Fretwell		George William	1918 03 28	DOW	
453743	Pte.	Friend		George Spencer	1916 06 14	DOW	
189881	Pte.	Fright		Edward James	1917 10 26	KIA	
453684	Pte.	Frissell		James Alexandeer	1917 11 15	DOW	

Service No.	Rank	Surname	Decorations/Alias	Given Names	Date of death	Cause of Death	Previous Unit
211217	Pte.	Frost		Percy	1916 10 08	KIA	98th
124420	Pte.	Fullsher		Edwin William	1916 09 22	DOW	
453037	Pte.	Gallagher		Oscar Edgar	1916 01 03	DOD	
445058	Pte.	Gallant		Israel	1918 08 27	KIA	55th
727212	Pte.	Gardiner		Earl Egbert	1917 06 26	KIA	110th
123205	L/Cpl.	Gardner		Louis Frank	1917 04 12	KIA	
210345	Pte.	Garster		Andrew	1916 10 08	KIA	
3314168	Pte.	Gatherum		David	1918 09 28	KIA	
445584	Pte.	Gendron		John	1916 06 07	DOW	
214199	Pte.	George		Pete	1916 09 26	DOW	
453260	Pte.	Gerrard		Frederick William	1917 10 26	KIA	
754325	Pte.	Gibb		George	1918 09 29	KIA	119th
452647	Pte.	Gibb		Robert	1916 11 01	KIA	
411041	Lieut.	Gibson		Harold Alexander Fraser	1916 10 08	KIA	PPCLI 38th
1066125	Pte.	Gibson		Walker George	1918 08 26	DOW	248th
451995	Pte.	Gilbert		Edward Albert	1916 06 07	DOW	
452564	L/Cpl.	Gilbert		Joseph Sidney	1918 02 22	DOD	
3050513	Pte.	Gildernew		James Francis	1919 05 19	Pneumonia	
124381	Pte.	Giles		George Thomas	1916 10 07	KIA	
249282	Pte.	Gillespie		Maurice	1918 10 13	DOW	208th
404841	Pte.	Gillon		Edward	1916 06 12	DOW	35th
451221	Pte.	Gilpin		Fred	1916 10 08	KIA	
210347	Pte.	Gilroy		Joseph Alysious	1916 10 08	KIA	98th
451222	Pte.	Gingell		Lawson Thomas	1916 12 19	DOD	36th BoR
444919	Pte.	Girard		Frank	1916 10 08	Missing	55th
451223	Pte.	Giroux		Edouard	1917 10 26	KIA	
453259	Pte.	Gist		Henry Jewell James	1916 06 06	KIA	
654240	Pte.	Glazier		Joseph	1917 10 26	KIA	161st
445344	Pte.	Glazier		William	1916 10 07	KIA	55th
452563	Pte.	Glen		John Frame	1917 07 23	KIA	
452434	L/Cpl.	Goff		Frank	1916 07 07	KIA	

Service No.	Rank	Surname	Decorations/Alias	Given Names	Date of death	Cause of Death	Previous Unit
451359	Pte.	Goheen	MM Walter	William	1918 10 01	KIA	
124309	Pte.	Golding		William Arthur	1917 06 15	KIA	
451360	Pte.	Gordon		Henry Hartley	1917 12 29	KIA	
727029	Pte.	Gorvett		Wilbert Roy	1917 06 28	KIA	110th
451850	L/Sgt.	Goss	aka Hanna, William Henry	William Henry	1918 09 30	DOW	
123211	Pte.	Gow		Thomas	1919 04 06	DOD	
451987	Pte.	Graham		Arthur William	1916 06 14	KIA	
451843	L/Cpl.	Graham		Fisher	1916 10 02	DOW	
453622	Pte.	Graham		Frank Richard	1916 04 04	KIA	
452436	Pte.	Graham		James	1916 05 01	KIA	
451845	Sgt.	Grainger		William Gilbert	1917 10 26	KIA	
727855	Pte.	Granger		Alfred E	1917 10 26	KIA	110th
654265	Pte.	Grant		Arthur Henry	1917 01 21	KIA	161st
451993	Pte.	Grant		George	1916 06 13	KIA	
654197	Pte.	Grant		William	1917 04 06	KIA	161st
648386	Pte.	Gray		Daniel Wilfred	1918 10 18	DOW	159th
453041	Sgt.	Gray		George	1921 10 06	Endocarditis	
	Capt.	Gray	MID	Harold Seward	1918 08 16	Drowned, att. GHQ	
171098	Pte.	Gray		Leslie Phillip	1916 09 20	Missing	
124654	Sgt.	Gray		Ronald Maxwell	1917 02 11	DOW	
249984	Pte.	Graysmark		Ernest Joseph	1918 08 07	KIA	
654604	Pte.	Grealis		Frank Clifford	1918 08 27	KIA	161st
839135	Pte.	Grieve		Annadale Gordon	1917 05 05	DOW	147th
453190	Pte.	Griffin		George	1916 06 12	KIA	
226837	Pte.	Griffin		Milton Frederick Burnham	1918 08 27	KIA	
123676	Pte.	Griffin		Orton West	1917 04 12	KIA	
211050	Pte.	Griffiths		Lloyd	1916 10 08	KIA	98th
755080	Pte.	Griffiths		George Alfred	1918 08 29	KIA	119th
727801	Pte.	Grimditch		George	1917 06 28	DOW	110th
727343	Pte.	Grindin		Thomas	1918 08 27	KIA	110th
	Lieut.	Groves		Harold Morton	1917 10 27	KIA	

Service No.	Rank	Surname	Decorations/Alias	Given Names	Date of death	Cause of Death	Previous Unit
451450	Sgt.	Groves	MM and two Bars	William John	1918 10 01	DOW POW	
210363	Pte.	Guido		Zanutti	1916 10 08	KIA	98th
453164	Pte.	Hackett		Charles Edward	1917 10 29	DOW	
453607	L/Cpl.	Hain		Alexander William	1916 10 08	KIA	
210439	Pte.	Haisley		William Norman	1917 02 15	DOW	98th
400524	Sgt.	Hall		Albert Frederick	1918 09 29	KIA	33rd
2562372	Pte.	Hall		David Wylie	1918 08 28	DOW	
445582	Pte.	Hall		Horace S	1916 10 08	KIA	55th
250007	Pte	Hamilton		Frederick Charles	1918 09 02	DOW	
452443	Pte.	Hamilton		Frederick George	1916 06 14	DOW	
249365	Pte.	Hamilton		James	1918 08 28	KIA	208th
727765	Pte.	Hammond		Albert Thomas Allan	1918 08 12	KIA	110th
210417	Pte.	Hammond		Herbert William	1918 08 28	Missing	98th
2507339	Pte.	Hanniford		James Rupert	1918 08 27	DOW	
249530	Pte.	Hardman		Edward	1918 09 29	KIA	
249139	Pte.	Harford		Ernest	1918 08 12	KIA	208th
451852	Pte.	Harling		Harry	1916 09 17	KIA	
452441	Pte.	Harris		Charles Victor	1918 10 01	KIA	
406103	L/Cpl.	Harris		Joseph H	1916 10 08	KIA	36th
785242	Pte.	Harrison		Albert Gordon	1918 10 01	KIA	129th
453045	Pte.	Harter		Edwin	1916 10 08	KIA	
754387	Pte.	Hartung		August John	1918 08 27	KIA	119th
727524	Pte.	Harvey		Ernest James	1917 06 17	Dow	110th
142354	Pte.	Harvey		Percy Egerton	1916 09 20	KIA	
754382	Pte.	Hatten		George Ortan	1918 08 28	KIA	119th
211222	Pte.	Hatton		John William Green	1916 10 08	Missing	98th
427150	Pte.	Haver		William Robert Chisholm	1916 10 08	KIA	46th
491226	Pte	Hayles		George	1917 06 26	DOW	33rd
127218	Pte.	Hemsworth		James Spencer	1916 06 13	KIA	
453818	Pte.	Henderson		Herbert	1916 08 27	KIA	
163836	Pte.	Henderson		Joseph	1916 10 08	Missing	84th

Service No.	Rank	Surname	Decorations/Alias	Given Names	Date of death	Cause of Death	Previous Unit
	Lieut.	Henderson		Maurice Russell	1916 06 13	KIA	33rd
2507396	Pte.	Hendry		John	1918 09 29	KIA	
444081	Pte.	Henry		Charles Edward	1916 06 01	KIA	55th
	Capt.	Henry		Lewis Brock	1917 08 30	KIA	76th
453581	Pte.	Higgins		Daniel	1916 04 25	KIA	
754994	Pte.	Higgins		James Edward	1918 07 15	KIA	119th
451858	Sgt.	Hill		Charles Hannaford	1916 10 08	KIA	
727163	Pte.	Hill		Edward Robert	1917 10 26	KIA	110th
210454	Pte.	Hill		Joseph	1916 10 08	KIA	98th
2304361	Pte.	Hill		Sydney George	1918 09 28	KIA	
451459	Pte.	Hillier		William Ernest	1916 05 03	DOW	
727554	Pte.	Hinscliffe		John Henry	1917 04 06	KIA	110th
2507412	Pte.	Hirst		Gilbert	1918 10 01	KIA	
451385	Cpl.	Hitchcock		Albert Edward Joseph	1916 06 13	KIA	
3030676	Pte.	Hoare		Francis Charles	1918 08 28	KIA	
124410	Pte.	Hobbs		John Henry	1916 10 08	Missing	
754423	Pte.	Hodder		Ernest George	1918 09 30	KIA	119th
453195	Pte.	Hollgerson		Sydney	1916 10 08	KIA	
142568	Pte.	Honey		David Frederick	1916 09 20	KIA	
210392	Sgt.	Hooton		Louis	1918 08 08	KIA	98th
3030126	Pte.	Hope		James Alfred	1918 08 28	KIA	
838881	Pte.	Hopkins		Austin Clarence Warren	1918 03 23	DOW	147th
453194	Pte.	Houser		John James	1916 04 03	KIA	
	Lieut.	Howard	MC	Charles Matthew	1916 10 08	KIA	
2562351	Pte.	Howard		George	1918 08 29	KIA	
3314125	Pte.	Howell		Reginald Arthur	1918 11 20	DOW	
210391	Pte.	Hubbard		Charles Ernest	1916 10 08	Missing	98th
451419	Pte.	Hubbard		Walter	1919 12 30	DOD Phthisis (TB)	
3317139	Pte.	Hudson		Russell James	1918 10 01	KIA	
427319	Pte.	Huntley		Sydney Leonard	1916 11 21	DOW	46th
453665	Pte	Hussack	MM	Ernest Edgar	1920 05 18	DOD Endocarditis	

Service No.	Rank	Surname	Decorations/Alias	Given Names	Date of death	Cause of Death	Previous Unit
211120	Pte.	Hutchison		William	1916 10 11	DOW	98th
400903	Pte.	Hutton		John	1916 10 04	KIA	33rd
451156	Lieut.	Ineson	MC MM	Dick	1918 08 27	KIA	
427805	Pte.	Irving		Thomas Herbert	1916 08 19	KIA	46th
727834	Pte.	Jackson		Charles	1918 08 27	KIA	110th
249615	Pte.	Jackson		William Clifford	1918 05 02	DOW	
1090391	Pte.	Jamieson		David Edward	1917 11 12	KIA	253rd
681673	Pte.	Jamieson		George	1917 10 26	KIA	170th
2507348	Pte.	Jamieson		Jesse	1918 08 28	DOW	
754465	Pte.	Jeffrey		Alexander Campbell	1918 04 16	KIA	119th
136067	Pte.	Jenkins		Thomas Richard	1917 11 12	KIA	
	Lieut.	Jensen		Ernest Peter Carl	1916 10 08	KIA	
451866	Pte.	Jessop		Arthur	1916 06 13	KIA	
445199	Pte.	John	aka Weouche, J.L.	Louis	1916 10 08	KIA	55th
654744	Pte.	Johns		Lawrence Earl	1917 09 12	KIA	161st
654594	Pte.	Johns		Norman Wellington	1917 10 26	DOW	161st
237112	Pte.	Johnson		George Harley Pears	1917 06 29	KIA	204th
654665	Pte.	Johnson		George Reginald	1917 04 12	KIA	161st
210476	Pte.	Johnson		Richard	1916 10 08	KIA	98th
681140	Pte.	Johnston		George William	1917 10 26	KIA	170th
727667	Pte.	Jolly		James Basil	1917 10 28	DOW	110th
123291	Pte.	Jones		William Albert	1916 10 08	KIA	
3025045	Pte.	Kane	aka Titterington, E.G.	John	1918 08 08	Missing	
210488	Pte.	Kean		John	1917 02 14	KIA	98th
451366	Pte.	Kearsley		Frederick	1916 05 01	KIA	
250142	Pte.	Keenan		William	1918 08 28	KIA	
654300	Pte.	Kellett		George Edward	1917 10 28	DOW	161st
654572	Pte.	Kemp		Ernest Albert	1917 10 26	KIA	161st
	Lieut.	Kemp		Croix de Guerre Sam	1918 12 07	DOW POW	
139127	Pte.	Kemp		William Henry	1916 05 05	KIA	75th
452005	Pte.	Kennedy		James	1917 10 24	KIA	

Service No.	Rank	Surname	Decorations/Alias	Given Names	Date of death	Cause of Death	Previous Unit
838311	Pte.	Kent		Alfred James	1917 10 26	KIA	147th
452367	Pte.	Kerr		Frank Lyons	1916 09 20	KIA	
452004	Pte.	Kerr		Harry	1916 09 20	KIA	
452607	Pte.	Kerr		James	1917 10 26	KIA	
643446	Pte.	Kidd		John Henry	1916 10 05	KIA	157th
249444	Pte.	Kidd		William George	1918 08 15	KIA	208th
3105404	Pte.	Kilgour		Robert	1918 08 15	KIA	
1066280	Pte.	Kincaid		John	1918 10 01	DOW	248th
451871	Pte.	King		Percival Albert	1916 09 18	DOW	
404538	Pte.	King		William	1916 06 13	KIA	35th
210493	Pte.	Kingston		Charles Rayburn	1917 04 06	KIA	98th
3310136	Pte.	Kneller		Robert Frank	1919 02 17	DOD Pneumonia	
654629	Pte.	Knight		Charles Edwin	1917 10 26	KIA	161st
727607	Pte.	Knipe		Henry James	1917 10 26	DOW	110th
727410	Pte.	Kress		Frank Lewis	1917 10 26	KIA	110th
455191	Pte.	Kuzima		Pavel	1916 12 29	KIA	59th
2527396	Pte.	Lacey		John Charles	1919 03 09	DOW	
633743	Pte.	LaFramboise		Georges	1918 10 01	KIA	154th
727162	Pte.	Laing		George Gordon	1917 10 26	KIA	110th
633009	Pte.	LaLonde		John George	1917 06 28	KIA	154th
123812	Pte.	Lamarre		Isidore	1917 10 26	KIA	
2265658	Pte.	Laricks		George Warren	1918 09 30	KIA	
451254	Pte.	Latter	MM	Percy Thomas	1916 10 08	KIA	
838534	Pte.	Lauder		Allister	1917 10 26	KIA	38th, BoR, 147th
839043	Pte.	Lawrence		William Leath	1917 11 12	KIA	147th
654677	Pte.	Lawson		Robert	1917 10 26	KIA	161st
727646	L/Cpl.	Lay/Leigh		Joseph	1917 10 25	DOW	110th
100865	Pte.	Leake		William George	1918 09 09	DOW	66th
	Maj.	Leckie		Norman Ewing	1916 04 23	KIA	
427791	Pte.	Lee		Frank	1916 09 24	DOW	46th
453754	Pte.	Lee		John	1916 08 02	DOW	

Service No.	Rank	Surname	Decorations/Alias	Given Names	Date of death	Cause of Death	Previous Unit
453631	Pte.	Leggott		Harrison	1918 03 28	DOW	
121672	Pte.	Lengowski		Stanislaw	1917 04 12	KIA	
427311	Pte.	Lewis		Daniel Andrew	1916 10 06	DOW	46th
527721	Pte.	Lewis		James Bernard	1918 08 27	KIA	
681484	L/Cpl.	Lewis		John Anson	1917 08 30	KIA	
210561	Pte.	Lickers		William	1916 10 08	KIA	98th
2562329	Pte.	Lickley		William	1918 10 01	KIA	
1066233	Pte.	Lobsinger		Edward	1918 08 29	KIA	248th
453266	Cpl.	Locheed		Thomas	1916 10 07	KIA	
126595	Pte	Lockey		Alfred	1917 06 28	DOW	71st
210515	Pte.	Logan		Robert Drummond	1917 10 26	KIA	98th
838873	Pte.	Lougheed		Wilson	1917 10 26	KIA	147th
400996	L/Cpl.	Lovelock		Gilbert Arthur	1917 10 26	KIA	33rd
225991	Pte.	Luscombe		Louis Kenneth	1917 11 13	KIA	
210548	Pte.	Lynch		John David	1916 10 08	KIA	98th
2537426	Pte.	Macdonald	aka McKinnon, Donald	John Cameron	1918 09 27	KIA	
427751	Pte.	Macdonald		Thomas	1916 09 20	Missing	46th
654131	Pte.	MacDonald		Thomas Todd	1917 11 13	KIA	161st
440086	Cpl.	Maciver		Evander	1916 07 09	DOW	52nd, 53rd
452013	Pte.	MacKay		John Alexander	1916 11 04	DOW	
	Lieut.	MacKendrick		Gordon King	1916 10 08	KIA	81st
189695	Pte.	MacKenzie		James William	1917 10 26	Missing	
1066199	Pte.	Mackey	MM	Arthur John	1918 10 02	KIA	248th
727616	Pte.	MacLean		Allan Duncan	1917 09 04	DOW	110th
453268	Pte.	Maginn		John Mitchell	1916 06 07	KIA	
868376	Pte.	Magnan		Allan Fainley	1919 02 18	DOD Influenza	182nd
654631	Pte.	Mahoney		Henry Roscoe	1917 06 28	KIA	161st
654380	Pte.	Maines		George Edward	1917 10 28	KIA	161st
838124	Pte.	Malcom		Allen Beatty	1917 08 17	KIA	147th
123836	Pte.	Mandeville		Verne Arthur	1916 09 18	Missing	
754672	Pte.	Manuel		Edward	1918 08 08	KIA	119th

Service No.	Rank	Surname	Decorations/Alias	Given Names	Date of death	Cause of Death	Previous Unit
654318	Pte.	Marshall		James Russell	1918 01 21	KIA	161st
3106747	Pte.	Martelle		Ernest	1918 10 01	KIA	
	Lieut.	Martin		Frederick John Strange	1918 08 30	DOW	119th
127135	Pte.	Martin		John Alexander	1916 06 13	KIA	
141961	Pte.	Martin		John William	1917 10 26	KIA	
727527	Pte.	Martin		Norman	1917 10 26	KIA	110th
649076	Pte.	Martin		Thomas Frederick	1917 09 13	KIA	159th
124692	Pte.	Mason		William Edward	1916 09 20	KIA	
2537432	Pte.	Mather		Ernest Oswald	1918 08 28	KIA	
3106812	Pte.	Matte		Alfred	1918 10 01	KIA	
654354	Pte.	Matthews		Bruce Herbert	1917 08 31	KIA	161st
451266	L/Sgt.	Matthews		Walter Franklin	1916 06 06	KIA	
451766	Pte.	Mauchan		Issac B.	1916 06 13	KIA	
135780	Pte.	Mawson		William Ewart	1916 06 10	KIA	
210599	Cpl.	Mayer		Louis John	1917 11 04	DOW	98th
654301	Pte.	Mayhew		Albert	1917 10 26	KIA	161st
226883	Pte.	Maynard		Jack	1918 09 29	KIA	
427765	Pte.	McAuliffe		William	1916 10 15	DOW	46th
654615	Pte.	McBride		George Henry	1917 04 12	KIA	161st
681827	Cpl.	McBride		Walter Campbell	1918 08 26	KIA	170th
3030169	Pte.	McCallum		Frederick William	1918 09 18	DOW	
654713	Pte.	McClinchy		Wesley	1917 11 11	KIA	161st
654636	Pte.	McCluskey		Joseph Arthur	1917 10 26	KIA	161st
228214	L/Cpl.	McComb		Thomas Allan	1917 08 30	KIA	210th
23297	Lieut.	McCord	MID	George Rankin	1919 02 02	DOD PPCLI, TMB	
727224	Pte.	McCutcheon		Edwin	1918 08 27	KIA	110th
633837	Pte.	McDermid		Earl	1917 10 26	DOW	154th
3030932	Pte.	McDonald		Angus	1919 02 28	DOD	
838767	Pte.	McDonald		Joseph	1917 10 27	DOW acc	147th
648587	Pte.	McDonald		Oscar	1918 10 01	KIA	158th
654066	Pte.	McDonald		Theodore StClair	1917 06 15	KIA	161st

Service No.	Rank	Surname	Decorations/Alias	Given Names	Date of death	Cause of Death	Previous Unit
401212	Pte.	McDonnell		Justin	1916 09 16	KIA	33rd
654287	Sgt.	McDougall	MM	Neil Gordon	1917 11 22	DOW	161st
754566	Pte.	McDowell		Henry Eldon	1918 08 08	KIA	119th
123839	Pte.	McEwan		Charles Robertson	1916 11 03	KIA	
427299	Pte.	McEwen		Albert	1916 10 08	KIA	46th
654816	Pte.	McFalls		Elmer	1917 10 24	KIA	161st
427790	Pte.	McGeorge		Thomas	1916 08 20	DOW	46th
727827	Pte.	McGillawee		Robert	1918 08 27	KIA	110th
124494	Pte.	McGinnis		Hugh	1916 09 20	KIA	
452478	Pte.	McGowan		Robert James	1917 09 17	KIA	
124472	Pte.	McIntosh		Andrew	1916 09 17	KIA	
452015	Pte.	McIntosh		Robert	1916 09 30	DOW	
452611	Pte.	McKellar		James	1916 06 13	KIA	
3030479	Pte.	McKenna		James	1918 09 12	KIA	
727542	Pte.	McKenzie		Malcolm Kenneth	1917 04 12	KIA	110th
654736	Pte.	McKinney		Thomas Leslie	1917 08 23	KIA	161st
1066284	Pte.	McLaggan		William	1918 08 08	KIA	248th
	Lieut.	McLaren		John Ferguson	1917 04 20	DOW	
	Lieut.	McLeish		Stuart	1917 09 02	KIA	
451889	Pte.	McLennan		Farquhar	1916 06 13	KIA	
648616	Sgt.	McLeod	MM	Duncan James	1919 02 05	DOW	159th
654425	Pte.	McLeod		Ogal	1917 04 18	KIA	161st
427793	Pte.	McMillan		James Alexander	1916 10 08	KIA	46th
	Capt.	McNair		George Orme	1916 05 01	KIA	
648618	Pte.	McNulty		Daniel	1917 08 30	KIA	159th
3107053	Pte.	McPhee		Harry	1918 10 01	KIA	
124756	Pte.	McQueen		Hugh Murray	1918 09 30	KIA	
838354	Pte.	McReynolds		William Cross	1917 08 30	KIA	147th
649459	Pte.	McTierman		William James	1917 06 29	KIA	159th
838945	Pte.	McVicar		Alexander	1917 11 01	DOW	147th
633040	Pte.	Mellor		Clifford William	1917 04 12	KIA	154th

Service No.	Rank	Surname	Decorations/Alias	Given Names	Date of death	Cause of Death	Previous Unit
453170	Pte.	Mellor		David	1916 06 13	KIA	
452612	Pte.	Mellor		Frederick	1918 08 07	KIA	
124110	Pte.	Menghette		Victor	1916 10 08	Missing	
444652	Pte.	Merchant		Vernon Keith	1916 06 06	KIA	55th
636344	Pte.	Merry		Benjamin	1917 11 13	KIA	155th
636351	Pte.	Merry		Elsie Gordon	1918 11 08	DOW	155th
123362	Pte.	Metcalfe		Richard Percival	1916 09 17	KIA	
451267	Pte.	Miles		Arthur Henry	1916 06 14	KIA	
124054	Pte.	Miller		James Arthur	1916 10 08	KIA	
141243	Pte.	Millican		Sidney Claridge	1916 09 21	DOW	
441637	Pte.	Milligan		Clinton Silas	1918 01 15	DOD	42nd
445036	Pte.	Mills		Clarence Lemuel	1917 07 24	KIA	55th
453760	Pte.	Mills		Norman Frederick	1916 08 19	KIA	
823028	Cpl.	Miner	VC, C de G	Harry Garnet Bedford	1918 08 08	DOW	
124723	Pte.	Minson		William	1917 11 11	KIA	
249822	Pte.	Mitchell		Bernard William	1918 09 08	DOW	
451079	Pte.	Mitchell		Daniel	1916 05 31	KIA	
228151	Pte.	Mitchell		Harold Bertram	1917 07 19	KIA	13 CMR
225227	Pte.	Mitchell		Robert William	1918 10 01	KIA	DBCMR
406357	Pte.	Mitchell		William	1917 04 12	KIA	36th
850761	Pte.	Moody		Robert Thomas	1916 10 06	KIA	176th
	Lieut.	Moore		William Ambrose	1917 10 26	KIA	
453086	Pte.	Morris		Leonard V.	1916 04 30	DOD	CASCTD
451901	Pte.	Morrison		James Allen	1916 10 08	KIA	
1066226	Pte.	Morrison		Russell Gordon	1918 10 06	DOW	248th
427192	Pte.	Morrison		Thomas Joseph	1916 10 08	KIA	46th
451902	Pte.	Morrison		William	1916 09 19	KIA	
649387	Pte.	Morrow		Orland James	1917 10 26	KIA	159th
126812	Pte.	Morse		Joseph	1916 06 02	KIA	
141731	Pte.	Mortimer		George James	1916 11 02	DOW	
114088	Pte.	Morton		William John S.	1916 06 02	KIA	9th CMR

Service No.	Rank	Surname	Decorations/Alias	Given Names	Date of death	Cause of Death	Previous Unit
654302	Pte.	Mugford		Jonathan Martin L.	1918 11 01	DOD	
1066089	Pte.	Mulcock		Arthur	1918 03 24	KIA	248th
1066247	Pte.	Mundle		Robert	1918 08 31	KIA	248th
1066259	Pte.	Mundle		William	1918 08 29	KIA	248th
210613	Pte.	Munro		Harry	1917 08 26	KIA	98th
427662	Pte.	Murdoch		George	1918 08 08	DOW	46th
2528508	Pte.	Murphy		Bernard	1918 08 27	KIA	
453089	L/Cpl.	Murphy		Frederick Lawrence	1918 08 08	DOW	
3107076	Pte.	Murphy	aka Schambach, Lyman	James	1918 10 01	KIA	
210571	Pte.	Murphy		John	1916 10 08	Missing	98th
141951	Pte.	Murray	aka Ritchie Wm H	Fred William	1916 10 08	KIA	
427297	Pte.	Murray		James	1916 09 20	KIA	46th
681716	Pte.	Murray		James	1917 06 28	KIA	170th
452055	Pte.	Murray		James Goudie	1916 06 13	KIA	
3106567	Pte.	Nadon		Eustache	1918 10 01	KIA	
654417	Pte.	Neely		Arthur Cecil	1917 06 26	KIA	161st
453271	Pte.	Newell		Joseph	1920 06 24	DOD	
754701	Pte.	Nicholas		Nathan Mansfield	1918 08 28	DOW	119th
	Lieut.	Nicol		Ewen Cameron	1916 06 13	KIA	
727759	Pte.	Nimmo		Lester Graham	1917 08 28	DOW	110th
681541	Pte.	Niquette		Eugene	1917 04 08	DOW	170th
228061	Pte.	Noble		Charles Gordon	1917 04 16	DOW	
654877	Pte.	Noble		Walter George	1917 04 08	KIA	161st
123109	Pte.	Norelius		Clarence	1918 12 11	DOD	
123649	L/Cpl.	Nurse		William John	1916 10 08	KIA	
754709	Pte.	O'Boyle		Desmond Gladstone	1918 10 01	KIA	119th
654319	Pte.	O'Brien		Ernest Patrick	1918 04 23	KIA	161st
727593	Pte.	O'Connell		James	1917 04 14	DOW	110th
452575	Pte.	Ogg		George William	1921 01 26	DOD	
124704	Pte.	Ogletree		William Tracy	1916 09 18	KIA	
727840	Pte.	O'Hara		Joseph Michael	1917 10 26	KIA	110th

Service No.	Rank	Surname	Decorations/Alias	Given Names	Date of death	Cause of Death	Previous Unit
2529303	Pte.	Oldenburg		George August	1918 08 27	KIA	
681139	Pte.	O'Leary		William Joseph	1917 10 26	Missing	170th
838366	Pte.	Orford		Charles Edgar	1917 10 26	KIA	147th
648689	Pte.	Ostrom		Frederick	1918 08 29	Missing	159th
2304306	Pte.	Page		Charles	1918 08 27	Missing	
838987	Pte.	Pallister		David Clifford	1917 08 31	KIA	147th
3105553	Pte.	Papas		Samuel	1918 09 29	DOW	
727587	Pte.	Park		John Maxwell	1917 10 27	DOW	110th
727317	Pte.	Park		Neil	1917 10 26	KIA	110th
681645	Pte.	Parke		William John	1917 10 26	KIA	170th
654074	Sgt.	Parker		Charles Arthur	1920 02 20	WG	161st
451020	Pte.	Parker		Hilton	1916 05 31	DOW	
715080	L/Cpl.	Parker		Norman McKelvie	1917 10 26	KIA	106th
453696	Pte.	Parkhurst		Leonard	1916 06 06	DOW	
452489	Pte.	Parkinson		John Henry	1916 06 13	KIA	
453274	Cpl.	Parks	MSM	Harry	1918 08 28	DOW	
2537377	Pte.	Parr		Albert	1918 10 04	DOW	
	Lieut.	Patten		Edgar William Galbraith	1917 10 26	KIA	215th
681368	Pte.	Payne		Alexander Richard	1917 10 26	KIA	170th
681577	L/Cpl.	Payne		Arthur Stacey	1920 11 14	DOD	170th
453218	Pte.	Pearson		John William	1917 11 13	KIA	
727818	Pte.	Pearson		Robert Harvey	1918 03 21	DOW	110th
210772	Pte.	Pedrick		Richard Albert William	1916 10 08	KIA	98th
648710	L/Cpl.	Pennell	MM	George Mathew	1918 08 27	KIA	159th
451283	L/Cpl.	Penton		John	1916 06 13	KIA	
451374	Pte.	Percival		William	1916 05 01	KIA	
427115	Pte.	Peterson		Gilbert Andrew	1918 08 27	Missing	46th
3106298	Pte.	Phillips		Edward	1918 10 02	DOW	
838620	Cpl.	Phillips		Harold Martin	1918 08 08	DOW	147th
427020	Pte.	Phillips		Harry	1916 09 22	KIA	46th
452022	Pte.	Pickett		Albert Ernest Edward	1916 05 11	DOD	

Service No.	Rank	Surname	Decorations/Alias	Given Names	Date of death	Cause of Death	Previous Unit
210737	Pte.	Pickworth		Rowland John	1916 10 08	KIA	98th
452069	Pte.	Pirouet		John	1916 06 13	KIA	
	Capt.	Pitts		Frederick	1917 06 28	DOW	
	Capt.	Pollock		Robert	1918 09 20	KIA	
141270	Pte.	Porter		Albert	1916 10 06	DOW	
427588	Pte.	Porter		Arthur William	1916 10 08	KIA	46th
451461	Pte.	Preston		George Struthers	1916 10 08	KIA	
754734	Pte.	Procter		John	1918 08 16	DOW	119th
754718	Pte.	Proulx		Franklin Ambrose	1918 08 27	KIA	119th
727059	Pte.	Puddle		Frank William	1917 10 26	Missing	110th
727514	Pte.	Pugh		Stanley	1918 08 07		110th
404917	Pte.	Pullar		Frank	1916 06 13	KIA	35th
451287	Pte.	Putt		Thomas Frank	1916 06 23	DOW	
453642	Pte.	Quance		Albert Thomas	1918 10 01	KIA	
453110	Sgt.	Quigley		William Edwart	1917 07 24	DOW	
648730	Pte.	Quinn		Isaac	1917 11 21	DOW	159th
838825	Pte.	Quinton		Robert Alexander	1918 09 05	SIW CFA	
636284	Pte.	Raber		William	1917 11 07	DOD Nephritis	
681141	Pte.	Ramsay		John	1917 07 01	KIA	170th
228166	Pte.	Ramsden		William Frederick	1917 04 15	KIA	13th CMR
451060	Bglr.	Rance		Harry	1916 01 06	DOD Meningitis	
491161	Pte.	Rathwell		Arnold	1916 10 08	KIA	33rd
453765	Sgt.	Ray		Ernest John	1916 09 17	KIA	
838169	Pte.	Rayner		Stephen	1917 08 30	KIA	147th
427039	Pte.	Rea		William Harold	1917 04 08	Missing	46th
210745	Pte.	Reakes		Victor Albert	1916 10 08	KIA	98th
427784	Pte.	Redford		Lewin Leroy	1916 10 08	KIA	46th
124152	Pte.	Redman		James Joseph	1917 07 23	DOW	
3107077	Pte.	Redmond		James	1918 10 01	KIA	
452621	Sgt.	Redpath		James	1916 09 20	KIA	
3030935	Pte.	Reid		Charles	1918 09 29	KIA	

Service No.	Rank	Surname	Decorations/Alias	Given Names	Date of death	Cause of Death	Previous Unit
	Maj.	Reid		George Alexander	1916 10 08	KIA	
453643	Pte.	Reid		Marshall William	1917 10 26	KIA	
451429	Pte.	Reid		Sydney Arthur	1916 05 01	KIA	
400868	Pte.	Reid		Thomas Campbell	1916 11 07	DOW	33rd
401331	Pte.	Render		Frederick	1916 07 09	KIA	33rd
727294	Pte.	Rendol		Arthur Gilbert	1917 08 30	DOW	110th
654618	Pte.	Renwick		Francis Melvin	1917 04 18	DOW	161st
453766	Pte.	Rice		Frederick Nelson	1916 09 20	KIA	
453275	Pte.	Richardson		John	1916 04 10	DOW	
491059	Pte.	Richmond		John	1916 09 20	Missing	33rd
3105575	Pte.	Risi		Francesca	1918 10 01	DOW	
141951	Pte.	Ritchie		William Hart	1916 10 08	KIA	
427995	Pte.	Rix		John Brown	1916 08 19	KIA	46th
401667	L/Cpl.	Roberts		William	1917 06 26	KIA	33rd
123298	Pte.	Robertson		Andrew	1916 09 16	KIA	
654788	Pte.	Robertson		Frederick Montague	1917 04 15	KIA	161st
124316	Pte.	Robertson		Harry	1916 10 08	KIA	
452498	Pte.	Robertson		James	1916 09 22	Missing	
135392	Pte.	Robertson		John	1916 07 09	DOW	
141758	Pte.	Robertson		Robert	1917 11 12	KIA	161st
451920	Pte.	Robertson		Thomas Walter	1916 06 13	KIA	
189980	Pte.	Robinson		Edward Arthur	1918 08 27	Missing	
452577	Pte.	Robinson		William	1916 05 31	KIA	
838573	Pte.	Robison		John	1917 10 26	KIA	147th
727122	Pte.	Roe		Walter Joseph	1917 02 11	DOD	110th
227085	Pte.	Rogers		Samuel	1917 11 12	KIA	
1066057	Pte.	Rolling		Dawson	1918 09 30	DOW	248th
451921	Pte.	Rollo		George Swan	1916 06 13	DOW	
453120	Pte.	Ronelson		Robert	1918 09 30	KIA	
141278	Pte.	Roper		Owen Valentine	1916 10 08	KIA	
452576	Pte.	Ross		Frederick	1916 06 13	KIA	

Service No.	Rank	Surname	Decorations/Alias	Given Names	Date of death	Cause of Death	Previous Unit
3031018	Pte.	Ross		James Rennie	1918 10 01	KIA	
427100	Pte.	Routledge		William	1916 09 20	KIA	46th
163680	Pte.	Rowe		Thomas	1916 10 08	KIA	84th
404765	Pte.	Rowland		John Wesley	1916 09 18	KIA	35th
654166	Pte.	Ruffell		Clifford William	1917 10 26	KIA	161st
249680	Pte.	Rumsey		Frederick Charles	1918 10 01	KIA	
123962	Sgt.	Russell	MM	William Clarence	1918 08 27	KIA	
3031110	Pte.	Ryan		Herbert Lewis	1918 08 28	KIA	
3031019	Pte.	Ryan		John	1918 09 29	KIA	
	Capt.	Ryerson	MID	John Egerton	1916 09 19	KIA	
3030166	Pte.	Ryle		Charles Carlyton	1918 08 27	KIA	
189443	Pte.	Sadler		Leslie Harold	1917 04 12	KIA	
427117	Pte.	Sanders		Percival Frank	1916 09 20	KIA	46th
451151	L/Sgt.	Sands		Francis	1916 06 06	KIA	
838402	Pte.	Saunders		Norman Russell	1918 09 06	DOW	147th
3106954	Pte.	Savard		Joseph	1918 10 01	KIA	
453126	Pte.	Schloss		Leo	1916 10 01	KIA	
727687	Pte.	Schotts		Roy Stanley	1917 10 26	KIA	110th
124102	Pte.	Schram		Ernest Herman	1916 09 16	KIA	
210799	Pte.	Schwab		William Edwin	1916 10 08	KIA	98th
	Lieut.	Scott		Andrew	1917 04 18	DOW	
453771	Pte.	Scott		Lionel	1916 04 23	DOW	
452505	Pte.	Scott		William	1918 08 08	KIA	
228382	Pte.	Searle		William John	1917 04 06	KIA	
452520	Pte.	Seden		Frederick William	1918 09 28	DOW	
648828	Pte.	Seguin		Arthur Joseph	1917 09 01	DOW	159th
452506	Sgt.	Selby		Benjamin	1916 07 08	KIA	
453128	Pte.	Seward		William	1916 04 10	DOW	
123329	Pte.	Sewell		Alfred William	1916 11 03	KIA	
451753	Sgt.	Sewell		Leonard	1916 06 13	DOW	
123910	Pte.	Seymour		George Peter	1917 04 19	DOW	

Service No.	Rank	Surname	Decorations/Alias	Given Names	Date of death	Cause of Death	Previous Unit
210845	Pte.	Sharp		Maurice	1916 10 08	KIA	98th
2562339	Pte.	Shaughnessy		William	1918 08 30	DOW	
838409	Pte.	Sheffield		James Dawson	1917 10 26	KIA	147th
453574	Pte.	Shepherd		Walter Waddington	1916 09 17	KIA	
754856	Pte.	Shewfelt		Roy Godfrey	1918 08 27	DOW	119th
452508	Cpl.	Shields		Richard S.	1916 10 08	KIA	
451305	Pte.	Shier		Thomas Edward	1916 05 02	DOW	
124103	Pte.	Shine		Edward Dennis	1916 09 21	DOW	70th
	Lieut.	Shortt	MC	Allen	1916 12 10	Missing	
123628	Pte.	Siebert		Charles Henry	1916 10 08	KIA	
451307	Pte.	Simons		Ernest Newton	1916 10 08	KIA	
451308	Sgt.	Simpson		Alfred Justice	1917 06 28	KIA	
681635	Pte.	Simpson		Edward	1917 04 15	KIA	170th
	Lieut.	Simpson		Ernest Alroy	1916 09 22	DOW	
727071	Pte.	Sinclair		Frank Raymond	1917 11 13	KIA	110th
3105065	Pte.	Sinclair		Jesse	1918 09 30	KIA	
3031083	Pte.	Skelly		John	1918 09 30	KIA	
681014	Cpl.	Skelton		Alexander DeVere	1918 08 27	KIA	170th
123293	Pte.	Skelton		Fred	1916 10 08	KIA	
	Lieut.	Skill		Albert Thomas	1917 10 26	KIA	
451934	Pte.	Skinner		Wilfred Thomas	1916 02 26	DOD	
210828	Pte.	Skuse		Martin	1917 01 27	KIA	98th
675332	Pte.	Slade		Thomas William	1918 10 28	KIA	168th
210811	Pte.	Slade		William Alfred Daniel	1917 10 26	KIA	98th
226921	Pte.	Slater		Percy	1918 08 29	KIA	
727830	Pte.	Small		Douglas James	1917 08 30	KIA	110th
2562353	Pte.	Smith		Albert Ernest	1918 08 29	DOW	
452029	Pte.	Smith		Alexander	1916 05 06	KIA	
681778	Pte.	Smith		Charles	1917 01 15	KIA	170th
123201	Pte.	Smith		Francis Henry	1916 09 21	DOW	
451311	Pte.	Smith		Frederick James	1918 09 13	DOW	

Service No.	Rank	Surname	Decorations/Alias	Given Names	Date of death	Cause of Death	Previous Unit
727596	Pte.	Smith	MM	George Christopher	1918 08 27	KIA	110th
453698	Pte.	Smith		George Henry	1916 09 20	KIA	
210853	Pte.	Smith		John	1917 06 28	KIA	98th
2562309	Pte.	Smith		Raymond Scott	1918 10 01	KIA	
654092	Pte.	Smith		Sidney Joseph	1918 09 29	KIA	38th
648824	Pte.	Smith		Thomas	1917 10 26	KIA	159th
451379	Pte.	Smith		William	1916 09 20	KIA	
249361	Pte.	Smith		William	1919 05 17	Phthisis(TB)	208th
3107095	Pte.	Smithson		George	1918 10 01	KIA	
123503	Pte.	Snowden		George Henry	1916 08 20	KIA	
451432	Pte.	Somerville		Philip	1916 10 08	Missing	
211271	Pte.	Souran		Labelle	1916 10 08	KIA	98th
225424	Pte.	Spain		George	1918 10 02	KIA	
1066069	Pte.	Sparrow		Henry Cecil	1918 08 27	Missing	248th
727748	Pte.	Spencer		Percival Franklin	1918 08 07	KIA	110th
452511	Pte.	Spragg		Walter	1918 01 05	KIA	
2438325	Pte.	Springgay		Percy Joseph	1918 08 08	Missing	
727535	Pte.	Squire		William John	1919 07 31	DOW	110th
727389	Pte.	Statton		Nelson	1917 10 28	DOW	110th
1066119	Pte.	Steele		Harold Gladstone	1918 08 27	KIA	248th
681867	Pte.	Stephenson		Robert John Stewart	1917 10 26	DOW	170th
426751	Pte.	Stevens		Sydney George	1916 07 31	KIA	46th
649136	Pte.	Stevenson		John David	1917 10 26	Missing	159th
681408	L/Cpl.	Stevenson		Robert Munro	1917 08 04	DOW	170th
451942	Pte.	Stirling		Alexander	1916 06 05	KIA	
	Lieut.	Stockhausen		Frederick Hope	1918 10 01	KIA	
649286	Pte.	Stoddart		Henry Robert	1917 10 26	KIA	159th
452515	Pte.	Stoker		Frederick	1916 05 28	KIA	
835209	Pte.	Strachan		James Russell	1917 10 26	KIA	146th
654817	Pte.	Strang		John Caldwell	1917 07 23	KIA	161st
648866	Pte.	Streeter		Frank	1918 04 13	DOW	159th

Service No.	Rank	Surname	Decorations/Alias	Given Names	Date of death	Cause of Death	Previous Unit
648868	Pte.	Streeter		Delbert	1918 08 14	DOW	159th
727568	Pte.	Struthers		Melville Henderson	1917 10 26	KIA	110th
727047	Pte.	Sugden		William	1918 08 28	KIA	110th
211299	Pte.	Sullivan		Thomas Joseph	1916 10 05	KIA	98th
410925	Lieut.	Sutherland		John Elliot	1916 07 29	KIA	PPCLI
127512	Lieut.	Swarts	MM	Jack Bertram	1918 09 30	KIA	
453136	Cpl.	Sweenie		William Ramsay	1916 10 08	Missing	
142577	Pte.	Sweeting		John	1916 10 08	KIA	
681308	Pte.	Taberner		William Henry	1917 06 28	KIA	170th
2507324	Pte.	Tattersall		John James	1918 09 29	KIA	
451462	Pte.	Taylor		Alfred Stephen	1916 09 12	KIA	
451949	Pte.	Taylor		Francis Price	1916 06 13	Missing	
838193	Pte.	Taylor		Frank	1917 08 30	KIA	147th
453774	Pte.	Taylor		Frederick	1916 10 08	KIA	
681738	Pte.	Taylor		Walter James	1917 06 30	KIA	170th
451339	Pte.	Taylor		William Irwin	1916 06 12	KIA	
453800	Pte.	Teal		John Stanley	1917 06 03	KIA	
850224	Pte.	Tell		Leonhart Henry	1917 02 05	KIA	176th
452036	Pte.	Terry		Arthur	1916 09 17	KIA	
654723	Pte.	Terry	MM	John Edward	1918 11 17	DOD	161st
654171	Pte.	Thamer		George Henry	1917 07 01	KIA	161st
189532	Pte.	Thompson		William Arthur	1916 10 08	KIA	
	Lieut.	Thomson		Henry Richard	1917 10 25	DOW	
210912	Pte.	Thorn		George	1916 12 19	KIA	98th
427708	Pte.	Tickner		Alfred Albert	1916 09 24	DOW	46th
838583	Pte.	Tindale		Harvey Richard	1917 11 13	DOW	147th
3025045	Pte.	Titterington		Edwin Groves	1918 08 08	Missing	
2507365	Pte.	Tolemy		James	1918 10 01	KIA	
453651	L/Cpl.	Tomlin		John Henry	1916 06 09	KIA	
727711	Pte.	Torrance		Lincoln Grimm	1917 10 26	KIA	110th
	Capt.	Torrance		Samuel Greenshields	1917 11 13	KIA	

Service No.	Rank	Surname	Decorations/Alias	Given Names	Date of death	Cause of Death	Previous Unit
451953	Sgt.	Trimble		Samuel John	1916 09 21	KIA	
643460	Pte.	Turner		Charles	1918 08 27	KIA	157th
839012	Pte.	Turner		William Henry	1918 09 12	DOW	147th
451384	Pte.	VanDuzen		Hugh	1916 09 18	KIA	
727474	Pte.	Vanstone		William Frederick	1917 10 26	KIA	110th
427774	Pte.	Varley		Samuel Mark	1916 08 19	KIA	46th
	Lieut.	Venn		Archie Valentine	1918 10 01	KIA	
838667	Pte.	Vernon		Frank	1917 10 22	KIA	147th
838992	Pte.	Vollett		Harry	1917 10 26	KIA	147th
427984	Pte.	Wadham		Frederick L.	1916 07 09	KIA	46th
228480	Pte.	Walker		Ephraim	1917 07 23	DOW	
	Lieut.	Walker		Henry Valmond	1916 10 08	KIA	81st
	Lieut.	Walker		Joseph Tackaberry	1916 09 20	KIA	
453708	Pte.	Walker		Roy Stanislaus	1916 09 17	Missing	
453176	L/Cpl.	Wallace		Alexander	1916 06 13	KIA	
427080	Pte.	Walley		John Albert	1917 04 07	KIA	46th
249376	Pte.	Walmsley		William John	1918 08 08	KIA	208th
453147	Pte.	Walpole		Stanley George Saunders	1916 06 13	KIA	
124326	Pte.	Walsh		Joseph Michael	1916 08 21	KIA	
838603	Pte.	Walter		Robert James Stanley	1917 10 26	KIA	147th
190039	Pte.	Ward		Ernest Sidney	1917 04 11	DOW ACC	
452530	Pte.	Wardle		Samuel	1916 03 18	DOD	34th
451099	Sgt.	Warwick		William Henry	1916 04 23	KIA	
427782	Pte.	Watson		Donald	1916 09 20	KIA	46th
63779	Cpl.	Watson		John Smith	1916 06 05	DOW	
654838	Pte.	Watt		Earl	1917 11 03	KIA	161st
142141	Pte.	Watt		George Somerset	1917 11 14	KIA	
	Lieut.	Way		John Hatherly	1918 08 27	KIA	
123146	Cpl.	Weatherill		Bertrand Peter	1916 09 17	Missing	
453802	L/Cpl.	Webb		Stanley Earl	1917 05 19	KIA	
681398	Pte.	Weldham		Ernest Henry	1917 01 30	DOW	170th

Service No.	Rank	Surname	Decorations/Alias	Given Names	Date of death	Cause of Death	Previous Unit
681292	Pte.	West		George William	1917 06 28	KIA	170th
654488	Pte.	West		Sydney	1917 10 26	KIA	161st
451463	Pte.	Weston		Frederick William	1916 06 13	KIA	
681674	Pte.	Whiston		Walter	1918 08 27	KIA	170th
681629	Pte.	White		John Arthur	1917 03 16	DOW	170th
453793	Pte.	White		Major Beverley	1916 09 18	KIA	
453231	Pte.	Whitehead		Edwin	1916 10 08	KIA	
427559	Pte.	Whitter		John Webster	1916 09 12	DOW	46th
427470	Pte.	Whittick		Harry	1916 09 21	DOW	46th
451968	Pte.	Wickens		Leonard	1916 08 19	KIA	
228102	Pte.	Wideman		Ernest Freeman	1917 10 26	KIA	13th CMR
654709	Pte.	Wightman		Charles Ivan	1917 10 26	KIA	161st
426715	Pte.	Wild		George Alfred	1916 10 08	Missing	46th
654306	L/Cpl.	Wilkinson		Thomas Harold Inman	1918 08 27	KIA	161st
220456	Pte.	Williams		Alexander Leonard	1916 11 16	KIA	
838232	Pte.	Willis		Harry Stanley	1917 10 26	Missing	147th
428000	Pte.	Wilson		Alexander Clark	1916 10 08	KIA	47th
838223	Pte.	Wilson		John Albert	1918 07 22	KIA	147th
453232	Pte.	Wilson		Melvin	1916 06 07	KIA	
452043	Sgt.	Wilson		Robert	1917 06 30	KIA	
453653	Pte.	Wiser		Oscar	1917 08 31	KIA	
681351	Pte.	Withington		William	1917 08 26	KIA	170th
643980	Pte.	Wood		Albert Vincent	1918 08 16	KIA	157th
452037	Pte.	Wood		Frederick	1916 09 17	KIA	
426892	Pte.	Woodbine		William Osborne	1916 08 18	KIA	46th
3030509	Pte.	Woodhouse		Joseph	1918 10 01	KIA	
401119	Pte.	Woodruff		Bert	1916 07 09	KIA	33rd
249288	Pte.	Woods		Bertram Thomas	1918 08 08	KIA	208th
452582	Pte.	Worrall		Squire	1916 09 25	DOW	
513186	Pte.	Wray		Henry Edward	1918 08 29	DOW	
123574	Pte.	Wray		Robert Wardle	1916 08 20	DOW	

Service No.	Rank	Surname	Decorations/Alias	Given Names	Date of death	Cause of Death	Previous Unit
142499	Pte.	Wretham		Alfred Ernest	1916 09 17	DOW	
727269	Pte.	Wright		Arthur Harold	1917 10 26	KIA	110th
451160	C.S.M.	Wright		Dudley Gordon	1916 06 13	KIA	
141818	L/Sgt.	Yakes	MM	Charles	1917 04 12	KIA	
434407	Pte.	Yaromich		Zachary (Zachaljasz)	1916 09 22	KIA	50th
211013	Pte.	Youlton		William Henry	1918 09 12	DOW	98th
2537451	Pte.	Young		John	1918 08 29	KIA	
838216	Pte.	Zimmerman		Arthur	1917 11 09	DOW	147th

Index

Adam, Capt. Herbert S., 34, 46, 52
Adamson, Lt. Col. Agar, 159
Affleck, Capt. Jack, 169, 181, 188, 196
Aircraft cooperation
  Klaxon horns, ground panels, flares, and lamps, 115, 227
Albert I, King of the Belgians, 277,279
Allen, Pte. Arthur A., 34
Allen, Lt. William A., 128, 132
Alexander, L/Corp., 63
Anderson, Lt. Andrew A., 110, 177, 179, 243, 252, 257,ph 258, 284,287,289
Anderson, Lt. J. F. W., 98, 144, 191
Anderson, Maj. , 81
Andrews, Lt., 261
ANZAC, Australian and New Zealand Army Corps, 222
  1st Division, Australian Imperial Force, 255
  Auckland Battalion, 172
Ashwell, Lt., 257
Avery, Lt., 257
Baker, Pte. Chester D., 16, 40, 93, 269
Baldwin, Lt. Henry W., 231, 233–235
Baldwin, Robert, 231
Ballachey, Maj. Panayoty P., 14, 63, 302
Bayley, Pte. Percy, 155
B.E.F. (British Expeditionary Force), 80, 249
  First Army, 123, 154, 255
  Second Army, 165
  Third Army, 127, 191, 217, 254
  Fourth Army, 240, 255
  Fifth Army, 93
  XI Corps, 232
  XIII Corps, 219
  4th Division, 262
  57th Division, 269
  2nd Dismounted Cavalry Brigade, 61
  3rd Tank Brigade, 256
  2/7 Duke of Wellington's Regiment, 218
  6th Sherwood Foresters; King's

Liverpool Regiment, 269
Newfoundland Regiment, 1st Battalion, 77
North Stafford Regiment, 226
Royal Engineers, 68, 85, 163
Royal Flying Corps, 27, 61
No.16 Squadron, 164
Royal Garrison Artillery, 164
Royal Tank Regiment, #9
Section Tanks, C Battalion, 168
A Company, 5th Battalion, 241
11th Tank Battalion, 223
Royal Warwickshire Regiment, 1st Battalion, 76
Seaforth Highlanders, 1st Battalion, 76

Bearman, Corp. F., 206.
Belgium
Aldershot Huts, 30, 31
Brussels, 278, 282
Derby Camp, 190
Fletre, 30, 31
Godersvelde (Godewaersvelde), 29–30, 169
Mons; 216, 276–278
Obourg, 277–278
Poperinghe, 76, 183, 185
Quaregnon, 276
St. Denis, 277–278
St. Sylvestre-Cappel, 29, 169
Waterloo, 278
Bell, Sgt. George Thomas, 10, 136, 265, 266, 296, ph 297
Bell, Lt. H.M., 202
Bennett, Sgt. John, 128
Bertram, Lt., 145
Bird, Pte. Will R., 240
Bishop, Sgt. Morden Lue, 116, 250
Bishop VC, Maj. W.A., 295
Borden, Prime Minister Sir Robert L., 21
Bramshott Camp, Hampshire, 25, 283
Brazill, Lt. R.F., 213
Brown, Lt. W.E., 266
Burrows, Capt. Charles S., 137, 241, 247, 250, 252, 272
Byng, Gen. Sir Julian , 56, 65, 74, 85, 94, 109, 125, 140, 191, 217, 255

Calver, Pte. Andrew J., 17
Calver, Emily, 17
Calver, Pte. Percy, 17
Calver, Ruth, 17
Cameron, Lt. Don, 178–9.
Campbell, Pte. Fred, 131, ph 298
Campbell, Pte. John “Pinky”, 20, 27, 45, 51, 62
Campbell, Pte. Lewis, 151–2, 297, ph298
Canada
Niagara-on-the-Lake, Ontario, 13, 17
Paradise Camp, 13, 17, 22
Toronto, Ontario, 14, 16, 17, 21, 22, 23, 32, 34, 103, 154, 198, 285, 287, 291, 296, 302
Argonauts, 41
Exhibition Grounds, 22, 287
St. James Cemetery, 198, 296, 302
Carmichael DSO and Bar, MC and Bar, Col. Dougall, 26, 105, 108, 116, 136, 144–5, 197, 202, 213, 229, 250, 251, 252, 265, 267, 272, 282, 285, 287, 289.
Carroll, Capt. L.J., 242.
Carter, Pte. John N., 85, 88.
Cassels, Col. George H., 14, 19, 26, 41, 89, 104, 108.
Catto MM, Pte., 207
C.E.F. Units
First Contingent, 13, 25, 26, 56
Canadian Corps, 64, 74, 79, 89,

93–4, 97, 127, 140, 149, 153, 154, 167, 171–2, 188, 207
Canadian Machine Gun Corps, 262
9th Machine Gun Company, 169
Canadian Corps Reinforcement Camp, 164, 169
Canadian Gas Service, 163
"Foch's Pets," "Salvation Army," 239
1st Canadian Division, 30, 31, 61, 94, 136, 140, 154, 209, 262, 263, 264, 271, 273, 278, 283, 300.
1st Canadian Infantry Brigade
2nd Battalion, 51, 84
4th Battalion, 165
2nd Canadian Infantry Brigade, 65, 266
8th Battalion, 65
10th Battalion, 185, 252
13th Battalion, 246
16th Battalion, 252
2nd Canadian Division, 44, 77, 80, 136, 263, 264, 281, 283
4th Canadian Infantry Brigade, 31, 117
3rd Canadian Division, 27, 56, 57, 140, 165, 183, 207, 211, 216, 218–219, 251, 255, 260, 263, 264, 271, 281, 283, 291, 296
7th Canadian Infantry Brigade, 55, 81, 123, 128, 233, 251, 260, 267,
Princess Patricia's Canadian Light Infantry, 27, 56, 57, 70, 128, 136, 158–160,180, 201, 218, 256.
Royal Canadian Regiment, 27, 75, 116, 128, 132, 149, 164, 190, 218
42nd Battalion, 27, 66, 139, 140, 240, 260, 261, 277
49th Battalion, 27, 233, 256, 276
8th Canadian Infantry Brigade, 27, 49, 56, 93, 132, 150, 255, 260, 269
1st Canadian Mounted Rifles, 27, 39, 41, 53, 132, 273
2nd Canadian Mounted Rifles, 27, 141, 150, 286
4th Canadian Mounted Rifles, 27, 49, 57, 70, 136, 140, 150
5th Canadian Mounted Rifles, 27, 57, 67, 70, 93, 216, 222
9th Canadian Infantry Brigade, 10, 26, 27, 50, 81, 82, 93, 117, 132, 154, 169, 183, 207, 215, 226, 260, 262, 265, 271, 283
Training Battalion, 164
43rd Battalion (Winnipeg), 26, 37, 39, 44, 50, 57, 60, 67, 68, 75, 82, 90, 95, 98, 100, 103, 108, 109, 110, 113, 114, 116, 131, 140, 141, 143–146, 163, 175, 188, 201, 216, 218, 221, 266, 271, 273.

52nd Battalion (Port Arthur, Ontario), 26, 31, 41, 49, 60, 81, 84, 113, 116, 131, 143–4, 155, 175, 198, 212, 218, 260, 266, 271.
60th Battalion (Montreal), 26, 81, 90, 118, 131, 132
116th Battalion, 119, 147, 150, 164, 169, 180, 181, 201, 202, 208, 213, 223, 236, 242, 244, 250, 251, 265, 267–272, 277, 289.
9th Field Ambulance, 118, 136, 196
4th Canadian Division, 25, 97, 141, 155, 175, 219, 251, 262,
10th Canadian Infantry Brigade, 265
44th Battalion, 155
47th Battalion, 265
54th Battalion (Kootenay Battalion, British Columbia), 23
12th Infantry Brigade, 140
73rd Battalion, 75
Royal Garrison Artillery, 164
No.1 Siege Battery of Halifax
No.2 Field Service Unit, 21
No.2 Field Ambulance, 21
5th Division, 192, 215–6
8th Reserve Battalion, 110th, 147th and 159th Battalions, 118
33rd Battalion, 50
34th Battalion, 21
35th Battalion, 21
37th Battalion, 21
74th Battalion, 23
75th Battalion, 22, 23
98th Battalion, 85, 93, 95
142nd Battalion, 151
158th Battalion, 154
161st Huron Battalion, 103, 151
123rd Canadian Pioneer Battalion, 164
127th Canadian Railway Troops, 186
Chown, Rev. Dr., Hon Lt. Col., 151
Church, Lt., 268
Church, Tommy (mayor of Toronto), 287
Clapperton, Lt. George, 63
Clare, L/Cpl. William, 32
Clarke MM, Pte., 207
Clayton, Sgt. Gerald, 50
Clinchett, Lt. F., 164
Collins, Pte., 259
Condie, Lt., 188
Cormack DCM, Scout F.W., 48, 203–7
Cosbie MC, Capt. Waring G., 14, 23, 24, 32, 34, 42, 52, 295–6
Courts martial
desertion, 126–7
commuted sentences, 165
Craig MC, MM, Lt. Lorne Bean, 16, 63, ph 268, 300
Croak VC, Pte. John, 246
Curtis, Lt. George Salmon, 27
Cusler, Jane, 12, 295
Cusler MC, Maj. Warner Elmo, 9, 12, 14, 25, 26, 27, 51–2, 59–60, 136, 146–7, 157–9, ph158, 191, 198, 222–3, 294–5

Dallyn, Lt. G.M., 191, 212, 269
Dalrymple, Lt., 216
Danbrook MM, Stretcher Bearer John S., 250
Dashwood MC, Lt.. J. L., 67, 76, 111, 120, 122, 130
Daw, Lt. Herbert, 44

Delamere, Lt., 216
Dempsey, Lt. James D., 129, 130
Dexter DCM, L/Corp. E. C., 160
Diseases
Gangrene, 35
Lice, 34, 47, 130, 151
Mumps, 114, 116, 154
Rats, 33, 51, 100
Shell shock (battle fatigue, post traumatic stress disorder), 41–3, 48, 52, 53, 63, 68, 76, 93, 98, 112, 166, 208.
Spinal meningitis, 26
Trench fever *Batonella quitana,* 35, 130
Venereal diseases, 212, 283
Dixon, Lt., 147
Doughty, Pte. Harold E. "Tiny", 93
Douglas, Lt. L. E., 164
Douglas, Sgt., 187
Doupe, Corp Ivan, 171
Drysdale, C.S.M. William B., 50
Duffett, Lt. M.G., 202
Dunham MC, Capt. F.H., 241, 252
Durie, Anna, 198, 302, 303
Durie, Helen, 37
Durie, Capt. William A.P., 14, 27, 35, 37, 39, 48, 197–8
Dyke, Lt., 213

Eager, Capt. King, 130
Edmison, Sgt. Harry G., 46,
Edward, Prince of Wales, 276, 277
Elver, Pte. Hubert, 253, 272, 298
Embree, C.S.M. David, 197
Empson, Lt. Lancelot W., 111
Enright DCM, MM, C. S. M. C. J., 206–7, 222, 250
Estaminets, 112
Ewens, Lt. G. A., 164, 173

Farr, R.S.M. James, 17, 188, 190, 282
Foch, Marshal Ferdinand, 225
Field MC and Bar, Capt. A.T., 116, 142, 177, 188, 222, 230, 261.
Finney, Lt., 268
Fitton MM, Sgt. George, 105, 108, 110, 121, 131.
Forwood, Capt. Thomas W., 48
France
Albert, 79, 84, 87, 255
Golden Virgin and Child, 87
Arras, 95, 97, 103, 109, 112, 114, 125, 127, 141, 149, 168, 217, 218, 219, 232, 233, 239, 254, 255, 262, 263, 264, 265
Avion, 143–5, 150, 151, 191, 202, 212, 290
Avion Road, 142
Avion Switch Trench, 142
Avion Trench, 142–4
Slag Heap, 145
Boiry-Notre Dame, 260–2
Artillery Hill, 260–1
Branch Farm, 261
Victoria Copse, 261
Bois de la Folie, 127–8, 130
Bray, 95, 100, 101, 108, 109, 112, 114
Cambrai, 190, 217, 239, 255, 263–4, 267–272, 287
Canal de l'Escaut, 271, 273
Pont d'Aire, 271
Canal du Nord, 264, 266, 272
Courcelette, 81, 84, 85, 89, 165
Sugar Refinery, 165
Courcelles, 242, 248
Demuin, 241–8, 252
Drocourt-Queant Line, 260, 262–3, 265, 272
Fresnes-Rouvroy Switch Line, 260, 262

Hamon Wood, 242, 250, 251
Hill 70, 147, 153–4
Hindenburg Line, 255, 264
Le Havre, 27, 29, 283
Le Pendu Camp, 164, 168, 169
Le Quesnoy, 251
Lens, 141, 144–7, 150, 153, 155, 161, 195, 197, 223
Cinnabar Trench, 157, 202, 223
Nun's Alley trench, 157–9
Marcoing Line, 264, 266–7, 269
Marquion Trench system, 264
Regina Trench, 88–92, 97, 299
Vimy Ridge, 97, 103, 125–133, 150, 154, 161, 164, 221, 255, 290, 296, 301
French Third Army, 254
French Tenth Army, 225, 255
Fretwell, Pte. George, 17, 33
Fretwell, Pte. George William, 17, fn 244
Frier, Nurse Dorothy, 146, 294
Frost, Pte. Art, 103
Frost, Arthur J. (florist), 103
Fulcher, Pte. Cecil, 171
Gallagher, Pte. Oscar, 26
Game MM, Pte., 207
Gauld, Lt. J. G., 116, 142–4
Geary, Maj. Reginald, 154, 287, 291
Genet DSO, Lt. Col. Henry Augustus, 13, 14, 23, 44, 77, 88, 95, 108, 112, 120, 123, 126, 136, 159, 184, 185, 191
George, Lt., 261
George, Donna (granddaughter of Hubert Elver), 298
George V, King, 191
German Units
7th Division, 84
165th Regiment, 143
365th Regiment, 159
464th Hanover Regiment, 175
Gibson, Pte. Walker G., 254, 261
Good VC, Corp. Herman, 246
Gooderham, Lt. Col. E.A., 291
Goodspeed, Maj. D.J., 10, 13
Gordon, Pte. Henry, 197
Gough, Gen. Hubert, 93, 172
Graham, Pte. Frank R., 37
Gray MC, Lt. Frank E., 117, 157, 159
Gunn, Gen., 287

Haig, Field Marshall Sir Douglas, 61, 80, 167–8, 222, 239, 254–5
Hanning, Lt. J.R., 202
Hardy, Sgt. J.C., 197
Harrison, Pte., 257
Hearst, Lt. H.V., 67, 81
Hedley, Capt. Chaplain, 150, 293–4
Helwig, Lt., 155
Henderson, Lt. Maurice R., 50, 63, fn101
Henry, Capt. Lewis B., 159
Hessian, Capt. (medical officer), 196
Hicks, Maj. Frank E., 57,
Hill Brig. Gen. F.W., 70, 79, 136, 159, 183, 211, 212.
Hitchcock, Corp. Albert, 63
Holden, Mary (daughter of Dougall Carmichael), 292
Hookey Jr., Pte James Henry, 17
Hookey Sr., Pte. James Henry, 17
Hooper. Lt. F.J., 136, 144, 224
Hooper MM, Corp. G., 206, 207
Horne, Gen. Sir H., 153
Horton, Lt. P.N., 191, 198, 208
Howard, Lt. Charles M., 33, 62–3, 90,92, 94
Hubbard, L/Corp. William, 63
Hughes, Maj. Gen. Garnet, 192, 216
Hughes, Lt. Gen. Sir Sam, 21, 22,

75, 192
Ineson MC, MM, Lt. Richard, 91, 191, 248, 252, 256–7
Jeakins, Hon. Capt. Charles, 24
Jennings, Pte.Harry, 208
Jensen, Lt. Ernest P. C., 67, 90
Johnson DSO, MC and Bar, Lt. Walter W., 183, 186, 188, 190, 206–7, 272, 289, 292
Joyce MC, Capt. Richard H., 14, 25, 26, 33, 39, 40, 41, 43, 50, 51, 62, 64, 295
Jucksch (Jukes) DSO and Bar, MC and Bar, Maj. Arnold Homer, 132, 142–3, 145, 155, 173, 180, 185, 202–7, 211, 241,fn 275, 252, 256, 257–60, 267, 273, 285, 294

Keevil, Benjamin (grandson of Thomas Skill), 299
Kemp, Lt. S., 272
Kerr, Lt. R.W., 191
King, William Lyon Mackenzie (prime minister of Canada), 235
Knight, Pte. Charles E., 137
Kress. Lt., 141, 147, 268

La Tour, Sgt. Harry Joseph, fn 97
Lamb MC, MM, Capt. Thomas F., 110, 191, 277, 289
Larivee, Sgt., 284
LeDoux, Pte. Leo E. 165, 208
Le Seur, Sgt, 63, fn 97
Leckie, Maj. Norman "Tout", 41
Legard, Lt., 268
Leggo, Lt. Ayton Ritchie, 14, 23, 27
Lipsett, Maj. Gen. Louis, 65, 85, 94, 117, 132, 139, 159, 165, 183, 226, 237, 266.
Lockwood, Lt., 233
Logie, Maj. Gen., 23
Loomis, Maj. Gen. F. O. W., 266, 271, 279, 283, 285.
Ludendorff, Gen.Erich, 236, 251, 255

Macdonald, Lt. Aubrey W.C., 27
Macfarlane DSO and two Bars, Lt. Col. Robert Alexander, 9, 45, 81, 126, 129, 158, 159, 168, 169, 177, 185, 188, 191, 197, 202, 209, 213, 229, 237, 253, fn 291, 257, 267, 273, 282, 284, 287, 289, 291, 293.
MacKay, Maj. John D., 14, 26, 57, 120, 137.
MacKendrick, Lt. Gordon King, 92
MacKinnon, Corp. Archie, 11,22, 27, 34, 42, 47–8, 61–2, 63, 81–2, 99–100, 298.
MacKinnon, Ronald, fn 141, 298
Martin, Pte. Clarence, 129–130, 151, 171
Martin, Lt. Fred, 227, 243, 257
Martin, Pte. Norman, 129, 151, 158, 160, 170–1, 181
Matthews, Sgt. Walter F., 16, 57, ph 58
McAdam, Lt. T.H., 261
McComb, L/Corp. Thomas A., 151, 159
McCord, Lt. George Rankin, 120
McCrimmon, Maj., 90
McGrath, Lt., 261
McGregor MM, Pte. Alexander D., 63
McHardy MM, Pte., 207
McKeand, Capt. David Livingston, 26, 44, 81, 295
McKechnie, Lt Neil K., 279
McKee, Pte. Robert Henry, 17, fn 127, 299
McKegney, Hon. Capt. S. E.
McKellar, Pte. James, 63
McLeish, Lt. Stuart, 141, 161
McNair, Capt. George O., 48
Mearns MM, Pte., 207
Mellor, L/Sgt. Frederick, 34

Mercer, Maj. Gen. Malcolm S., 56, 65
Military units, miscellaneous
38th Dufferin Rifles, 14
48th Highlanders, 14
97th Regiment 154
Governor General's Bodyguard, 17, 32
Queen's Own Rifles of Canada, 14
Miner VC, C de G, Corp, Harry G.B., 151, 198, 244–5, 248, 250, 252, 302–3
Mitchell, Capt. George Gooderham, 41
Montgomery, Lt., 141
Moore, Lt William Ambrose, 178
Murdoch, Agnes wife of David Waldron, 300

Nicol, Lt. Ewen C., 63
Nivelle, Gen. Robert, 149, 168

Oliver, Capt. Edmund H., 197, 201
Ormond, Brig. Gen. Dan, 237, 253–4, 261, 262, 278
Orr, Maj., 141–2, 145, 155

Parke, Lt. Roy W., 84
Parsons, Capt., 64, 68, 87
Patten, Lt. Edgar "Pat", 178–9
Pearce MC, Lt. Joseph A., 62, 68
Pearkes VC DSO MC, Lt. Col. George, 265
Pedley MC, Lt. James, 165
Perritt, Sgt., 284
Petain, Marshal Henri, 236
Phin, Lt., 219
Pillboxes (bunkers), 172
Piper, Lt., 132
Pitts, Lt., 128
Platoon organization, 117, 141, 196, 211, 217
Training, Divisional Demonstration Platoon, 117, 119, 209, 211, 216
Plumer, Gen. Herbert C., 172
Pollock, Capt. Robert, 191, 268
Priaulx, Lance Sergeant Reginald, 187

Quinn, R.S.M. Richard H., 31

Railways
broad-gauge, 185
Grand Trunk, 23
Inter-Colonial, 23
narrow-gauge, 41, 186, 216.
Rance, Bugler Harry, 26
Raspberry DCM, A/Sgt Joseph C., 105, 116
Rawlinson, Pte. James H., 139, 286, 303
Reid, Maj. G. A., 91
Render, Pte. Fred, 68
Richardson, Lt. F. H., 67
Rollo, Pte. George, 40
Rose, Maj. Henry E., 9, 14, 123, 126, 131, 132, 135, 241, 246-8, 252
Ross, Maj. Arthur, 130
Ross, Mrs. Duncan, 130
Ross, Lt. William G., 130
Rosser, Pte Frederick G., 17, fn89, fn194, 299
Rosser, Margaret, 299
Royal Grenadiers, 291
Royal Highness, Duke of Connaught (governor general of Canada), 95
Royal Regiment of Canada, 10
Russell, Sgt. William, 257
Rutherford, Sgt. James Douglas, 16, 23, 24, 25, 251, 265, 296
Ryerson, Lt. John E., 14, 82
S.S. *Saxonia*, Cunard Liner, 23–25, ph 24
Sadler, Acting Corp. Leslie, 128
Scott, Lt., 129

Scott, Pte. Herbert R., 16, 40
Settle, Pte. Findlay, 154
Shortt, Lt. A., 104–5, 106–7
Simms, L/Corp., 107
Simmonds, Pte. Lawrence M., 91
Simpson, Lt. E. A., 67, 84
Skill, Lt. Albert Thomas, 154, 181, 299
Smith, Lt., 136
Smith, Lt. W.H., 198
Smith, Lt. W.R., 191
Smythe DSO, MC, Maj. Rolsa Eric, 95, 121–2, 170, 174–5, 178, 188, ph209, 252, 260–1, 273, 278, 293
Springford, Lt., 257
Stevenson, Lt., 257
Stockhausen, Lt. Fred, 268, fn304, 297
Strathy, Lt. Elliot G., 183–9
Strathy MC, Lt. J. G. H. "Harry", 109, 116, 142, 183, 223
Swarts, Lt. J. B., 269
Sutherland, Lt. J. E., 67, 70
Sutherland, Col., 271
Taylor, Brig. Gen. William (chaplain general), 284
Thomson, Lt. Henry R., 49, 141, 181.
Thorold, Pte. Henry, 121
Thorpe MC MM, Lt. Henry Leroy, 122, 284
Torrance, Capt. Samuel G.
Tryon, Capt., 75
Turner, Maj. Gen. R.E.W., 77
Trywhitt, Miss (friend of Elliot Strathy), 186

Venn, Lt. Archie, 267, 269
Vimy University, 197, 281
Khaki University, 281
Vipond, Capt. Frank (chaplain), 150

Waldron, Pte. David, 11, 16, 29, 30, 33, 37, 40, 48, 50, 57, ph 58, 59, 63, 69, 84, 85, 93, 113, 116, 119, 222, 224, 269, 297, 298, 299–301
Waldron, Ian (son of David Waldron), 11
Walker, Lt. Joseph T., 27, 84
Wallace, Lt., 84, 91, 144
Warwick, Sgt. William, 41, 44
Way, Lt. John H., 227, 248–50, 257
Weapons
  Ammonal tube, wire cutting, 104–6, 203–6
  Grenades
    Hairbrush, Jam Tin, 25
    Mills Bombs, 25, 113, 117, 121, 206
    Stick, 122, 203
  Lee-Enfield rifle, 74–5
  Lewis Gun (light machine gun), 39, 90, 92, 94, 104, 105, 113, 121, 158
    firing from the hip, 117, 195
    in anti-aircraft role, 218, 234.
  No. 106 fuse, 127, 263.
  Oliver harness, 22, 26.
  Rifle grenades, 49, 195, 207
  Ross rifle, 22, 40, 74–5.
  Web equipment, 26
Webster, L/Corp., 108
Welch MM, Pte., 207
White, Pte. John A., 120
Wilhelm II, Kaiser, 28, 251, 276.
Williams, Lt. A. C., 67
Williams, Brig. Gen. Victor, 56–7
Woodyatt, Lt., 269
Wright, C.S.M. D.G., 63

Yates MM, Corp., 122
Ypres Salient, 30, 95, 168, 171
  Bellevue Spur, 174, 178, 180
  Clonmel Copse, 37, 50

Dad Trench, 178
Lamkeek Farm, 177, 180
Maple Copse, 57, 60
Menin Gate, 179, 301
Passchendaele, 167, map 176
Sanctuary Wood, 57, ph 60, 61, 62
Stirling Castle, 37
Third Battle of, 176
Vindictive Crossroads, 188, map 189
Young, Pte., 126–7
Young, Sgt. J., 284